DESIGN & DESIGNING

Ian Burden
John Morrison
John Twyford

Longman
London and New York

Acknowledgements

We wish to thank the following teachers for their help and assistance with the book:

Anne Agger, Tony Bailey, Diana Beeden, Dane Froggatt, Alec Ingle, Debbie Langar, Sue Manley, Lesley Tyers and Ernie Williams.

We also wish to thank the pupils of Burleigh Community College, The City of Leicester School, Hamilton School and Lonside Community College including:

Sandra Begnor, Helen Bexley, Andrew Carr, Jonathan Christian, Geoffrey Coleman, Stuart Crawford, Geoffrey Curwen, Louise Dobson, Simon Donoghue, Margaret Hall, Naomi Howitt, Rizwan Jasat, Sarah Lindley, Ian Oakley, David Palfreman, Rajesh Patel, Sanjay Patel, Shakti Patel, Parvin Ragaqne, Lesley Read, Justine Sterland, Nicola Sturgess, Joanne Tailby, Richard Webster, Louise Wells, Louisa Willoughby.

We are grateful to the following for permission to reproduce photographs:
Advertising Standards Authority, pages 25 *above right*, 25 *below*; Airship Industries, page 57 *left*; Amstrad, page 27 *below*; Asmer Seeds, page 68 *below*; Aspect Picture Library, page 66 *above*; BBC, page 72 *centre*; Lesley Robson-Foster/BBC Television, pages 86–89; Barclaycard, page 24 *below*; British Aerospace, pages 65 *above left*, 158 *above*; British Gas, page 23 *below right*; British Standards Institution, page 30; Paul Broadhurst/Janet & Colin Bord, page 66 *below right*; Margaret Bruce, pages 44 *below centre* & *right*; Bulmers, page 93 *above*; Ian Burden, pages 37 *below right*, 40 *above*, 42 *above*, 124, 128, 110 *above*; Cambridge University Press, 'The Wheelwrights Shop' by George Sturt, painting by Mike Nicholls, page 10 *above*; Camera Reproductions, page 17 *above left*; Central Electricity Generating Board, page 73 *above*; The Conran Foundation, page 76 *below*; Consumers' Association, page 45; Cordless Iron Co, page 44 *below left*; Crafts Council, pages 34 *above* (photo: Karen Norquay) & *centre* & *below*, 35 *above* (photo:Karen Norquay) & *below*; Creed Lane Studio, page 61; A.P. Davey, Royal College of Art, page 78; Design Council Picture Library, pages 7 *below left*, 19 *centre* (photo:Sam Lambert) & *below left*, 21 (Designing (photo:Gary Childs)), 29 *below*, *centre*, *above left* & *above centre*, 52 *above* (Design Magazine), 109 *below*, 148, 152 *above*; Duracell, page 48, 49, 50, 51; Electricity Council, page 9 *below right*; English Grains, page 23 *below left*; Courtesy of Eon Productions Ltd © 1983 Danjaq S.A, page 147 *above right*; Ford Motor Company, pages 6 *centre left* & *below left*, 20, 62 *below*, 112 *below*, 113 *below*, 114 *above*, 156, 157 *above left*; General Motors Corporation, pages 114 *below*, 115; Bob Gordon & Shire Publications, page 12 *below*; Stephen Green, pages 47 *below left* & *below right*; Greenpeace, page 91 *below*; David Grewcock, pages 40 *below left* & *below right*, 55 *above*, 69 *centre*; Health Education Council, page 24 *above*; Hoechst UK, page 23 *below centre*; Illustrated London News, pages 38 *right*, 62 *above*; Alex Ingle, page 113 *above right*; Institute for Consumer Ergonomics, page 109 *above left*; Institute of Civil Engineers, page 7 *above right*; Intasun, page 56 *centre left*; Ironbridge Gorge Museum Trust, page 14; Jaguar, page 53 *above left*; Kellogg Company, page 22 *below*; Kenwood, page 57 *right*; Leicester Mercury Picture, page 38 *left*; Leicestershire County Council, page 32 *below*; Leicestershire Museum Service, page 43; London Underground, page 77 *right*; Longman Photographic Unit, pages 7 *above left*, 36, 83, 94, 97 *left*, 100, 101, 117 *below*, 118 *below left*, 152, 166, 169, 170; Copyright © by Universal City Studios, Inc. Courtesy of MCA Publishing Rights, a Division of MCA Inc, page 67 *above*; McDonald's Hamburgers, page 56 *above left*; John Makepeace, page 33; Marley Floors, page 23 *above*; Mercedes Benz, page 77 *left*; Metal Box, page 37 *above right*; The William Morris Gallery, Walthamstow, London, pages 18 *above left* & *above right* & *above centre*; John Morrison, pages 100, 101, 107, 117 *below left* & *below right*; Mothercare, page 7 *below right*, 9 *below centre*, 139 *centre*; NASA, page 71; Office of Fair Trading, pages 31, 32 *above*; The Robert Opie Collection, Gloucester, page 52 *below*; Christine Osborne, page 68 *above*; Parker Pen, page 39; Philips Electronics, pages 6 *below right*, 7 *centre*, 136 *below left*, 139 *below*; The Picture Place, page 17 *above left*; *Punch*, page 60 *below left*; Renault UK, page 72 *below*; Richard Shops, page 72 *above*; Robinson State Museum, Pierre, South Dakota, page 67 *below*; Rochdale Library, page 17 *below*; Royal Institute of Builders & Architects, page 19 *above*; Rutland County Museum, page 10 *below*; Salford Local History Library, page 17 *above right*; Hans Schlegers/Design Magazine, page 112 *centre right*; Science Museum, pages 8 *below left*, 12 *centre*, 15 *above*; Sommer Allibert (UK), pages 162, 164; Sporting Pictures (UK), pages 59 *below*, 60 *above*; Sunderland AFC, pages 147 *centre right* & *below right*; Tate Gallery Publications, page 64 *above*; Norman Thelwell, Brat Race, Methuen, London, page 139 *above*; Thompson Holidays, page 55 *centre* Twyfords, pages 75 *above* & *below*; Lesley Tyers, pages 105, 176, 177; Van den Bergh, page 73 *below*; Victoria & Albert Museum, pages 13 *above*, 16; Volkswagen, pages 53 *below left*, 70; Volvo, page 26; West Midlands Consumer Services Department, pages 46 *above* & *centre* (photo:D.W Jenkins); *Which?*, pages 28, 74, 80, 123; John Whybrow, page 4 *below right*; Terry Williams, page 171 *above*; York Archaeological Trust, page 8 *above*, 8 *below right*; Yorkshire Post, page 42 *below*.

We are grateful to the following for permission to reproduce the following artwork:
Diane Beeden, page 146; Sandra Begnor, pages 113 *above left*, 180; Helen Bexley, pages 126, 127; Katie Burden, page 46 *below left*; Burleigh College, page 122 *below*; Jonathon Christiary, page 163; Geoffrey Curwen, page 168; A P Davey, Royal College of Art, page 79; Bill Frindall, page 60 *below right*; David Froggatt, page 118 *above*; General Motors Corporation, page 63 *below*; Kenneth Grange, page 47 *above*; Mr Gregory and Mr D Jones, 'Polegate Windmill Guidebook', page 65 *below*; Margaret Hall, pages 150, 151; Naomi Howitt, pages 134 *below*, 135; Design Students from City of Leicester School, (Geoffrey Curwen, Paul Jagger, Ian Staniland, Alan Stephens), pages 82, 142, 143; Sarah Lindley, pages 125, 152, 153; Ian Oakley, pages 110, 111; David Palfreman, page 165; Rajesh Patel, pages 116, 117 *above*; Karen Preedy & Pamela Chandler, page 109 *above right*; A Shaft, page 16 *above*; Nicola Sturgess & Lesley Read, page 172; Ernie Williams, pages 122 *above*, 134 *above*, 174, 175; Roger Warren, pages 41 *above*, & *below left*, 44 *above*; Louisa Willoughby, pages 102, 103, 104. All other artwork drawn by Ian Burden, John Morrison & John Twyford.

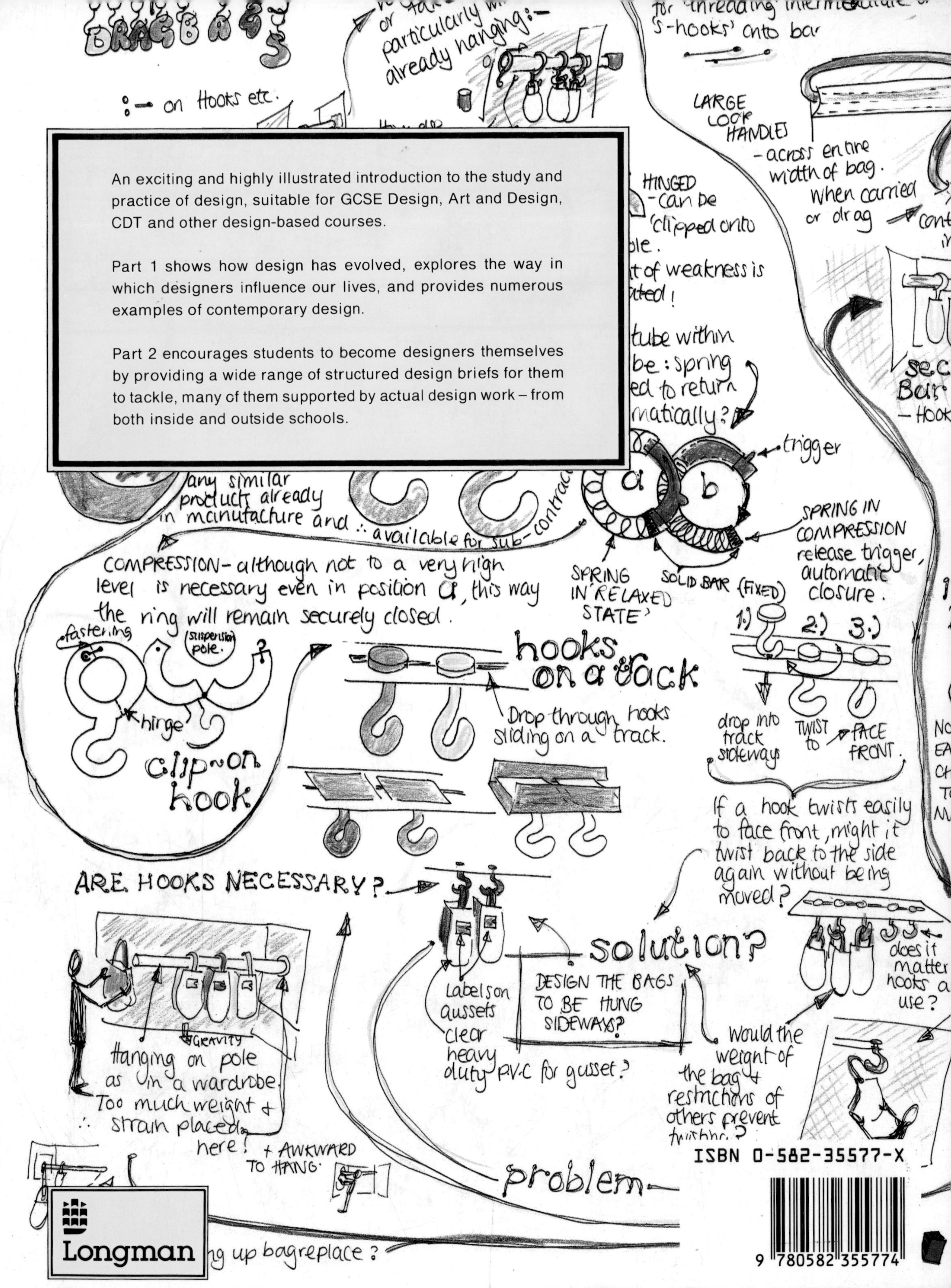

An exciting and highly illustrated introduction to the study and practice of design, suitable for GCSE Design, Art and Design, CDT and other design-based courses.

Part 1 shows how design has evolved, explores the way in which designers influence our lives, and provides numerous examples of contemporary design.

Part 2 encourages students to become designers themselves by providing a wide range of structured design briefs for them to tackle, many of them supported by actual design work – from both inside and outside schools.

Longman

ISBN 0-582-35577-X

9 780582 355774

Y COLEG NORMAL
ADRAN
ADDYSG
CDT
BANGOR

Contents

Introduction

Design in general education is crucial to every child's experience because it is essential to the development and promotion of enquiry, emotional growth, creativity and expression. How children learn about design depends on how they are taught and the selection of appropriate knowledge and experiences for them to explore.

Recent consideration of a National School Curriculum promotes the need to develop within pupils "their capacity to adapt and respond flexibly to a changing world". (The National Curriculum Consultation Document D.E.S. July 1987.) This is at the heart of design and designing. Many curriculum initiatives such as T.V.E.I., coupled with an increased interest in technology based courses, have design related activities as a central part of their philosophy.

In the report *Design Education at Secondary Level*, the Design Council suggests that courses should have the aim of giving pupils experience of:

- Examining a given problem or situation in order to identify and state the opportunities and difficulties involved.
- Understanding research and compiling data on the problem or situation and the factors affecting it.
- Analysing the information gained.
- Preparing a brief against which design proposals can be tested, so as to overcome the difficulties identified.
- Proposing responses to the brief and choosing the most appropriate.
- Developing this response and where appropriate bringing it to some practical conclusion.
- Analysing and evaluating the result and communicating this to others.

The thrust of the Design Council's report was the need for secondary school courses to move away from a separate subject approach, based largely on craft skills, to a curriculum approach which uses the design concepts listed above to form the framework upon which specialist teachers can develop the wide range of activities unique to their subject disciplines.

The aim of this book is to introduce students to the study and practice of design and designing. This approach is becoming increasingly important for the new design orientated GCSE examinations. Through a series of structured design briefs, the reader will experience the problems of designing whilst studying the solutions of others. By the end of their course, students should be trying to identify their own design problems in areas which are of special interest to them. Recent entries in the Design Councils Schools Design Prize show the enormous variety of ideas, and the ingenious solutions which can result, if examination courses are a vehicle to creativity rather than a deterrent, as many courses have proved to be in the past.

As well as their activities in the 'classroom' young people growing up in a modern technological world should be required to look at the influences which designers have upon the world in which they live, and display a critical awareness of their observations.

Design courses at secondary schools should, therefore, promote within students the confidence and capacity to carry through design projects and come to terms with the work of all types of designers who seek to shape our way of life.

For these reasons this book is organised into two sections. The first part of the book emphasises the way designers influence our way of life and the second section encourages students to become designers themselves.

The philosophy of the book is aligned to the principle of encouraging design enquiry in all its aspects, and in particular the idea that students should be organising tasks related to their projects.

For this reason this book is not intended as an encyclopaedia of practical skills, but is a guide to help staff and students through a variety of challenges – giving sufficient direction without being prescriptive, always acting as starting points which may be modified in line with individual needs.

Design education is an investment in the future, and it is vitally important that secondary school students understand the need for design to infiltrate all aspects of industrial society. By giving them a foundation in the activities of design and designing we are making a most positive contribution to the future economic performance of this country and the quality of life within it.

Section One: ***Design***

The world of design

Architecture

Meal Planning

Design is . . .
'The imaginative jump from present facts to future possibilities.'
(Page)

Mechanical Engineering

'Engineering design is the use of scientific principles, technical information and imagination in the definition of a mechanical structure, machine or system to perform a pre-specified function with the maximum economy and efficiency.' (*Fielden*)

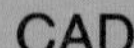

CAD

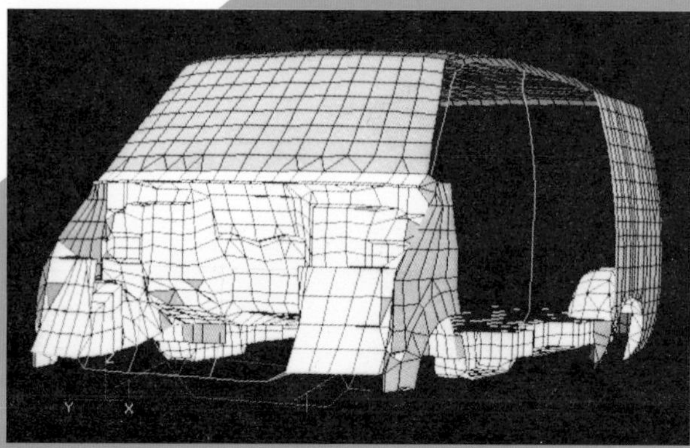

Design is . . .
'The performing of a very complicated act of faith.' (Jones)

Product Design

Art

Civil Engineering

Design is . . .

'Decision making in the face of uncertainty with high penalties for error.' (Asimov)

Electronics

'Design is what occurs when Art meets industry, when people begin to make decisions about what mass-produced goods should look like.' (*Art and Industry Boilerhouse inaugural exhibition*)

Graphic Design

Fashion

How design influences our lives

The changing nature of design

Ever since the beginning of civilisation men and women have produced items of usefulness, interest, beauty and destruction. A few of these are illustrated opposite, though visits to museums, art galleries, stately homes and antique shops will reveal many more.

Certain names stand out in history – Michaelangelo, Leonardo da Vinci, Christopher Wren and many others worked on very special and prestigious products, though there have always been lesser known artists and craftsmen working in and around local towns and villages throughout the world.

Today, because our lifestyles have become more specialised, we talk about architects, fashion designers and product designers. Although these people work in different media and to different scales, they are all concerned with *designing* and *making*. The products of their work are found in our homes and communities, although, unlike the great designers of the past, most of our modern masterpieces of design are made by machine rather than crafted by hand.

The turning point was the Industrial Revolution of the eighteenth and nineteenth centuries: the birthplace of modern design methods. The Industrial Revolution changed the shape and form of objects and more and more they were made by machine. This process, once started, steadily evolved to the present methods of production, often relying on sophisticated technologies and modern materials.

The first section of this book traces the changing nature of design and, more importantly, looks at the consequences of design on people's lifestyles.

An Anglian helmet circa AD 750.

The interior of a Viking household from the Jorvik centre in York.

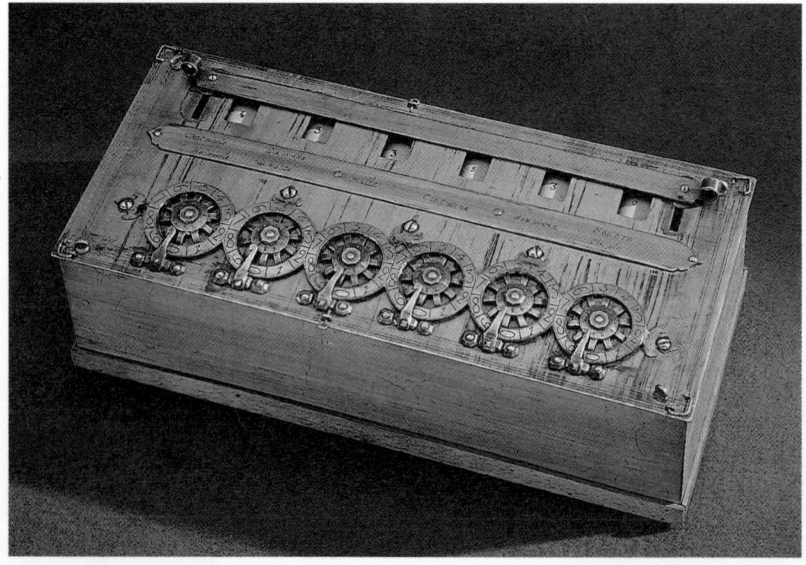

A Pascal calculating machine.

Periods of design

If we try to place work into particular periods of design, the following three categories may be useful, although exceptions to the rule always exist.

Craft oriented design

These are usually the products of a pre-industrial society where production is limited to the output of individual craftsmen using muscle power and hand tools.

The modern design process

The products of an industrial society based on the factory system using mechanisation and mass-production techniques.

Hi-tech design

The products of the new technological revolution. Computers may be used to aid design and manufacture, and certain parts of the production process may be semi- or fully automated.

The Pompidou centre of Art and Culture in Paris.

The Eiffel Tower was built for the World Fair of 1889 to see how tall a structure could be made from steel. It is 320 metres high.

Mothercare carry cot and transporter.

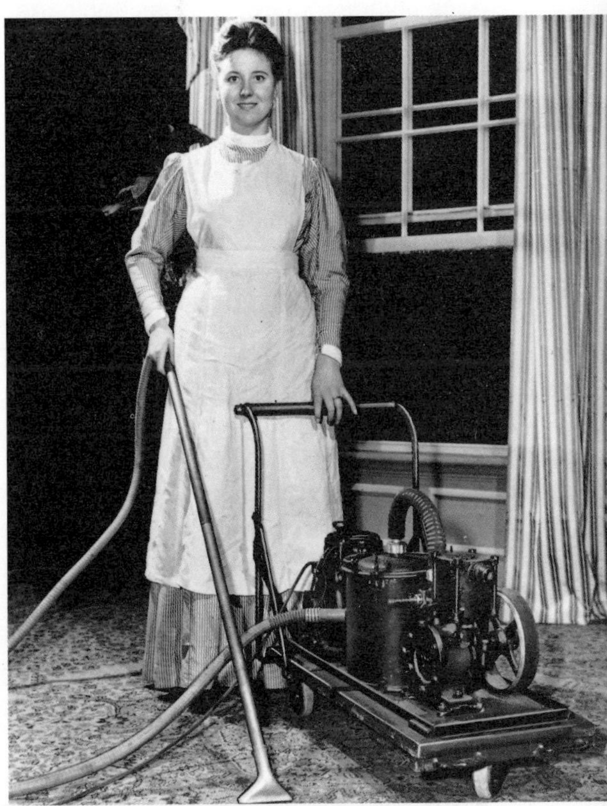

The 'Maid of All Work' vacuum cleaner was built by the British Vacuum Cleaner Company about 1914.

> *From which periods of design might the examples on this page belong?*

Craft oriented design

There are certain features which make these items stand out as different from many of the items we produce today. These features include:

The shape and form of products developed over a long period of time. For example, the barrel with straight sides and wooden hoops appears on Egyptian tomb paintings as early as 2690 BC. Yet with very little change and development it was being traditionally crafted by some cooperages for brewers right up to the 1950s.

Artist Mike Nicholls captures the atmosphere of the old country crafts in his paintings.

In the world of the artist/craftsmen, the designer and maker were very often the same person. The village blacksmith was much more than a farrier. He was very often the main metalworker in the area, taking on commissions to produce fittings for farm wagons and carts, as well as ornamental work such as screens, garden furniture, gates, fences and fire irons. He served the whole community; nobility, the Church and the local villagers.

The skills and knowledge acquired were passed on by word and example from one generation to the next. Very little, if anything, was ever written down.

The Rutland farm wagon now in the county museum at Oakham is one of the last remaining wagons in the region.

George Sturt was the son of a village wheelwright, who left the family business to teach. Returning to the wheelwrights' shop in 1884 he explains this transmission of knowledge:

"It was set out in no book. It was not scientific. I never met a man who professed any other than an empirical acquaintance with the waggon-builders lore. My own case was typical. I knew that the hindwheels had to be five feet two inches high, and the fore wheels four feet two; that the 'sides' must be cut from the best four inch heart of the oak and so on. This sort of thing I knew, and in vast detail in course of time; but I seldom knew why. And this is how most other men knew. The lore was a tangled network of country prejudices, whose reasons were known in some respects here, in others there, and so on. In farm-yard, in tap-room, at market, the details were discussed over and over again; they were gathered together for rememberance in village workshops; carters, smiths, farmers, wheelmakers, in thousands handed on his own little bit of understanding, passing it on to his son or the wheelwright of the day linking up the centuries. But for the most part the details were but dimly understood; the whole body of knowledge was a mystery, a piece of folk knowledge, residing in the folk collectively, but never wholly in any individual."

Extract from The Wheelwrights Shop *by George Sturt.*

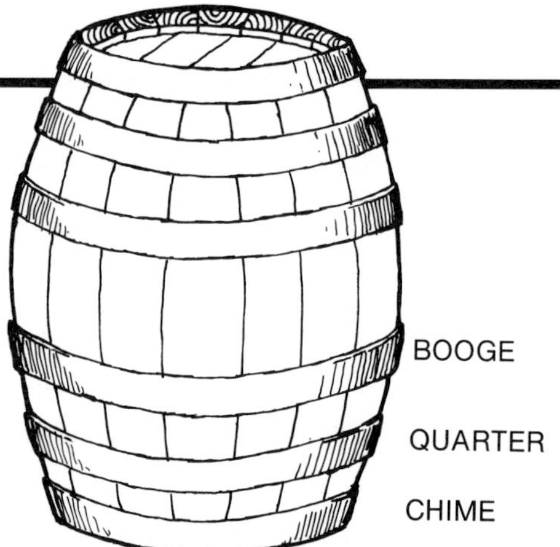

The cooper's craft

The cooper mainly used oak, beech and chestnut for water, milk, butter or cheese barrels where care had to be taken in case the wood gave any taste to the contents. The wood used for the staves had to be seasoned for between 2 and 5 years. Before filling an oak cask with beer it needed to be soaked in a solution of salt and sodium bicarbonate to counteract the acid taste of tannin from the timber.

The development of the barrel was just as important as that of the wheel. Why? Because barrels were extremely strong, with hoops binding the joints into a form of double arch; because they were themselves a wheel, a means of movement at a time when power was dependent on the muscles of man, and because certain goods kept much better in a barrel.

Without containers such as barrels, most goods would not have been transported. Few inventions have prompted such demand over so long a period of time.

Nineteenth century farm dairy. There was little use of machines, the equipment was mainly wooden and consisted of pails, bowls, churns, and small utensils for butter making, and cheese vats and presses for cheese production.

Even the early electrical domestic appliances such as the Beatty wooden tub electrical washing machine with power wringer, show how their design had been influenced by the cooper (circa 1916).

What examples can you find of people working today in the style of the traditional craftsmen, producing original articles of a limited number?

For more information about the work of practising Artists and Craftsmen contact:
The Crafts Council,
12 Waterloo Place,
London SW1.

The British Craft Centre,
43 Earlham Street,
London WC2.

The craftsmen designer

Thomas Chippendale (1718–1779) was without doubt one of the finest craftsmen that England has produced. He was a master wood carver who was at the same time an excellent cabinet maker. In addition he had an inventive mind. This combination, together with his design ability, contributed to his success. He published his design drawings in a 'catalogue' which he circulated to wealthy potential customers. Chippendale and his craftsmen then made the furniture when orders or 'commissions' were received.

Chippendale armchair (1765) pierced and carved back with cabriole legs, very similar to the design drawing below (Victoria and Albert Museum).

A reprint from the third edition of The Gentleman and Cabinet-Maker's Director *published by Thomas Chippendale in 1762.*

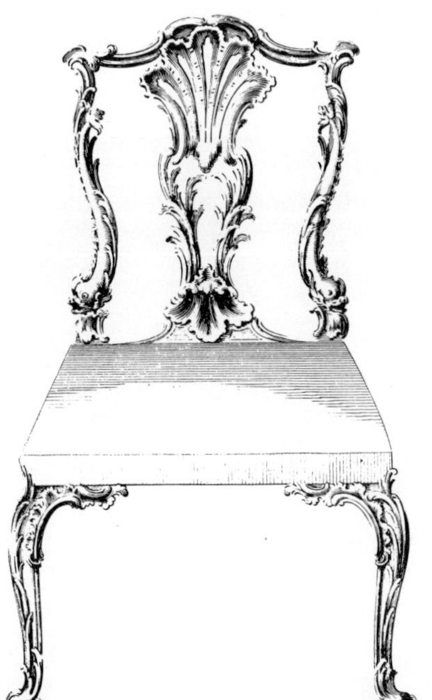

The modern design process

Towards the end of the eighteenth century developments were taking place in the organisation of industry which were to transform the role of the craftsman and the shape and form of future products, as well as the lives of the people engaged in the work. Slowly the features of this new industrial system were to emerge:

- Many craftsmen were gathered together in factories, usually under the pay of an owner who provided the necessary financial investment to set up initial production.
- The craftsmen often became responsible for producing only a part of the overall product and their tasks became more specialised. This became known as *division of labour*.
- As tasks became more specialised, machines were introduced to improve efficiency, and replace muscle power. This became known as *mechanisation*.

The new industrial factories became more organised and management methods tended to separate the activities of designing and making in order to increase efficiency.

One of the consequences of this separation was that drawings needed to be formalised before designs were put into production. This allowed the designer to 'communicate' what needed to be made to the craftsmen, and it also allowed new ideas to be devised and tested before costly manufacturing expenses were incurred.

Whilst the Industrial Revolution may have begun amidst the rolling hills and valleys around Ironbridge, its full impact was to be found in the larger towns and cities. The landscape became dominated by chimneys, factories, and 'dark satanic mills'. Men, women and children worked long hours in poor conditions for very little reward. The quote on page 15 illustrates some of these early developments.

Coalport china was made here until 1926 when the company moved to Staffordshire. The old works have now been restored to a museum of china, showing the technique of manufacture and the products of Coalport.

Cast in 1779, this was the world's first cast-iron bridge. It is now the focal point of the gorge.

The effects of the Industrial Revolution

Some dates may illustrate the rapid industrial growth which formed a world capable, a century later, of creating the Modern Movement. As England was leading in the Industrial Revolution nearly all these early dates are English. In 1709, Abraham Darby made cast iron with coke instead of wood . . . about 1810 the decisive improvements in the use of the blast-furnace took place (Aubertot) . . . J. Watt invented the steam-engine with separate condenser (1765) . . . and the railway engine was invented in 1825. The principal dates in the spinning and weaving industries are . . . 1733 fly-shuttle (J. Kay), 1760 shuttle drop box (R. Kay), 1764–7 spinning jenny (Hargreaves), 1769–75 water frame for spinning (Arkwright), 1774–9 spinning mule (Crompton), 1785 power loom (Cartwright), 1799 Jacquard loom.

The immediate consequence of this precipitous development was a sudden increase in production . . . leading to an equally fast increase in population. Towns grew up . . . new markets had to be satisfied, an even bigger production was demanded, and inventiveness was stimulated.

In the midst of this breathless race, no time was left to refine all those innumerable innovations which swamped producer and consumer. With the extinction of the medieval craftsman, the shape and appearance of all products were left to the uneducated manufacturer. Designers of some standing had not penetrated into industry, artists kept aloof, and the workman had no say in artistic matters. Work was bleaker than ever before in European history. Working hours were between twelve and fourteen, doors and windows in factories were kept locked. Children were employed from their fifth or sixth year on. Their hours of work were reduced in 1802, after long struggles, to twelve hours a day. In 1833, 61,000 men, 65,000 women, and 84,000 children under eighteen years of age worked in cotton mills. In mines no inquiries into accidents were held before 1814.'

From *The Pioneers of Modern Design* by Nikolaus Pevsner

'Coalbrookdale by Night' painted in 1801 by Philip James de Loutherbourg RA, captures some the early industrial atmosphere of the Ironbridge gorge.

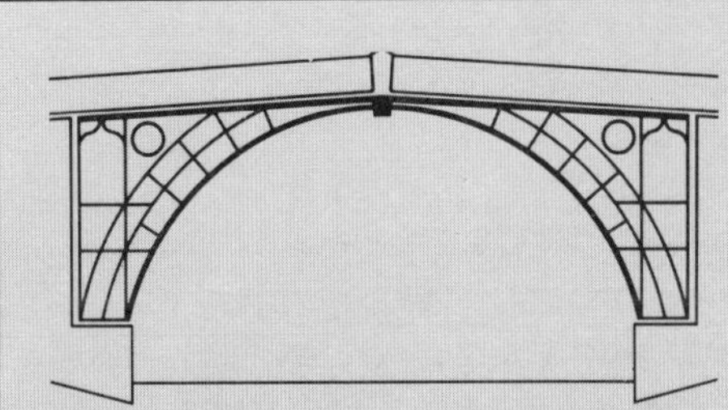

Ironbridge Gorge Museum

The Ironbridge Gorge Museum

Situated in the Severn valley in Shropshire and centred on the areas of Coalbrookdale, Coalport and Ironbridge, this is an outstandingly important area where many of the key events which shaped the world's first Industrial Revolution took place.
Contact:

Ironbridge Gorge Museum,
Ironbridge,
Telford,
Shropshire TF8 7AW.

The Great Exhibition

By the middle of the nineteenth century Victorian industrialists were anxious to promote trade on an international scale. In 1851 Prince Albert, along with Sir Henry Cole and his group of commissioners, planned 'The Great Exhibition of the works of industry of all Nations'. This festival of industry was to include every process of manufacture then known.

The Exhibition was open for 141 days between 1 May and 14 October, 1851. It attracted over 6 million visitors and made a profit of £86,000. The exhibits were varied and unusual, ranging from 'cuffs, hand-spun and knitted from the wool of French poodle dogs' to 'hats made from the leaf of the cabbage-tree by Australian prisoners'!

Sportsman's knife with eighty blades and instruments. By J. Rodgers and Sons, from the 1851 Exhibition catalogue.

View of the Eastern or Foreign Knave looking west, from a rare contemporary photograph in the Victoria and Albert Museum of the Great Exhibition.

The Great Exhibition building was taken down during the summer of 1852 and re-built in a much modified form in Sydenham. Opened by the queen in 1854 it was burnt to the ground on 30 November 1936.

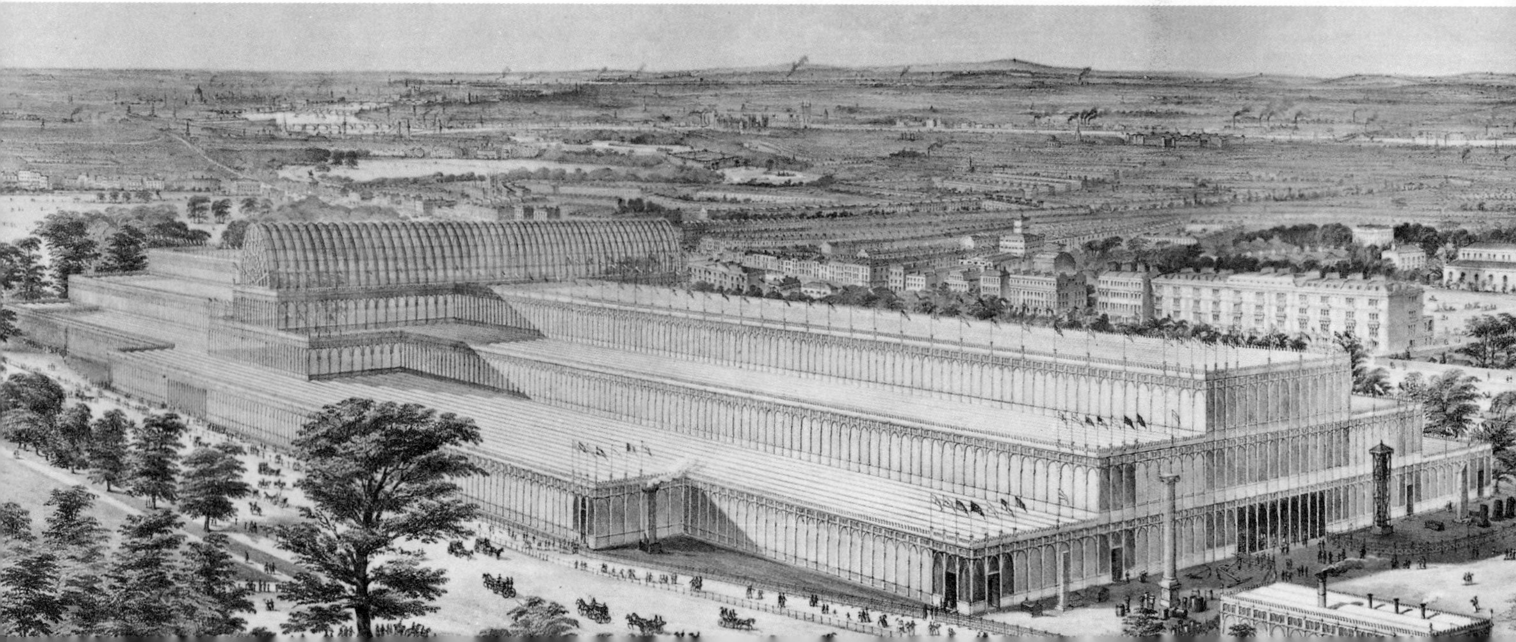

Lifestyles in the cities

Children: 'Our own family was in the slum, but not, we felt, of it; we had "connections". Father, besides, was a skilled mechanic. . . . At the age of eight, he took up education and, twelve months later, put it down, despite the new fangled compulsion Act, to find, his mother said "summat a sight better to do at the blacksmiths".'

'As a child my mother had been something of a prodigy and was hawked from one local school to another to display her talents; but, her father dying, she got work, at the age of nine, helping in a weaving shed.' (From *The Classic Slum* by Robert Roberts)

Life in the cities for Edwardian slum children.

Women: Industrialisation had a profound influence upon the role of women and work. Prior to the Industrial Revolution women either worked on the land or were tied to the home, where they looked after the family, or in certain districts such as the textile areas of Lancashire and Yorkshire were part of a home-based method of production.

The concentration of work into factories took women away from the home and they became an essential part of the industrial workforce. Once begun this trend continued, with the war periods further accelerating the numbers of women in industry.

As the textile industry of Lancashire and Yorkshire became mechanised, women became an essential part of the work-force.

Reactions to the industrial revolution

Looking back . . .

William Morris (1834–96)

William Morris's sketch of his wife Jane, who he believed was the ideal of pre-Raphaelite theories of feminine perfection.

Many of the Morris designs for wallpaper and tiles used nature as a source. The trellis print above is typical.

Prince Albert's Great Exhibition of 1851 launched Britain as the 'workshop of the world', and whilst the exhibits were varied and indeed inventive, the aesthetic quality of the products was criticised as being very poor. Unfortunately, mechanisation had undermined the visual quality of the products rather than adding to it. This was mainly because production methods had developed at such a rate that output was the overriding factor and little time and effort was put into refining the products.

The reaction of many artists and designers to this vast output of tasteless artefacts was to reject totally industry and the social evils it represented. Individuals such as *Pugin, Ruskin* and *Morris* who were both intellectuals and artists attempted to set up an alternative method of manufacture based on skills and techniques where the dignity of the craftsman would be restored to the level it had been prior to the machine. This reaction became known as 'The Arts and Crafts Movement' and whilst its motives were praiseworthy, in practice its members looked back into the past for inspiration, rather than into the future. They failed to take on the challenge of the machine and the opportunities this offered for good quality mass produced goods.

By the end of the nineteenth century there was confusion and little realisation of the role of art and design in British industry. Our artists and designers stood aloof from industry and mass production: a mixture of good taste, social criticism, nostalgia and fear of the future limited their minds and restricted their vision.

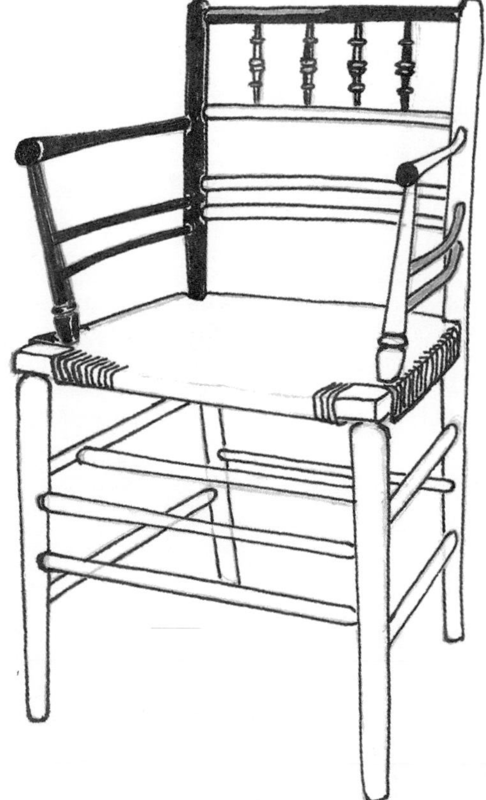
Sussex chair made by Morris and Company in 1865 (ebonised beech with rush seat).

Looking forward . . .
The Bauhaus and the development of a 'modern' style

In Britain, art and industry seemed to be pulling in opposite directions, while in Germany an organisation was set up in 1907 called the 'Deutscher Werkbund' with the specific aim of trying to unite artists, craftsmen and manufacturers to improve standards of design. As a result German schools of Art and Design began to develop the idea of designing for industry, harnessing the powers of production whilst trying to develop a style for a modern age – a machine age.

Gropius's design for the Fagus factory in 1911 used glass and steel as it had not been used before. In order to emphasise the light and airy feel to the building there were no supports in the corners, as can be seen from the illustration.

Amidst this climate of opinion emerged an architect, Walter Gropius, who was to take over the school at Weimar in 1919. His philosophy was to develop an all-embracing course for architects and designers which would deal with all aspects of the home. He renamed his school Das Staatliches Bauhaus (House of Building), soon shortened to *Bauhaus*.

Gropius taught that objects should function well and that their beauty should not rely on additional decoration, but that a shape should be expressive of its purpose and the technology that produced it.

The Bauhaus was one of the first centres of design that took the machine seriously. As Gillian Naylor in her book *The Bauhaus* explains:

> '. . . the school set out in a resurgence of optimism and idealism after the First World War, to train a generation of architects and designers to accept and anticipate the demands of the twentieth century, and to use all its resources, scientific, intellectual and aesthetic, to create an environment that would satisfy man's spiritual as well as material needs.'

Walter Gropius (right) visiting the Design Centre in London prior to its opening in 1956. Gordon Russell, then chairman of the Council of Industrial Design, is on the left.

In 1933 the Bauhaus was closed down by the Nazis. However, its influence has become legendary in developing a style and trend that is true to materials, simple and elegant.

The sofa shown below was designed by Le Corbusier in 1928 and is still being produced today by an Italian company.

First chair using tubular steel (Marcel Breuer 1925).

Products of an industrial society

The Ford motor car

As methods of production steadily increased and the twentieth century arrived, it gradually became clear to certain manufacturers that it was as important to look into the techniques of production as it was to improve manufactured goods.

Henry Ford had been building cars since 1897 and, convinced that the car was here to stay, he began to think about ways in which he could produce a reliable and reasonably-priced vehicle which might 'change motoring from a rich-man's hobby to an average man's pastime'.In 1907 he began designing such a vehicle and by 1910 it was in production at the company's new Highland Park plant in Michigan, USA.

To improve output and increase worker efficiency, Ford subdivided work tasks, delivered parts to workers, and finally devised a moving assembly line.

The results were dramatic. Initially it took 12 hours and 28 minutes to assemble a Model T. The time was cut to 5 hours and 28 minutes, and then to 93 minutes. Eventually Model T's were rolling off the production line at one every 10 seconds of the working day. Increased efficiency also reduced the price: in 1910 the Model 'T' touring car cost $950; six years later it cost only $360!

These price cuts created such tremendous demand that when production of the Model 'T' ended in 1927, over 15 million cars had been sold.

Flywheel and magneto assembly . . .

Fitting fuel tanks . . .

Testing the chassis . . .

Hi-tech design

Most industries followed in the footsteps of the early production engineers like Henry Ford. In particular there was a significant increase in mechanisation. However, the human contribution to the production line was essential as the worker had to control and sense the quality of manufacture throughout production. The disadvantage of this set-up was that the quality of the finished goods was only as high as the standards of the people operating the line.

What is the difference between mechanisation and automation?

As technological developments have advanced, new methods have emerged which can replace many of our human senses. In particular, electronic components have evolved which can sense light or heat, can count rapidly or accurately measure parts of components. Consequently, *automation* is with us, and the human senses are replaced by electronic, pneumatic or mechanical devices which can act upon information received either to rectify production problems or to control output quantity and quality.

In some machine tool factories in Japan, efficiency is higher than any other part of the world. Automated robots not only manufacture the tools but also service and repair any part of the automated set-up which may break down.

An essential part of this technological revolution is the use of computers to watch over and control automated plants. Workers replaced by these systems must either learn new skills or face redundancy.

The long term implications of these developments are only just emerging. However, patterns of work and employment prospects are changing rapidly. Traditional crafts such as typesetting and printing are being replaced by word-processors and computer controlled newspaper output. Information technology is infiltrating education, banking, administration and all forms of commercial life at an unprecedented pace.

We are in the throes of a new technological revolution offering fresh challenges on the one hand, but threatening to change the face of society even more radically than the first industrial revolution.

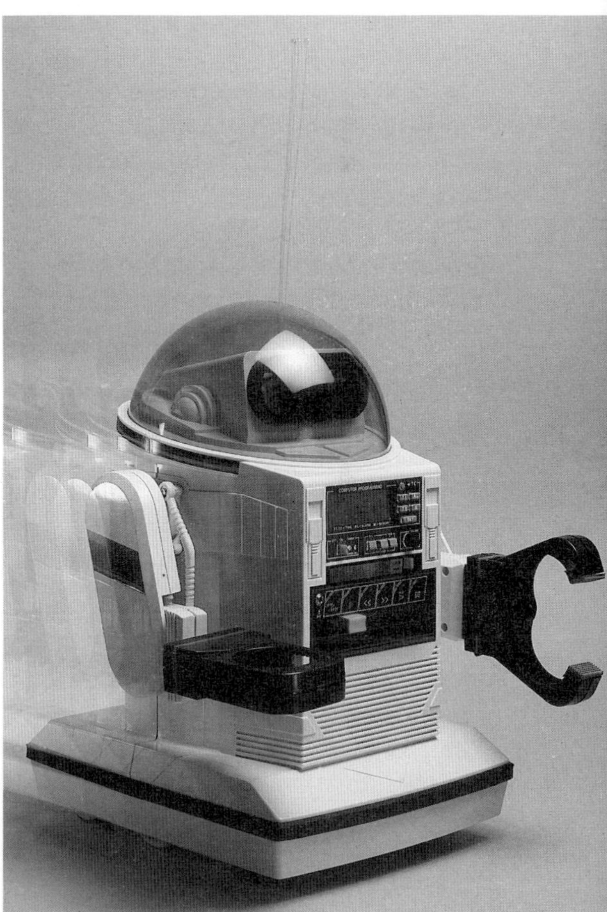

Is Tomy, the small servant robot, a forerunner of the domestic robot of the future?

What are the consequences of the increased use of automation in industry?

Can you give examples of industries in which automated production lines have replaced skilled workers?

How 'design' may influence our lifestyle

There are many examples of the way design influences our lives today. In this section we will look at four specific examples.

1 Advertising
2 Fashion and 'obsolescence'
3 Consumerism
4 The craft approach to design

One of these topics may form the basis for your own personal study, or you may find other examples of how the 'man-made' or 'designed' world influences our lifestyles.

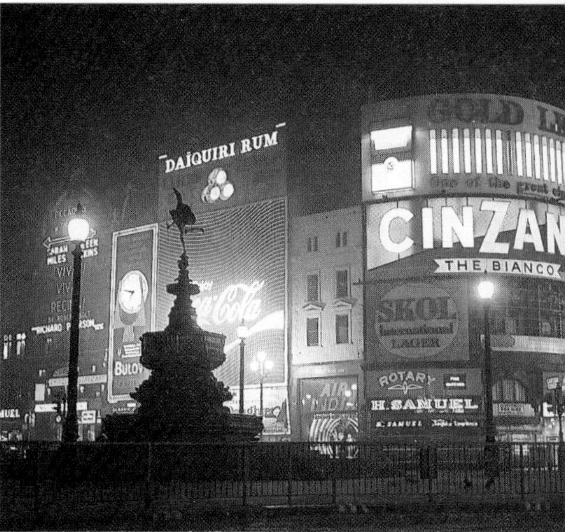

Advertising – so much a part of our surroundings

Advertising

The world of advertising is really concerned with buying and selling, regardless of whether the advert is a simple 'classified' placed in your local newspaper or an expensive commercial produced for television.

Advertising may influence us in one of several ways:

- We may be designing the advert.
- We may be designing a product or service which will require advertising skill to promote and sell it.
- We may be the target of advertisers as potential customers.

Advertising surrounds us, whether we are aware of this or not. Our senses are constantly bombarded with 'catchy slogans' and visual images are carefully designed to encourage us to buy products and services. Advertising today is a multi-million pound industry which promotes anything from frozen peas to political parties, from continental holidays to public corporations and from soap powders to savings accounts.

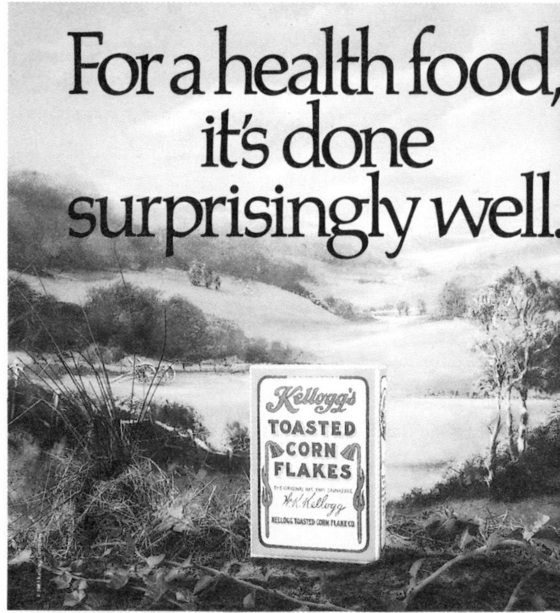

For a health food, it's done surprisingly well.
Kellogg's
TOASTED CORN FLAKES
KELLOGG TOASTED CORN FLAKE CO.
William K. Kellogg first started to produce cereal foods in ready-to-eat form in 18
He firmly believed that people accustomed to a heavy diet would benefit from a lighter, more easily digestible food.
Eventually, as a result of his long dietary research, he was able to gain a patent on "flaked cereals and process of preparing same."
The result was Kellogg's Corn Flakes.
The rest is history.
The best to you. Since 1894.

The power of persuasion

Advertising often uses very clever forms of persuasion to create the right image for the product, trying to make us believe that by acquiring these products we will improve our status. Consequently, *persuasive advertising* is the most common form of advertising, urging the consumer to buy new products and services as well as promoting and maintaining existing sales.

Building an image around a product is an important part of persuasive advertising. 'Snob-appeal', 'sex appeal', 'nostalgia' and 'comedy' are techniques which advertisers use to promote a desirable image and make us, the consumers, look more favourably on their products.

What are the positive economic benefits which advertising bestows on society

Informative advertising

These types of adverts are usually designed to sell long-term and often expensive purchases such as cars, central heating, double glazing, fitted kitchens or computers. They often appear in magazines and newspapers where they can be surrounded by a great deal of technical information and data. They also use persuasive methods of advertising: the consumer will be encouraged to find out more by the inclusion of a customer liaison form, with the promise of a free brochure or the visit of a salesperson.

Commercial advertising

This is where 'industry' tries to sell its raw materials, products or services to other sectors of industry. Sales in this sector of the market are often generated by trade fairs and specialist exhibitions at places such as the National Exhibition Centre in Birmingham, as well as trade publications and journals.

Corporate advertising

Large companies like to promote a favourable image of themselves by explaining either their technical successes or perhaps their interest in conservation. Oil companies are good examples of multi-national corporations who spend vast amounts of money convincing us of their value and good intention, and the benefits they bestow on the community.

What images are the advertisers trying to create in the examples on this page?

The emphasis is on persuading people to use the design potential of vinyl flooring in living rooms, rather than confining it to kitchens and bathrooms. Marley Floors of Lenham, Kent, the UK's largest manufacturer of resilient floorings for the retail and contract markets, get the message over with style and panache, with the slogan: 'Nothing Touches A Marley Floor', to illustrate 2m and 3m wide 'Sorrento' from the company's Supasoft range.

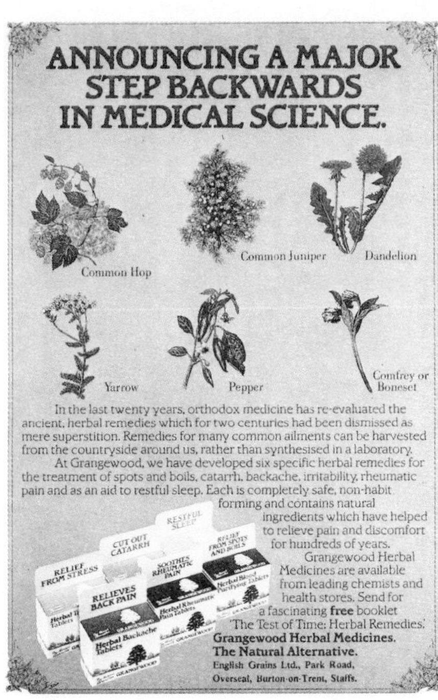

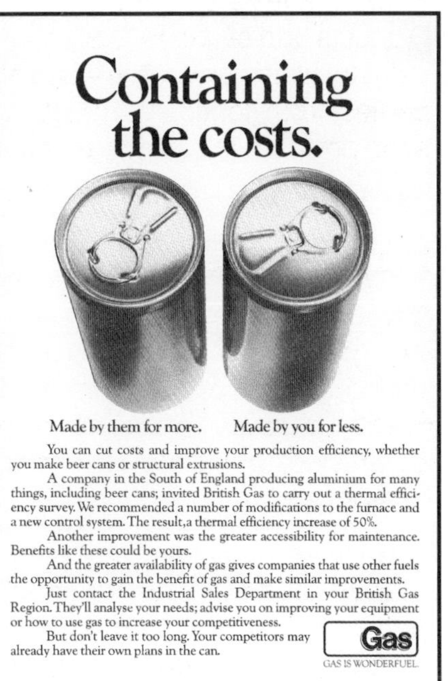

Government advertising

This type of advertising is paid for by the government and can include Health Education Council Publicity, Road Safety Campaigns, DHSS services and grants and many other informative types of promotional material. During times of war governments may use 'propaganda' to promote their ideas and beliefs.

Classified advertising

If you wanted to sell something 'second-hand' such as a bicycle, gas cooker, or computer, you may place an advert in the classified section of your local paper. However, many other forms of advertising and announcements appear in the classified section of newspapers. Can you identify them? Why is classified advertising so popular?

Financial advertising

Banks and Building Societies spend a great deal of time and money on trying to attract our savings and investments. They sometimes use persuasive forms of advertising to build up their 'image', offering the consumer security, extra interest and special terms.

TOTAL ADVERTISING EXPENDITURE BY MEDIA (£m) 1982–85

Media	*1982*	*%*	*1983*	*%*	*1984*	*%*	*1985*	*%*
Television	928	29.7	1109	31.0	1245	30.7	1376	31.0
Poster and transport	124	4.0	137	3.8	150	3.7	164	3.7
Cinema	18	0.6	16	0.4	16	0.4	18	0.4
Radio	70	2.2	81	2.3	86	2.1	82	1.8
National newspapers	515	16.5	584	16.3	678	16.7	747	16.8
Regional newspapers	737	23.6	817	22.8	921	22.7	1003	22.5
Magazines and periodicals	209	6.7	224	6.3	250	6.2	253	5.7
Business and professional	247	7.9	276	7.7	311	7.7	344	7.7
Directories	124	4.0	154	4.3	182	4.5	209	4.7
Press production costs	154	4.9	181	5.1	216	5.3	245	5.5

Source: Advertising Statistics Yearbook 1986

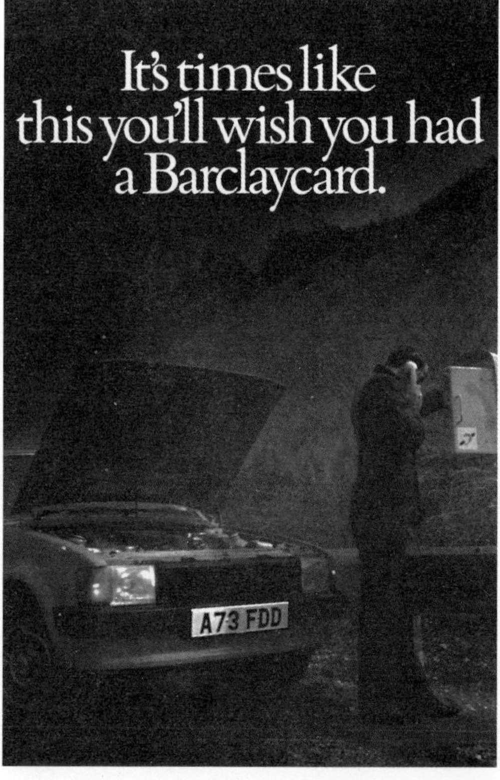

'Advertising encourages us to buy things we don't really want and can't really afford'

Do you agree with this statement?

What is the difference between advertising and propaganda?

Perhaps your parents or grandparents can tell you about examples of propaganda used during the Second World War.

Can you think of modern examples of propaganda?

'All adverts should be legal, decent, honest and truthful.'

The quote above is an extract from the British Code of Advertising Practice, and implies that sometimes adverts can be misleading, because they do not all come up to this standard.

In this competitive industry for an advert to be successful, it should:

- attract attention
- command interest
- create the desire for purchase
- inspire the conviction of the product or service to the consumer
- provoke the consumer to purchase the product or service.

In such a high risk business adverts may mislead and make promises that the products and services cannot fulfil. This may be done intentionally or accidentally.

Whatever the intent the consumer must be protected. The Advertising Standards Authority is the industry's own self-regulating body which maintains a code of practice as well as enquiring into complaints from the public. Each month the ASA receives hundreds of complaints, and where there are grounds for complaint an investigation takes place. The results of these are then printed in the association's monthly case reports as below.

If an advertisement is wrong we're here to put it right.

If you see an advertisement in the press, in print, on posters or in the cinema which you find unacceptable, write to us at the address below.

The Advertising Standards Authority.

ASA Ltd, Dept 3
Brook House, Torrington Place,
London WC1E 7HN

Examples of the ASA complaints procedure.

HEARING AIDS OF SWITZERLAND
165 Hamilton Road
Taunton
Somerset TA1 2EU

Complaint from: North Devon

Basis of Complaint: A member of the public challenged the claim in a local press advertisement for hearing aids that users would be "... free from disturbing noises". (Section II.4.1)

Conclusion: Complaint upheld. The Authority was concerned that the advertisers did not submit substantiation, but noted that the claim would be deleted from future advertisements.

BRITISH AIRWAYS
Speedbird House
Heathrow Airport (London)
Hounslow TW6 2JA

Agency: Saatchi & Saatchi Compton Ltd

(Previous complaints upheld during last 12 months: 4)

Complaint from: Linlithgow, Scotland

Basis of Complaint: A member of the public objected to a national press advertisement claiming "Edinburgh–Dusseldorf direct". The complainant maintained that the flights went via Birmingham where passengers were obliged to leave and then re-board the aircraft for emigration and customs purposes. He considered that this should have been made clear. (Section II.3; II.4.2)

Conclusion: Complaint upheld. The advertisers stated that flights which had one or more stops but used the same flight number throughout and involved no transfer of aircraft or luggage, were commonly known within the air travel industry as "direct" flights. The Authority accepted that this was generally the case but considered that in the context of an Edinburgh–Dusseldorf "direct" flight readers would not expect to travel via Birmingham. The advertisers were requested to clarify the situation in future advertising material.

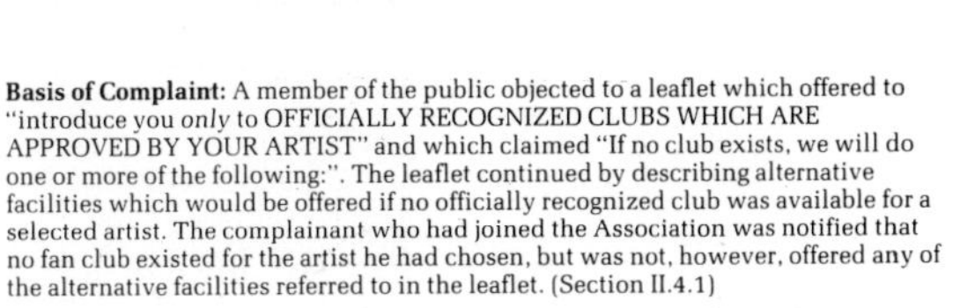

INTERNATIONAL ASSOCIATION OF FAN CLUBS
478 Fulham Road
London SW6 1BY

Complaint from: Aintree, Liverpool

Basis of Complaint: A member of the public objected to a leaflet which offered to "introduce you *only* to OFFICIALLY RECOGNIZED CLUBS WHICH ARE APPROVED BY YOUR ARTIST" and which claimed "If no club exists, we will do one or more of the following:". The leaflet continued by describing alternative facilities which would be offered if no officially recognized club was available for a selected artist. The complainant who had joined the Association was notified that no fan club existed for the artist he had chosen, but was not, however, offered any of the alternative facilities referred to in the leaflet. (Section II.4.1)

Conclusion: Complaint upheld. The advertisers failed to comment on the circumstances of the complaint. The Authority was notified that the advertisers had ceased to trade.

DO SOME ADVERTISERS GO TOO FAR TO ATTRACT YOUR ATTENTION?

Every week many hundreds of thousands of advertisements appear for the first time.

Some stand out from the multitude by virtue of their relevance, wit or charm.

Others for less creditable reasons.

It is our job as the Advertising Standards Authority to look into any serious malpractices, and make sure they don't happen again.

HOW FAR CAN AN ADVERTISER GO?

This is a vexed question because sometimes there is a very fine line between what is above board and what is below the belt.

One rule in our Code states, 'Advertisements should contain nothing which is likely, in the light of generally prevailing standards of decency and propriety, to cause grave or widespread offence.'

There is no doubt at all what we would do with an ad for a 'video nasty' that depicted someone being eaten alive.

But what about a car advertisement which addressed the reader as 'Ye of little faith'?

A few people might regard it as offensive, but not, we think, the majority.

Although the phrase is of biblical origin, it has slipped into common usage as a metaphor for the sceptical.

PREVENTING UNDERHAND TACTICS.

Another rule states, 'Advertisements should not without justifiable reason play on fear.' What is 'justifiable', and what isn't?

Again we take the view we think the majority would.

We might regard an ad acceptable if it showed how a widow and her children were able to survive on the proceeds of her deceased husband's life assurance.

While offering an answer to a frightening problem it does not in itself induce fear.

But suppose a security firm sent a leaflet through the post that said 'I'm a burglar, and I can get into your house as easily as this leaflet.'

This could terrify an old person living alone, and we would do all we could to put a stop to it.

WHO CAN WE THROW THE BOOK AT?

The British Code of Advertising Practice covers newspapers, magazines, cinema commercials, posters, brochures, leaflets, circulars posted to you, and now commercials on video tapes.

It does not cover TV and radio advertising.

Though the rules are very similar, they are administered by the Independent Broadcasting Authority.

WHY WE ASK YOU TO GRAB A PEN.

Unfortunately some advertisers are unaware of the Code, and breach the rules unwittingly.

Others forget, bend or deliberately ignore the rules.

That is why we keep a continuous check on advertising.

But because of the sheer volume we cannot monitor every advertiser all the time.

So we encourage the public to help by telling us about advertisements they think ought not to have appeared.

Last year over 7,500 people wrote to us.

WHAT WE DO TO THE BULLY BOYS.

If we decide there has been a breach of any rules we ask the advertiser to amend the advertisement.

If he cannot, or refuses, we ask him to withdraw it completely.

Nearly all agree without further argument.

In any case we inform the publishers, who will not knowingly accept any ad which we have decided contravenes the Code.

If the advertiser refuses to withdraw the advertisement he will find it hard if not impossible to have it published.

CAN ADVERTISERS PUSH US AROUND.

The ASA was not created by law and has no legal powers.

Not unnaturally some people are sceptical about its effectiveness.

In fact the ASA was set up by the advertising business to make sure the system of self control genuinely worked in the public interest.

For this to be credible, the ASA has to be totally independent of the business.

Neither the chairman nor the majority of ASA council members is allowed to have any involvement in advertising.

Though administrative costs are met by a levy on the business, no advertiser has any influence over ASA decisions.

Advertisers are aware it is as much in their interests as the public's to uphold advertising standards.

If you would like to know more about the ASA and the rules it seeks to enforce you can write to us at the address below for an abridged copy of the Code.

The Advertising Standards Authority.
If an advertisement is wrong, we're here to put it right.

ASA Ltd, Brook House,
Torrington Place, London WC1E 7HN.

Fashion & obsolescence

'Buy more, consume more, throw-away more . . . but what about our vanishing resources?'

To generate sales and profits, new markets need to be created and new products must be introduced to the consumer. We have already seen how advertising can play an important part in this exercise. Consumers must also be made to believe that new products are an improvement upon what they have already. Often clever and sometimes unscrupulous marketing tries to manipulate our feelings about how goods can improve our image and lifestyle, by encouraging us to feel unhappy with what we already have.

The term *obsolescence* was used by Vance Packard in his book *The Waste Maker*, published in 1960. He described the situation in America where products had been prematurely outdated by either the use of 'built-in' design weaknesses or marketing methods which created new products at such a rate that the status-conscious American public always felt 'out of date' unless they had the very latest product.

Built-in obsolescence. During the 1960s and '70s American car producers developed models with a limited life expectancy and poor corrosion treatment. This was coupled with the frequent introduction of cosmetic changes aimed at outdating models much more frequently. Whilst production levels stayed high and business was brisk for the manufacturers, it was very poor service for the customer. Gradually through increased awareness the consumer hit back, boycotting the 'rust-box, gas guzzlers' in favour of models with a longer life expectancy. The trend has now gone full circle with Volvo claiming a life expectancy of 17 years on some of their models.

A 17 YEAR-OLD VOLVO AND TWO OF ITS CONTEMPORARIES.

The Volvo has an average life expectancy of 17.9 years.

According to the Swedish government, who keep records, that's longer than any other car.

Longer than Mercedes. Longer than Volkswagen.

In fact, in Sweden, 47% of the Volvos registered in 1961 are still on the road.

Which makes them nineteen years old.

Of course, not everyone wants to keep a car that long, but a car that's built to last seventeen years or more has certain short-term advantages, too.

Check the re-sale value of a 6-year old Volvo and you'll begin to see our point.

A Volvo that cost £2,155 new in 1974 can still command £2,050. (Parker's Car Price Guide.)

And as you'd expect, a car that's built to last is also built well.

Every weld on the Volvo's body is strong enough to support the weight of the entire car.

The zinc coating we use is about 4 times thicker than that used by many other car makers.

(Which means 4 times more protection from rust.)

Our bumpers can soak up 3 mph knocks without damage to the bodywork.

And every working day, we take engines at random from the production line and give them 7 hours bench testing at full loads.

We even use twin fan belts to halve the risk of being caught with a broken one.

Not surprisingly, in survey after survey, the Volvo emerges as one of the most trouble-free cars on the road.

So whether you plan to keep your car for 2 years or 17, no car will keep better than a Volvo.

Please send me the 1980 edition of 'Volvo Facts'.
To: Volvo Concessionaires Ltd., London W13 9JQ.
Name
Address

VOLVO. A CAR WITH STANDARDS.

What examples can you think of where products have 'built-in obsolescence'?

With the increase in unemployment is 'built-in obsolescence' such a bad idea after all?

'Out with the typewriter, in with the word processor' obsolescence by technical improvement

As technologists develop new materials, processes and techniques of manufacture, improvements take place which outdate some of the products we take for granted. Many traditional fabrics have been replaced by synthetic materials with improved properties, particularly for sports and leisure wear.

In the area of electronics, changes take place so rapidly that often the consumer has great difficulty in keeping pace with these new technologies. The meteoric rise of the home computer in recent years is a good example of how technologies overtake one another at an alarming rate. Products have improved and prices have fallen: in 1978 the most competitively priced home computer was the Apple II selling at £995; by 1983 the Sinclair Spectrum with a comparable 16K memory was £99!

'Fashion, fashion, fashion'

As consumers we become aware of 'trends' or 'fashions' in clothes, furniture, electrical products, cars, colour schemes, or anything which may be promoted. Sometimes we may not be aware of the origin of these trends, though we do react to them, buying new trousers because this year they are perhaps narrower in the leg, or trying longer or shorter skirts, whichever happens to be 'in' at the present time.

Different youth cults play an important part in fashion, offering identity and acceptance within a particular group.

How many people have perfectly good clothes hanging up in wardrobes which they would not wear now, because they are 'old fashioned' even though they may only be a couple of years old? The clothing industry in particular uses our vanity to promote sales and profits.

What examples can you think of where products have become obsolete due to technical improvements?

Can you identify the present trends in youth culture and their influences upon fashion?

Consumerism

When we pay for a product or a service we become a 'consumer'. In today's complex world we often have to purchase sophisticated technical equipment, or require detailed and specialised services which we may not fully understand. How do you choose the best video recorder, or the most reliable washing machine when perhaps you have little, if any, understanding of how they work? Industrial designers are constantly developing and upgrading the technical specification of products from cassette recorders to microwave ovens. Accountants develop new ways of trying to stimulate sales by different types of credit arrangements, encouraging us to buy now and pay later.

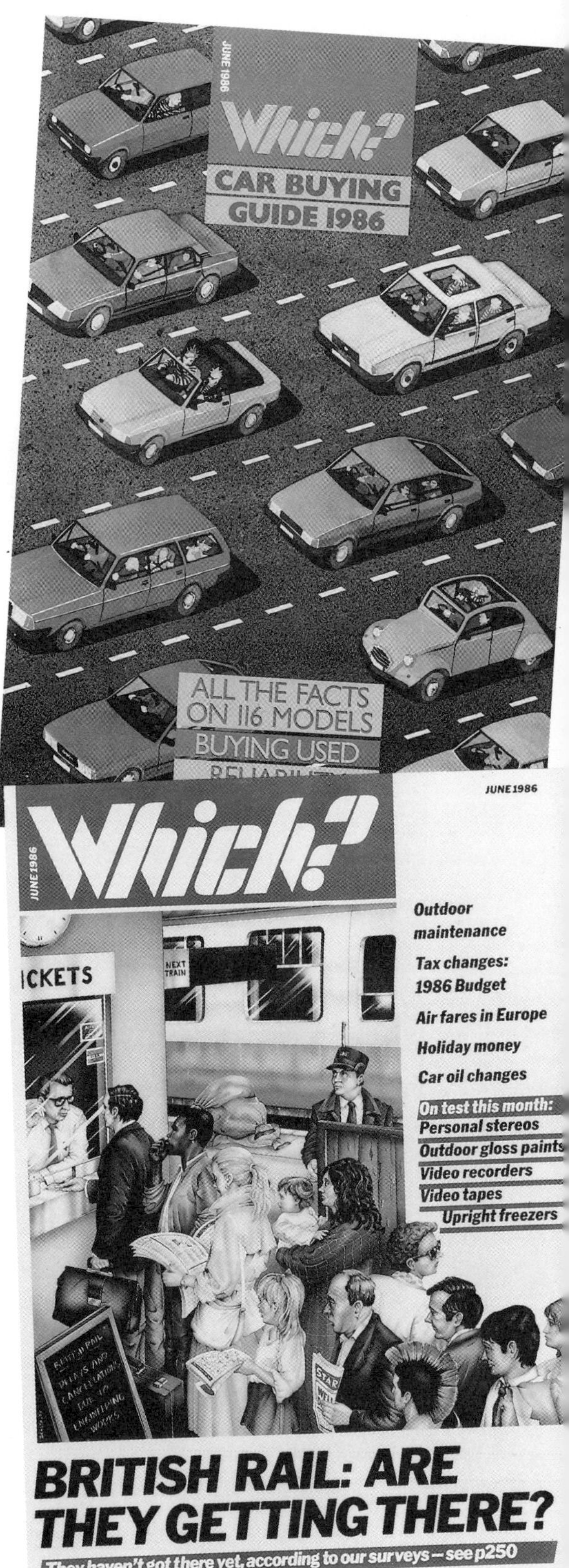

Making the right choice?

The best way to protect yourself from making a poor purchase is to try and gain as much information as you possibly can about the range of products on the market. Study the alternatives and try to decide which is going to be the most suitable for your needs. You will usually have a limited amount of money to spend and this will obviously restrict your choice. Above all you will be looking for 'value for money'. You can read reviews of products and services in magazines such as *Which?*

Which? magazine

Which? magazine is published monthly by an independent organisation called the 'Consumers' Association' which reports on household products and services. Reports in *Which?* test and compare products for 'performance', 'reliability', 'safety' 'ease of use', 'value for money', and always include current prices to help you make an informed choice. The aim of the magazine is to help you to find your own best buy, by giving you acts and impartial advice and saving you the time, trouble and money of undertaking the research yourself.

Most public libraries keep back copies of 'Which?' *magazine and they will help you find reports for the particular goods or services you may be interested in.*

'Which?' *magazines are not sold through your local newsagents but are sold through subscription. Contact:*
Consumer Association,
Subscription Dept.,
Castlemead,
Gascoyne Way,
Hertford SG14 1YB.

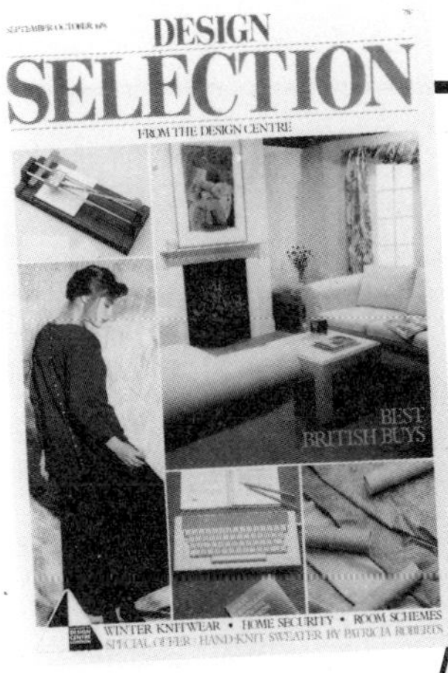

The Design Council

The Design Council is a Government funded body set up to promote the improvement of design in the products of British Industry. The Council does this by:

- Advising companies on the solution to particular design problems.
- Publishing information on well designed British goods. This includes the awarding of The Design Centre Label to those products which comply with the relevant British Standards and Safety regulations as well as having an overall high standard of functional and visual appeal.
- Encouraging improvements in the training of designers.
- Stimulating interest in design among schoolchildren and their teachers.

Exhibitions: The Design Centres in London and Glasgow provide continuing but changing exhibitions of new developments in consumer design and engineering design. Admission is free.

Publications: *Design* magazine is concerned with the latest development in industrial design of all kinds from Britain and overseas. *Engineering* publishes technical information, and highlights the importance of good design in the engineering industry. *Designing* is a magazine for pupils in secondary schools, covering all aspects of Art, Design and Technology.

Design prizes: Two annual design prize schemes are specially useful in strengthening the links between education and industry; the Schools Design Prize, sponsored by a major industrial company, and the Molins Design Prize, for engineering design students at universities and polytechnics.

For more information about the work of the Design Council, or details about the current Schools Design Prize contact:

The Design Centre, 28 Haymarket, London SW1 4SU,	*or*	*The Design Council, Scottish Design Centre, 72 Vincent Street, Glasgow G2 5TN.*

Design Council offices also exist in Wales, Northern Ireland and the Midlands.

'Designing' the termly newspaper for students and teachers.

DESIGNING

THE TERMLY PAPER FOR STUDENTS & TEACHERS
Published by the Design Council and the Crafts Council

Autumn 1985 — Number 10

With a new school year ahead, you probably have many things to plan. Those of you starting on design-based examination courses will be considering project work, while younger students may be thinking of things to make for Christmas or for a school play. This issue of DESIGNING aims to help you with your decisions, offering a variety of ideas and information to spark your imagination. Some of the articles may also inspire you to take up new interests or hobbies to occupy your spare time. The topics covered range from crafts to technology, in some cases with projects for you to follow up. On pages 2–3, for example, we look at the various uses of holography as an up-to-the minute modelling and testing device. By comparison, the feature on stone carving traditions in Ladakh in Northern India on page 5 glimpses an ancient ethnic craft. More modern crafts are reviewed on pages 10 and 15 where we highlight students who have just completed crafts degrees, while our poster on pages 12–13 combines crafts and technology, exploring the development of musical instruments over the years. The same sort of mix of skills is shown in the work of banner artist John Dugger, whose work is featured on page 19. For a general view of what is happening in design, turn to our Update section for news, book reviews and listings of events.

Design for less developed countries – a review of appropriate technology on pages 6–7 to coincide with the Design Council's current exhibition. The designers' alphabet quiz on page 8. Laying the foundations – a special course for design-minded sixth formers on page 9. Craft, design and technology – a glimpse behind the scenes of Thames TV's schools series on page 16. Exploded view – the British Aerospace Giotto spacecraft explained on page 17. Making faces – make-up trends for stage, screen and street wear on pages 20–21. Save it – energy conservation in house design on page 22. Off the beaten track – animated trails as environmental education on page 23. Flipside – designs from the Design Council's new Innovation Centre on page 24.

The Design Centre index houses records of over 7 000 well designed products from British industry – helping you to find out more about design.

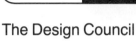

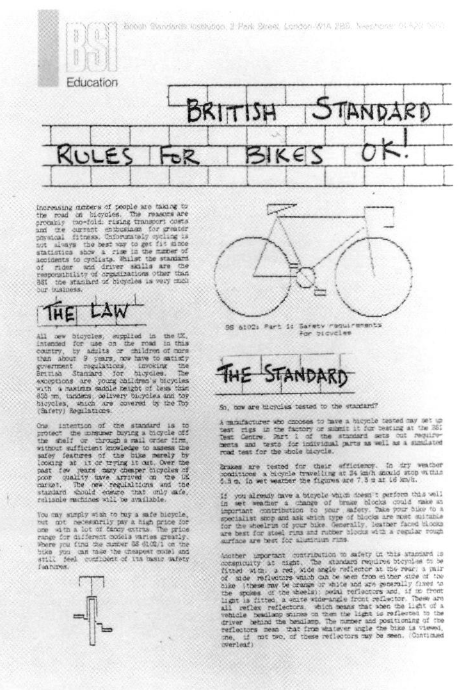

BSI Education

BRITISH STANDARD RULES FOR BIKES OK!

Increasing numbers of people are taking to the road on bicycles. The reasons are probably two-fold: rising transport costs and the current enthusiasm for greater physical fitness. Unforunately cycling is not always the best way to get fit since statistics show a rise in the number of accidents to cyclists. Whilst the standard of rider and driver skills are the responsibility of organizations other than BSI the standard of bicycles is very much our business.

THE LAW

All new bicycles, supplied in the UK, intended for use on the road in this country, by adults or children of more than about 9 years, now have to satisfy government regulations, invoking the British Standard for bicycles. The exceptions are young children's bicycles with a maximum saddle height of less than 635 mm, tandems, delivery bicycles and toy bicycles, which are covered by the Toy (Safety) Regulations.

One intention of the standard is to protect the consumer buying a bicycle off the shelf or through a mail order firm, without sufficient knowledge to assess the safey features of the bike merely by looking at it or trying it out. Over the past few years many cheaper bicycles of poor quality have arrived on the UK market. The new regulaitons and the standard should ensure that only safe, reliable machines will be available.

You may simply wish to buy a safe bicycle, but not necessarily pay a high price for one with a lot of fancy extras. The price range for different models varies greatly. Where you find the number BS 6102/1 on the bike you can take the cheapest model and still feel confident of its basic safety features.

BS 6102: Part 1: Safety requirements for bicycles

THE STANDARD

So, how are bicycles tested to the standard?

A manufacturer who chooses to have a bicycle tested may set up test rigs in the factory or submit it for testing at the BSI Test Centre. Part 1 of the standard sets out requirements and tests for individual parts as well as a simulated road test for the whole bicycle.

Brakes are tested for their efficiency. In dry weather conditions a bicycle travelling at 24 km/h should stop within 5.5 m. In wet weather the figures are 7.5 m at 16 km/h.

If you already have a bicycle which doesn't perform this well in wet weather a change of brake blocks could make an important contribution to your safety. Take your bike to a specialist shop and ask which type of blocks are most suitable for the wheelrim of your bike. Generally, leather faced blocks are best for steel rims and rubber blocks with a regular rough surface are best for aluminium rims.

Another important contribution to safety in this standard is conspicuity at night. The standard requires bicycles to be fitted with: a red, wide angle reflector at the rear; a pair of side reflectors which can be seen from either side of the bike (these may be orange or white and are generally fixed to the spokes of the wheels); pedal reflectors and, if no front light is fitted, a white wide-angle front reflector. These are all reflex reflectors, which means that when the light of a vehicle headlamp shines on them the light is reflected to the driver behind the headlamp. The number and positioning of the reflectors mean that from whatever angle the bike is viewed, one, if not two, of these reflectors may be seen. (Continued overleaf)

Free leaflets such as the one illustrated are available from the British Standards Education Department.

British Standards Institute

The British Standards Institute is an independent national organisation concerned with publishing technical documents called British Standards. By testing, inspecting and issuing certificates to products and companies they help to make sure that what the consumer puchases will do the job for which it is required.

At BSI's Test House, 132 technicians and engineers work in 17 laboratories testing products from pushchairs, to motor-bikes and from babies' dummies to electric drills.

BSI is a centre for discussion on national standards, which help manufacturers, consumers and Government agree on levels of quality and safety. There are thousands of specific standards, here are a few:

- BS 5665 – Safety of toys
- BS 4467 – Dimensions in designing for the elderly
- BS 5799 – Children's highchairs
- BS 5568 – Folding wheelchairs
- BS 3939 – Electrical and electronic graphic symbols
- BS 3121 – Flammable children's nightdresses.

When designing, or making purchases it is important that you are aware of the relevant BS. Some standards are embodied in consumer legislation: if you set up a small company making children's nightdresses and the fabrics you used did not conform to BS 3121 (requiring you to use material which does not flare up or burn easily) you would be liable to prosecution by your local Trading Standards Dept.

Playing safe with British Standards
Although this colourful booklet is primarily aimed at the buyers of nursery products it is proving very useful for design students.

The description below sets out part of the requirements which reclosable drug containers such as paracetamol bottles must meet if they are to be awarded BS 5321. (The sample is of 200 children aged 42–51 months.)

- *At least 85% of the test panel of children shall be unable to open the containers prior to the demonstration.*
- *At least 80% of the same children shall still be unable to open the containers after the demonstration.*
- *At least 90% of a panel of adults shall be able to open and properly reclose the container by following written instructions but without having received a demonstration.*

Many libraries keep stocks of British Standards. For further information contact:
The Education Dept.,
British Standards Institution,
2 Park Street, London W1A 2BS.

The law and the Office of Fair Trading

Even in Saxon times it was recognised that there needed to be a uniform system of weights and measure to avoid misunderstanding and cheating. However in the twentieth century the manufacturing of goods has become so complex that apart from weights and measures, laws have had to be passed to include quality, quantity, prices, safety, labelling, description and money lending or 'credit' as it is usually known.

These laws and your rights as a consumer or trader are promoted at a national level by the Office of Fair Trading and enforced at a local level by your city or County Trading Standards Dept.

The Office of Fair Trading is a Government department which keeps watch on trading matters in the United Kingdom and protects both consumers and business people against unfair practices. Part of the responsibilities of the OFT are:

- To publish information to help people know their rights and obligations (as illustrated).
- To collect information about trading practices which can then be used to suggest changes to the law.
- To make sure that large companies 'act within the public interest'.

In what ways do you think large companies may not act within the public interest'?

If you cannot obtain the OFT leaflets locally contact:
Room 310c,
Office of Fair Trading,
15–25 Bream's Buildings,
London EC4A 1PR.

How to avoid consumer problems

- Always try to make informed purchases. Do not simply rely on advertising or promotional information to make your choice.
- Keep any receipt of purchase, you may need this to return goods.
- Return faulty goods as soon as possible to the place of purchase.
- Check before you purchase to find out the full terms of the guarantee.
- Read all the small print on agreements, particularly those involving 'credit terms'. Once you have read the agreement do not sign anything unless you fully understand it.

If you are uncertain as to the trustworthy nature of an individual or company always seek the advice of an independent agency such as your local Trading Standards or Consumer Protection Dept, Consumer Advice Centre, or Citizens Advice Bureau. They will advise you as to your rights. Consumer laws are complex, and information can be obtained in greater detail from the agencies above. However here are a few examples:

The sale of goods act: Goods must be of 'merchantable quality', 'as described' and 'fit for their purpose'.

The trade descriptions acts: Makes it an offence for a trader to describe falsely goods or services. Goods not produced in Britain, but bearing a British name or mark must be marked with an indication of their country of origin.

Consumer protection act: Safety regulations are laid down for electrical appliances, toys, prams, nightdresses, upholstered furniture, and many more.

Food act: This covers labelling, composition, contaminants and the use of additives in produce.

Your local Trading Standards Department will provide a variety of information in leaflet form.

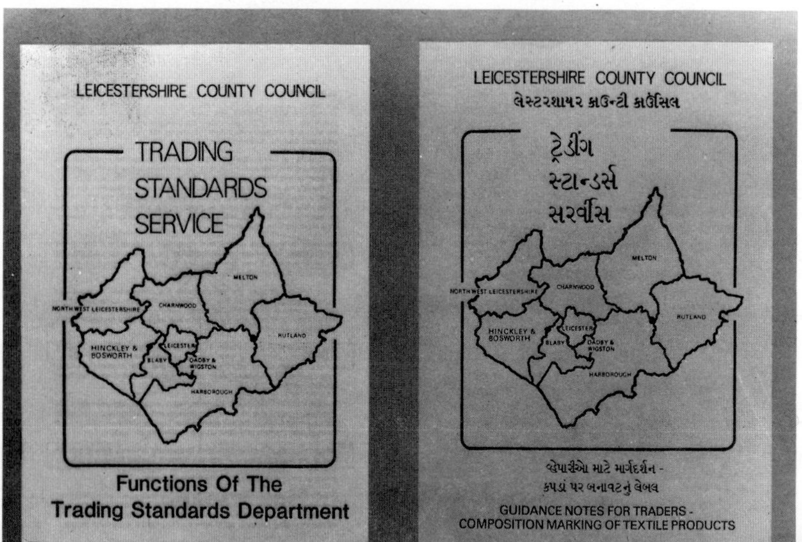

Many towns and cities have Consumer Advice Centres.

Remember it is the responsibility of your local Trading Standards Officers to 'police' and enforce the laws as they apply to trading.

If you have a justifiable grievance:

- *Check your rights and responsibilities under the law.*
- *Seek further advice from the Citizens Advice Bureau who will advise you on your best course of action.*
- *Report any dangerous products or illegal practice to your Trading Standards Department (address and telephone number in the 'phone book').*

The 'craft' approach to design

Despite modern methods of production there are still many craftsmen and women who design and make their own products, often using old established techniques with the minimum amount of mechanisation. In this section we shall look at some examples of their work and their sources of inspiration.

A cabinet of English yew.

John Makepeace

John Makepeace runs a very successful venture at Parnham House near Beaminster in Dorest. The main activities involve him in the design of furniture for individual clients, which is then made in the Parnham workshops by dedicated craftsmen and apprentices. The School for Craftsmen in Wood, founded by the Parnham Trust in 1977 educates those who intend to run their own woodworking business. A programme of demonstrations, lectures and exhibitions acts as a stimulus both to the public and students.

John Makepeace gave up an academic career in favour of a workshop training in cabinet making. In the 1950s this was not an easy thing to do, but he persuaded an excellent small workshop to take him on as an apprentice, a privilege for which he had to pay. After two years learning the practical skills, he realised the need to direct this new found ability through design. He then began an intensive period of travel through Europe, Scandinavia and America. In 1963 he converted a derelict barn near Banbury into his home, workshop and gallery. By 1976 his business had outgrown its premises and there was increasing pressure to train more young people. Setting up, and directing a school, teaching practical and business skills had long been one of Makepeaces' ambitions. Parnham presented the ideal opportunity to run his own workshop alongside a residential school.

A stool carved from an elm trunk.

Janice Tchalenko at work.

Janice Tchalenko

Decided to become a potter after starting a career in a completely different profession. She developed her craft by study and by working in a variety of pottery workshops around London.

As her work has developed she has concentrated on decoration, becoming more and more involved with the style and techniques associated with the decoration of pots. Bright colours feature in her work, inspired by her travels and observations in Russia, Central Europe and Persia.

An example of Janice Tchalenko's use of decoration on her work.

Wendy Ramshaw

Studied in illustration and fabric design at Newcastle College of Art and Design. However, she is best known as a jeweller, linking her mastery of technical processes with the development of ideas often based on her own themes.

She is particularly well-known for her exciting range of designs for rings which stretch the traditional idea of this piece of jewellery, and her collaborative work with Wedgwood which utilises ceramics as an essential part of her designs. The Wedgwood collection includes designs for necklaces, pins, brooches and earrings where she has drawn upon the use of fine-grain stoneware, in particular jasper and black basalt combined with precious metals.

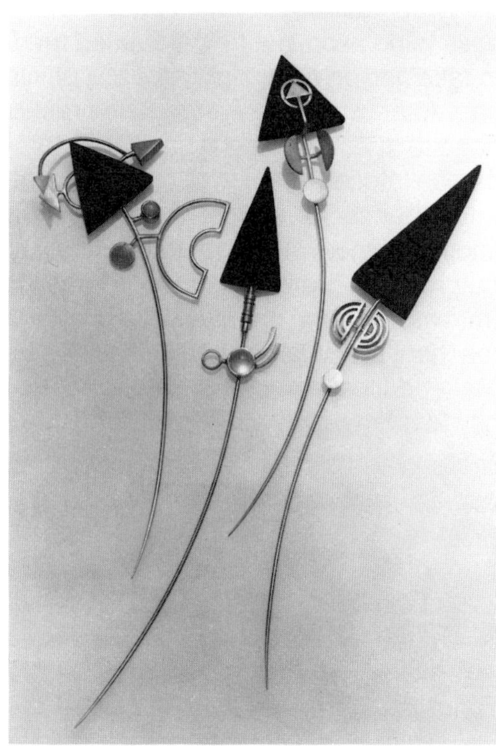

Set of four pins. Gold with carved black basalt arrow heads with opal and moonstone. Part of the Wedgwood and Wendy Ramshaw collection.

Pauline Solven at work in her studio in Gloucestershire.

Pauline Solven

Was one of the first students on the glass blowing course at The Royal College of Art. She now has her own highly successful glass blowing workshop in Gloucestershire, producing a range of domestic glassware as well as individual pieces.

She uses a variety of techniques for introducing colour into the glass, many of which require a great deal of planning in order to visualise the end result and control the process. Sources of inspiration for her work have included the Malvern Hills, patterns of light and colour created by the sun, and sailboards at sea. Many of these images she records by photography.

Coloured glass bowl by Pauline Solven.

Being aware of how design affects you

We have seen that everything around us that has been made by man has been designed.

As a student you will be designing your own work from beginning to end. Your ideas will be influenced by your experience of other people's design work. As a designer faced with a problem you are most likely to research it thoroughly before thinking through any ideas. A useful aspect of this research is to evaluate existing solutions to similar problems. For example, to design a soft toy for a small child it would be useful to examine existing soft toys very carefully and evaluate their design, particularly as regards safety.

Even people who are not active designers – your parents, for example – need to be concerned about design if they care about the quality of their lives. We are all consumers, choosing, buying and using goods and services. In the western world most of us live in houses and in streets, many in towns and cities. If we are at all concerned about the quality of life in our homes and cities, we must be concerned about **design**.

> ***Looking around yourself***
>
> *Select a design.*
>
> *What is its purpose?*
>
> *Does it fulfil the purpose well?*
>
> *List all the qualities and functions such a design should have.*

Problem: how to open a can

In 1824 an Arctic expedition took with them veal sealed in cans to preserve the meat; to open the iron cans, they were instructed to use a hammer and chisel!

Below is a 'Bully' can opener. It was designed and then marketed by Gustavus F. Swift in the late nineteenth century to enable people to open the newly invented Corned Beef, often called 'Bully Beef'. It remained the only available effective can opener for many years, but as a design it had many drawbacks.

Can you think what they were?

What improvements have been made in recent can opener designs?

There are electric ones available – do these have any advantages over hand operated ones?

The 'Bully' can opener. There are similar designs available today!

Collect several different types of can opener and make a list of desirable qualities of any can opener design. For example:

It should be easy to clean
It should leave no sharp edge on the opened can or lid.
It should . . .

To evaluate fully the openers as solutions to the problem of getting food out of a can, it is useful to study the technologies involved.

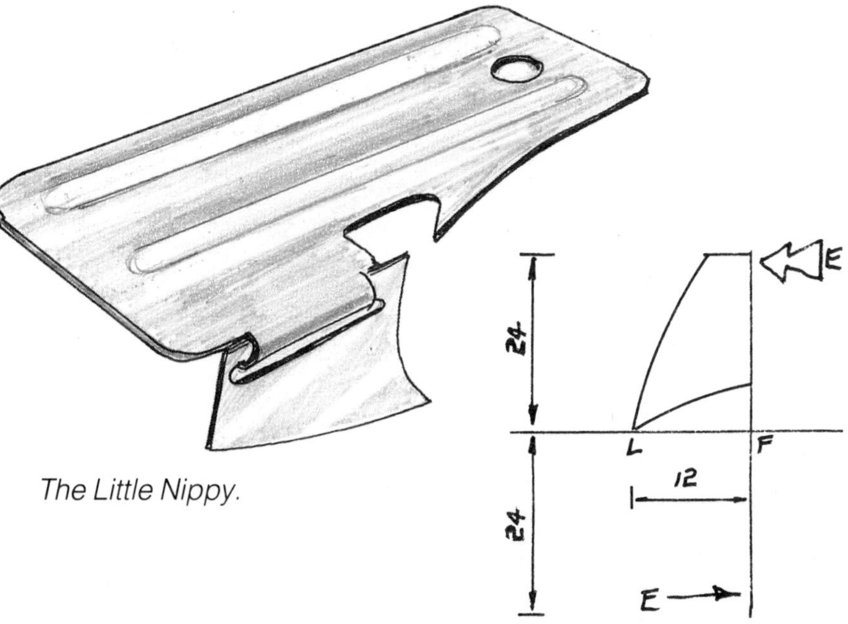

The Little Nippy.

This design is claimed to leave no sharp edge on either can or lid.

Many designs use the principle of the lever to give the user mechanical advantage. The drawing above is of a very compact opener; the diagram analyses it in use.

Can you calculate the mechanical advantage to the user? What might be the particular advantage of this design over others you have seen or used? Might there be drawbacks to the design?

Analyse others in a similar way and make comparisons.

Have you considered all probable users of can opener designs – children and old people for example?

Evaluating can openers. Questionnaires with careful analysis of all results will help you come to informed conclusions.

Other ideas

You could conduct other consumer tests on products such as:
cutlery
paint
clothes pegs
envelopes
Can you think of others?

Analyse a design of your choice

Market research into consumer needs, preferences and complaints assists designers in their work. Feedback after a design has been used gives additional information. Manufacturers often produce new versions of a product incorporating improvements based on the findings of researchers. However, there is another reason for marketing a 'new' model; can you think what it is?

Select a design, perhaps in your own home.

- First, list all the ways in which ideally it should perform.
- Second, list the ways in which it meets your critieria for success.
- Third, list the ways in which it does *not*.

This baby's rattle contained small steel balls which easily came out.

A garage to hold 700 cars, with spiral driveways for London's congested city areas.

Useless or dangerous objects

Collect together some objects that in your opinion are useless or unsafe to use.

- *Designs that do not work properly or perhaps not at all.*
- *Designs that have ceased to work or have broken in normal use or in an unreasonably short time.*
- *Designs that are simply awful to look at.*

In each case, can you say why? How could they be improved?

Claims to design perfection.

Look around your own environment and consider each item that you see:

1 What is the purpose of the design?
2 Does it fulfil this purpose well?
3 Are there other designs available that are intended to meet the same need?
4 What are, in your opinion, all the desirable qualities that such a design should have.

Example: a handwriting pen

If we consider the ideal qualities of an everyday item such as this, we might include:

the capability of producing clear lines
leakproof
price
attractive appearance
comfortable to hold
shaped to avoid rolling
colour of ink
long lasting

Would you wish to modify or add to this list?

Research

In considering the design of a modern handwriting pen, it will be helpful to find out about the history and development of writing and writing implements. For example:

- Investigate man's need to write and how this was achieved in ancient civilisations.
- The word 'pen' derives from the Latin, 'penna'. What did this word mean?
- Discover what materials have been used for pens and pen nibs.
- Trace the development of the fountain pen. Can you explain how it works? A diagram might be useful in doing this.
- When was the ballpoint pen first designed and manufactured? How does it work?
- What other types of pen are there today? You could find out how they work, conduct comparative tests of performance and price, and carry out market research establishing what consumers need and what they actually buy and use.

Ways in which you can be aware of design

In previous pages we have looked at how our lives have been strongly influenced by the design work of others. We could of course ignore such design work. We could give no thought to the quality of manufactured goods, to the planning of our towns and homes, to the 'persuasion' of advertisements.

However, it is more likely that you *are* concerned about the designed world around you. To discover how much, consider the following questions:

1 Think of the street in which you live or one that you know well. What aspects of that street do you particularly like? What aspects do you dislike? Can you say why?

The photograph on the right illustrates how the appearance of houses changes over the years. What changes have been made? In your opinion, what has been gained, and what has been lost?

The two photographs below are of the same street. What can you deduce about the probable lifestyles of the people for whom the houses were designed? How do the probable lifestyles of the inhabitants of today compare?

Change – for better or for worse?

The changing face of a street; how has your street changed?

Find out how alterations and improvements to your own town are controlled. Is the control strict enough – or do you think there should be less restrictions?

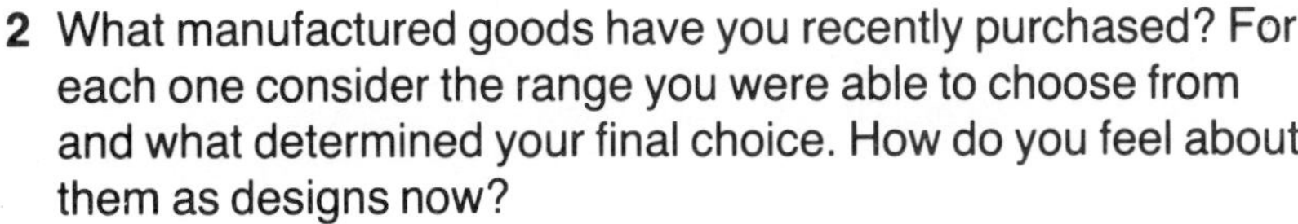

2 What manufactured goods have you recently purchased? For each one consider the range you were able to choose from and what determined your final choice. How do you feel about them as designs now?

3 Think of something that you, or someone you know, has purchased which has broken or ceased to function as it should? Can you say why it no longer works as intended?

4 Think of a painting or picture you like. Can you say why?

5 Think of other questions about designs and how you feel about them.

How we feel about design depends on many variable factors, for example: our experiences, our education, our culture, our moods, our age, our prejudices. What influences you and your opinions?

What criteria would you use to evaluate a picture or sculpture? Are these examples of non-functional design? Should they be judged purely in terms of how we feel or respond to them?

'A New Digester or Engine for Softening Bones' – the first pressure cooker – Denis Papin's 'digester' of 1679. Although something of a monstrosity and highly dangerous, it really did work. Compare it with a pressure cooker of today and note improvements, particularly in respect to safety.

Forming opinions about design

Your opinions and feelings matter a great deal. The quality of our lives – our homes, our towns, things we buy – depends on people: the designer, the maker and the consumer. Consider the following:

In a group of designs like toys, why is it that some toys are poorly designed or manufactured? Try to list qualities that make a toy a bad design. How can we as consumers reduce the number of badly designed toys available?

We can evaluate and test a product which has been designed to meet a particular need. In doing so, it is important to remember that our opinions and feelings, both as consumers *and* designers, matter.

A cast-iron apple peeler and corer – an elaborate design of circa 1900. 'The Bonanza' by Godell & Co.

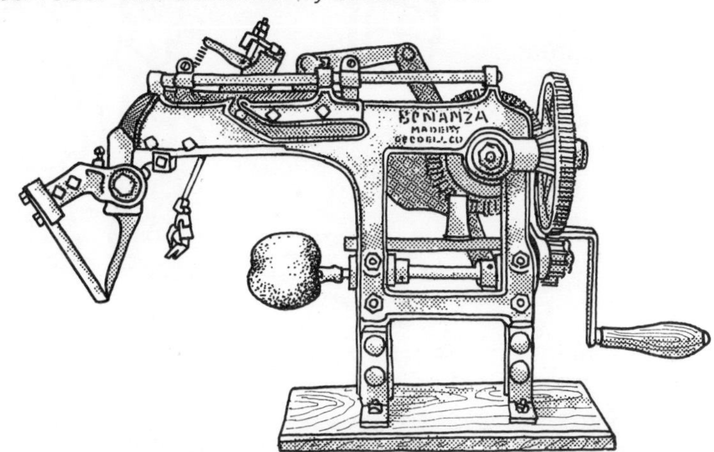

King Kong – not in the flesh, but GRP.

Example: buying a pair of jeans

Imagine that you want to buy a pair of jeans and that you have the money to do so. Would you:

1 Ask your mother to choose a pair for you?
2 Ask your friends to guide you in your choice?
3 Browse in shops hoping to find a pair that you like?
4 Buy a pair advertised in a teenage magazine?
5 Buy the cheapest available?
6 Select from a mail-order catalogue?
7 Make your own?

American Corn

You may have responded 'yes' to one or more of the above – or you may have a method of selection that is not listed. Most of us have feelings about the clothes we wish to wear. Many of us can identify with the people in advertisements, for example, or we may be anxious to be fashionable. Often we cannot say why we make one choice and not another.

There is another method of making a decision. We could randomly list aspects related to the design of a pair of jeans. Designers often adopt this method of 'brainstorming' when thinking about their own work. Here is a list:

value for money	seams	pockets
baggy	faded	strong zip
belt	rivets	colour
hard wearing	dye-fast	belt loops
stretch	brand	corded
washable	well constructed	tear resistent
advertised	comfort	clinging

Try making your own list. Some needs will be definite, others you may be less certain about. If you were then to go out to buy your jeans, your problem would be in finding a pair that came nearest to matching your list of considerations. You would be able to make judgements about the garments you see based on the factors you have already decided are important. Further information will help; for example, asking questions of shop assistants, discussing with friends. You could seek product research information such as that published by the Consumer Association in the magazine *Which?*

Careful selection will lead to better designing. Better designing will lead to better quality in our lives. The quality of design will be influenced by all of us if we are careful in the way we select.

'Bet my mom gets that one – it's the Which? *Best Buy'* Yorkshire Post.

How aware of design are you?

Investigating a household appliance: The domestic iron

Investigate the design of the domestic iron by considering the following questions. Examine your iron at home to assist your investigations.

1 Some of the pictures on this page give us clues about the origins of the domestic iron. Find out about the first irons and how they were used.
2 Look at your iron at home. What materials are used in its construction?
3 How is the heat produced and how is it controlled?
4 How is the heat prevented from burning the hands?
5 Does the handle get hot in use?
6 What provision is made in the design to stand the iron whilst hot? Is it stable?
7 How effective is the heat control?
8 Does the shape of the iron help in use e.g. around buttons?
9 Is it heavy in use? Decide whether an iron should be heavy or light.
10 Is there any visual indication that the iron is on?
11 Some irons produce steam. Why?
12 What problems might arise with using water in a steam iron? Is there any provision in the design to cope with this?
13 If a steam iron, is there any way of telling the water level?
14 Look at the cable inlet to the iron. Is it in the best place? Does it prove awkward in use?
15 Is the mains cable long enough in use?
16 Do you think any real thought has been given to styling of the iron to make it more attractive or functional? Are these two considerations complementary or in conflict?
17 How could your iron be improved to make it function better in use?
18 How long have you had the appliance? Has it broken down – if so give details?

What can you say about these irons?

Consumer Association testing

You may be able to find out more. You could do the family's ironing to evaluate properly the design of the appliance. You could talk to other users. You could even plan and conduct a questionnaire to discover the reactions of a group of consumers.

When testing irons, the Consumer Association listed the considerations that they thought should be included in the design of a successful model. See the list at the bottom of page 45.

Do you agree with these? Have you any to add? What does BEAB approved mean? What other standards must a manufacturer of electrical appliances abide by?

Look up the most recent *Which?* report on irons. Which model would you buy? Is the cheapest a good buy? Look at irons in the shops and decide which you would choose on appearances alone, then refer back to the report and see how it fared in the CA test.

Are domestic irons used more by either men or women? Designs such as irons and other domestic appliances are designed by professional industrial designers and yet less than one in every hundred industrial designers are female. Do you think this is important?

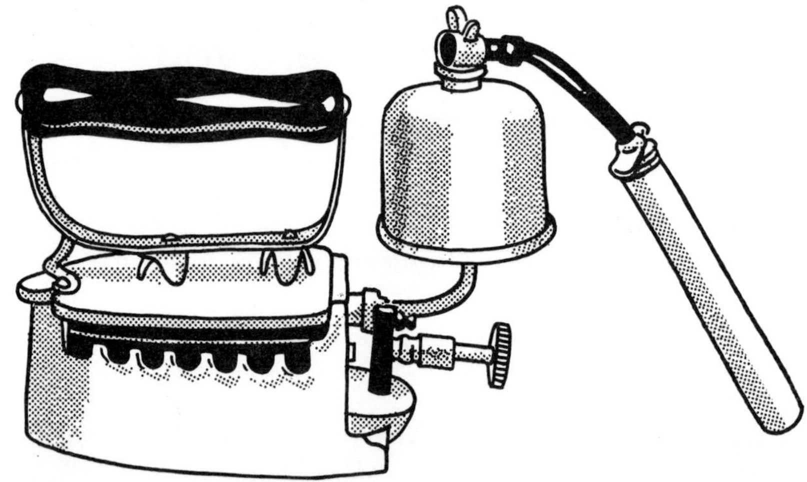

How do you think this appliance worked?

How do todays irons work?

The cordless iron. This is filled with butane gas from a canister and has temperature control. What do you imagine are its advantages – and disadvantages – as a design?

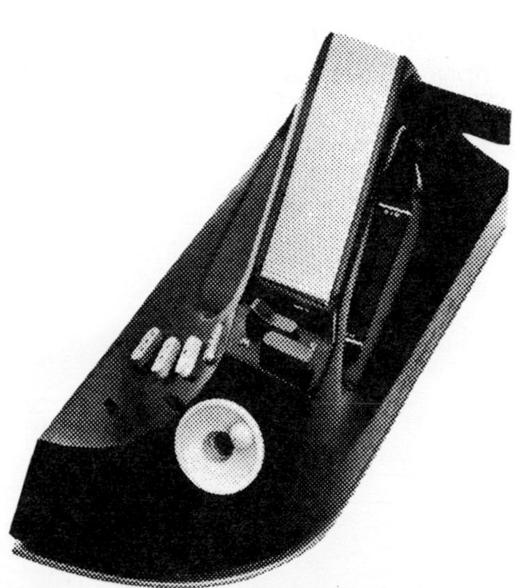

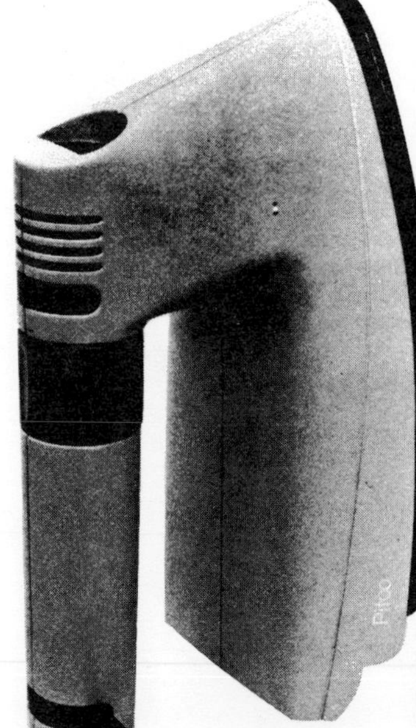

These irons were designed, one by a man, the other by a woman.

Safety

The baseplate of this iron melted when the thermostat failed. In 1966 an eight year old girl lost a hand when she tried to catch a melting baseplate. In 1984 a family of six died in Wales, almost certainly because an iron was left on overnight and the thermostat failed to cut out. Numerous other incidents in which the baseplates of irons have melted have been recorded, usually when the user's attention has been distracted.

It is a fact that manufacturers have known about this problem for years and at the same time have known how to overcome it by including in the design a simple and inexpensive thermal cut-out device.

A consumer unit officer in the West Midlands continually campaigns for designers and manufacturers to be responsible in this respect:

> In my view, the fundamental principle of 'fail safe' should have been employed originally in the design of such products and this move is long overdue. British and international standards will be amended in due course. The Government has told manufacturers that if they do not act quickly, mandatory requirements will be introduced.
>
> The main argument or justification put forward by the makers is of nuisance tripping.
>
> I find the attitude of manufacturers worrying, as in my view they cannot justify inaction over five years.

Can you say why manufacturers are sometimes reluctant to make even small changes to their products.

Some designs of iron are now available with a safety cut-out built in. Would *you* buy one without?

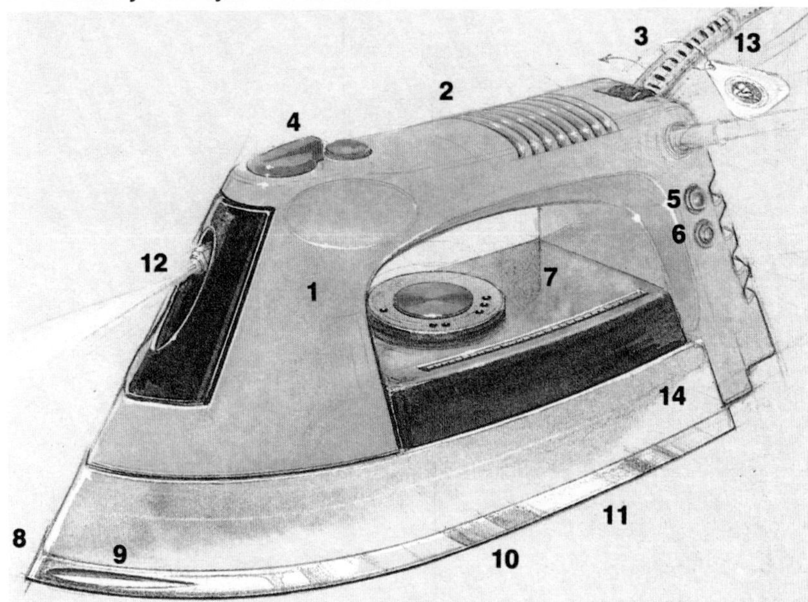

A melted soleplate.

The Consumer Association thoroughly tests products it investigates. Here steam irons are tested continuously whilst set to 'steam', a tough but realistic test according to the Association's survey of members. What problems do you think the steam might give?

A Which? *report on the domestic iron.*

The CA recommended to readers that they consider the following when buying an iron:

1. *Weight*
2. *Handle*
3. *Flex length*
4. *Extra controls*
5. *Indicator light*
6. *Mains on light*
7. *Water reservoir*
8. *Well-pointed front*
9. *Button grooves*
10. *Soleplate*
11. *Steam production*
12. *Spray*
13. *Electrical safety*
14. *Thermal cut-out*

For information on the BSI, turn to page 30.

A deadly design

Do you put absolute trust in every product that you buy? You could be buying potential killers when you purchase some designs.

The domestic iron illustrated above was discovered by the West Midlands Consumer Services Department to be very unsafe. The British Standards Institute declared it to be the worst electrical domestic appliance they had ever examined, noting many dangerous faults, including the fact that it had no earth, despite being made entirely of metal.

Another example, the 'Crown Travel Iron TR3', was found to have 20 faults, including: substandard insulation, no earth or additional insulation, access for a finger of the user to touch live parts and an inadequate cord restraint. Both of these products were on sale in the shops as recently as 1985.

Two dangerous products.

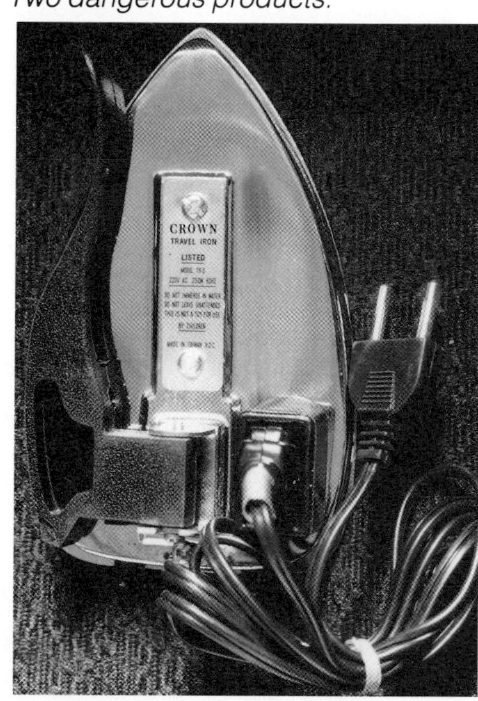

Who do you think is responsible for ensuring safe designs:
The Government? *The manufacturer?*
The shopkeeper? *The importer?*
The designer?

Write to the Consumer Services Department or Trading Standards Officer in your locality and ask for information on the design aspects of the consumer products that are supported by standards and regulations enforceable by law.

Meeting consumer needs: the left-handed iron

Detailed research is undertaken by designers and manufacturers, especially when the products are potentially dangerous.

Kenneth Grange, an experienced professional designer of numerous well-known products, is keenly aware of consumer needs, as the rough sketch from his design pad indicates.

He explains:

> 'To help left handed users of the Morphy Richards irons, we devised a method of changing the cable exit and therefore the handling of the iron. There were no extra parts: the retailer had simply to remove the backpanel and swap over the lamp and the cable.'

This idea, although an attempt to meet the needs of the 10% left handed users, has not been taken up by the retailers. Can you suggest why?

What other ways have designers of irons attempted to consider the needs of left handers? Can you find examples in the shops?

The iron illustrated below is by a student of design. It is a prototype model rather than a working appliance: designers often make models so that they and their clients can evaluate ideas. How do you think this example is adaptable to left and right handed people?

Working out a problem – a professional designer's sketch.

A design student's answer to left and right-handed users. This is a full size model rather than a working prototype. Some designers work finishes at this point.

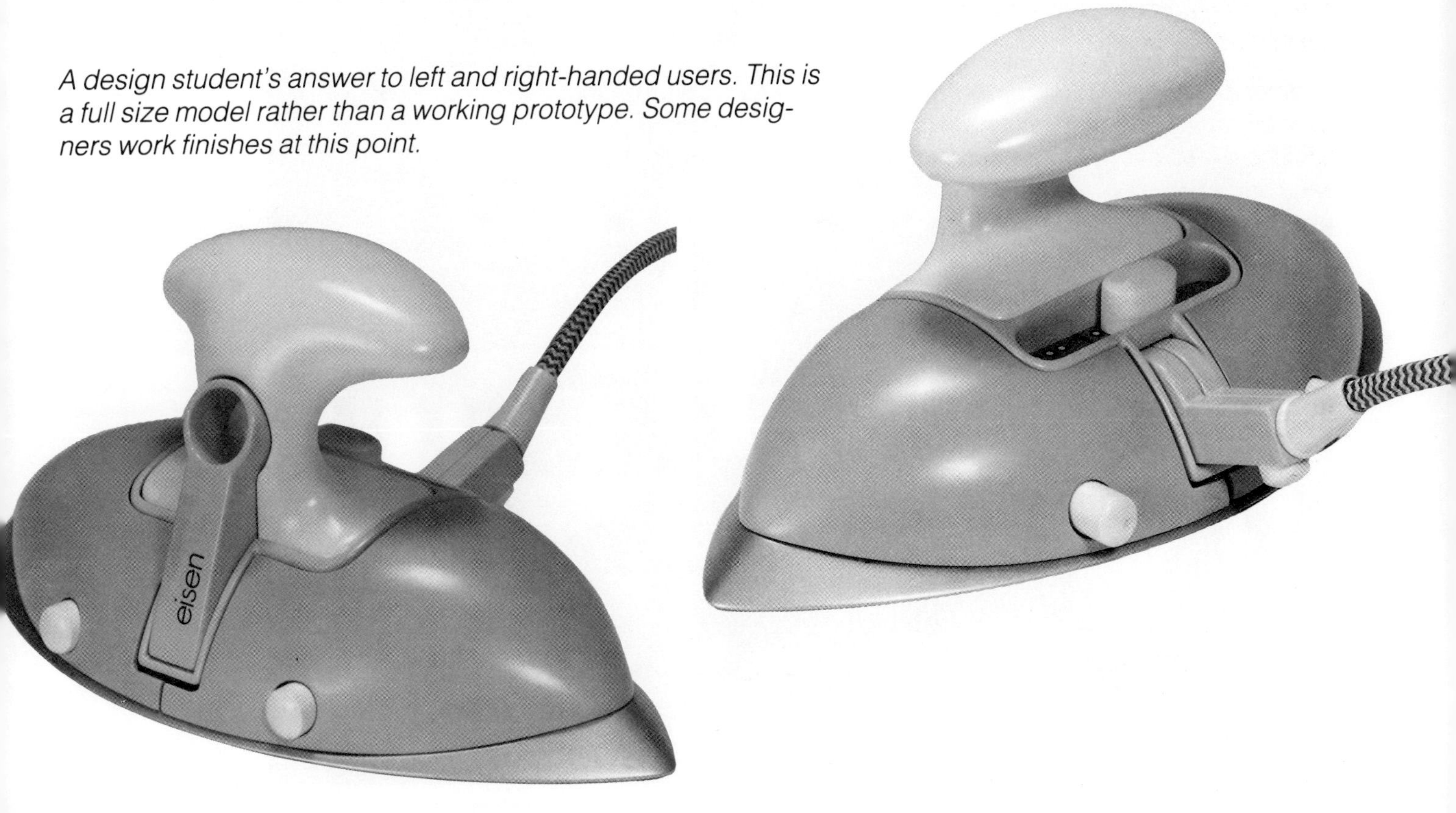

Investigating industrial design

Most of the goods that are available for us to purchase have been designed – that is clear and obvious. We have already examined how in the case of the traditional craftsman, the design of his or her work has been passed on from generation to generation. Often designs that are new are designed by the maker and can be very successful. You might have experienced this sort of designing yourself, for example: when you were younger you may have needed to build a hutch for a pet rabbit, to make clothes for a doll, to build a plane from a construction kit, and so on. When you made any of these items, you were manufacturer and designer. You may well have been dissatisfied with your first attempts, and have re-made the item, with modifications to improve the design.

Many manufactured goods around us have been designed in this way. Unfortunately this sometimes results in poor design, in the functioning or appearance of the goods.

High quality in manufactured goods is usually the result of work by *industrial designers*, the professional designers employed by manufacturers. Just as you in your own design work will start from a *brief*, so will the industrial designer.

> *Can you name an industrial designer or perhaps a design consultancy in your area?*
>
> *Use the* Yellow Pages *and look under 'Design Consultants' and 'Designers – Industrial'*

The Durabeam torch

A successful industrial design: The Durabeam torch

The Durabeam torch is a good example of a product designed so well that it completely outsold the manufacturer's expectations. It was launched in September 1984. By December 1984, 450,000 had been sold and by mid 1985, sales topped 3 million. It also won a Design Council award for design excellence.

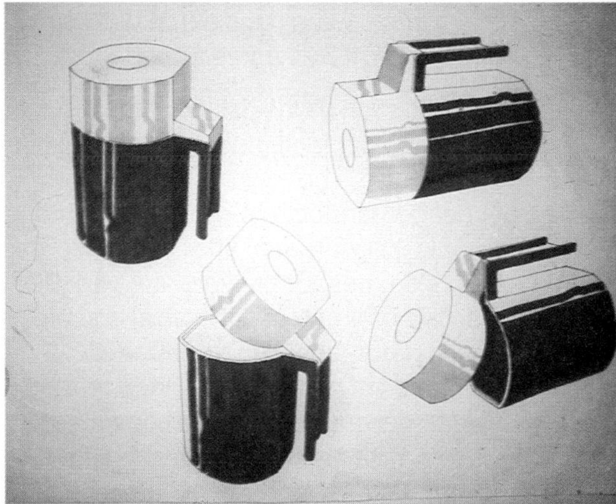

The Duracell Company is a major manufacturer of alkaline batteries that have a reputation for long life and high quality. In order to diversify its range of products and to increase the demand for the batteries, the Duracell Company decided to manufacture and market a torch. However, the company had no experience in this area, nor did it have the necessary design skills. It therefore undertook the following before launching the new product:

1 Consumer Research

Duracell was able to state clearly its needs after conducting its own market research. This research identified a potential market for a small portable light source which could:

- satisfy short range portable lighting needs in a flexible and versatile way
- provide a free standing and directional beam, enabling both hands to be left free
- provide an attractive and appealing personal possession
- provide an interesting and worthwhile gift
- have a modern and technological style appropriate to the Duracell corporate image
- meet specified standards of high quality and performance
- meet specified price limitations.

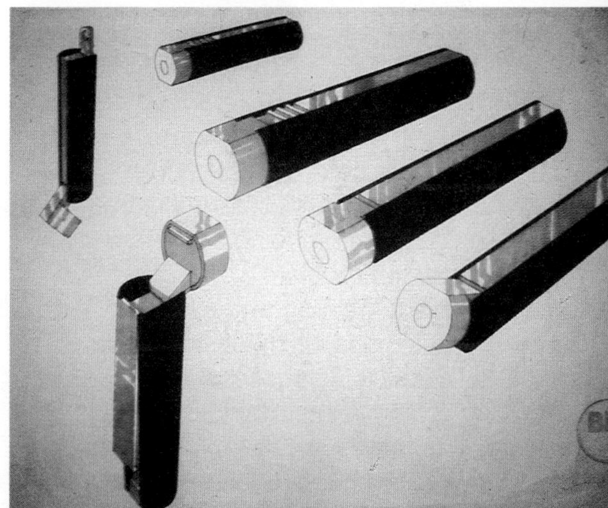

2 Commissioning a design consultant

In selecting a suitable designer, Duracell invited design consultancies to explain how they would go about designing the product. The consultants who won the contract gave a detailed budget and timescale. The development programme they suggested was:

1. concept design
2. client approval
3. market research
4. design revision
5. client approval
6. design development
7. prototype manufacture
8. prototype proving
9. production drawing and tooling
10. liaison with manufacturers during production

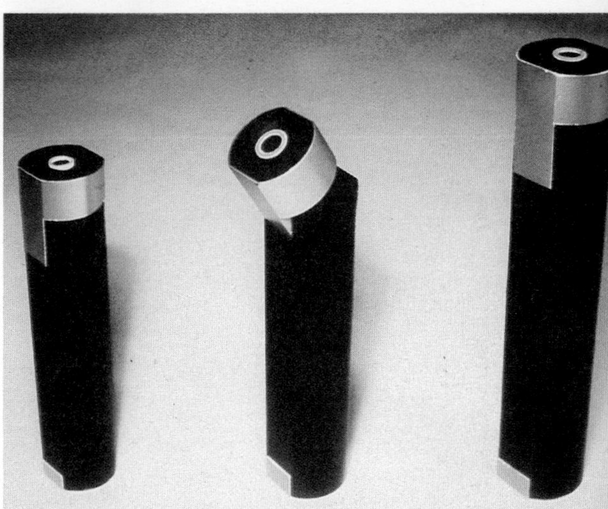

Concept models and sketches

3 The design and development of the Durabeam Torch

As in all good designing, several concept ideas were considered before the final design was agreed upon.

Details such as the design of the electrical switch contacts had to be exhaustively planned. The specifications in the brief demanded a reliable switch that would still work well after being used 25,000 times. Because of the variable factors of pressure, chemical and electrical properties of materials and methods of manufacture, independent electrical engineers were consulted. Alternative methods of pivoting the torch head were investigated, also of creating a snap fit to the top, of moulding a battery carrier, of assembling the torch, and of avoiding moulding defects spoiling the outer surface.

Altogether, the design took 2 years to complete before production could begin. The exercise clearly illustrated that:

- there is no one right solution to any design problem
- there are stages in the process of designing which designers need to follow to be successful
- styling is important but so are other aspects such as function, cost, ease of manufacture, ease of use, suitability of materials, etc.
- professional designers often need other skills that will assist creation e.g. technical knowledge, management skills, accountancy skills, and so on.

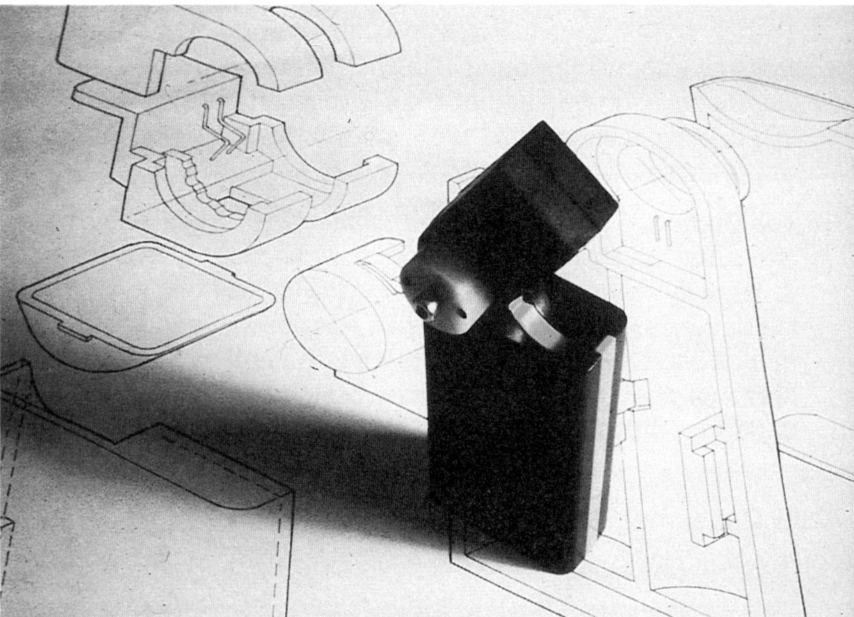

Designer's detail and adjustable ratchet test rig.

Concept model

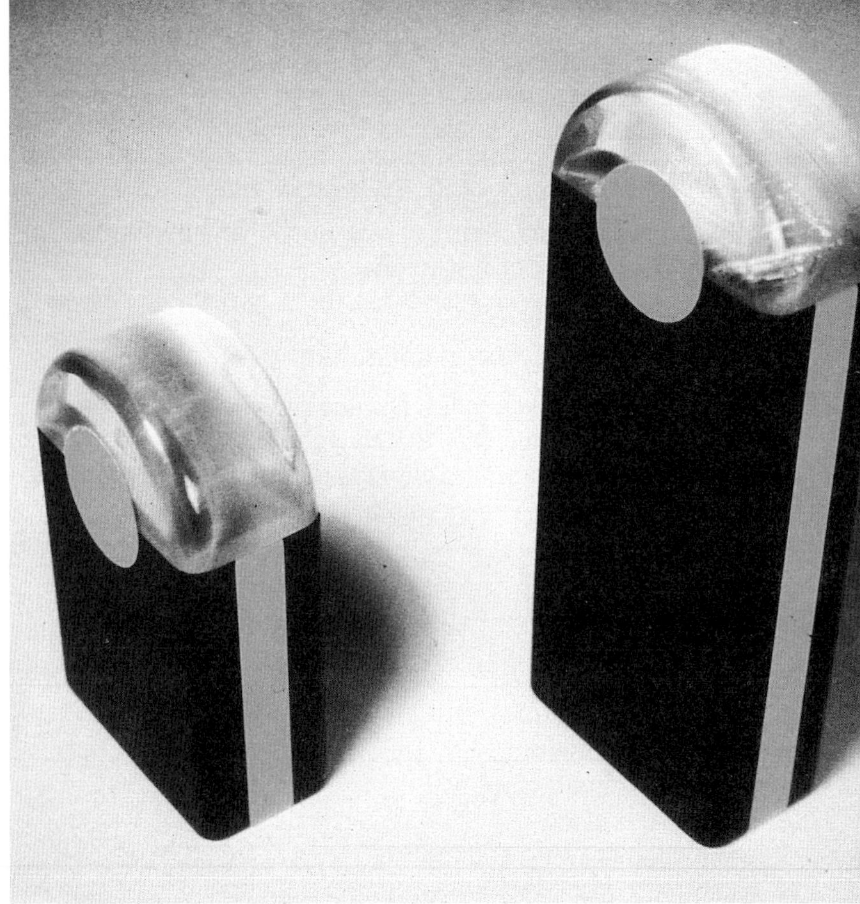

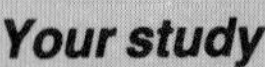

Your study

Choose a product and try to find out who designed it.

Find out all you can about how the designer approached the work.

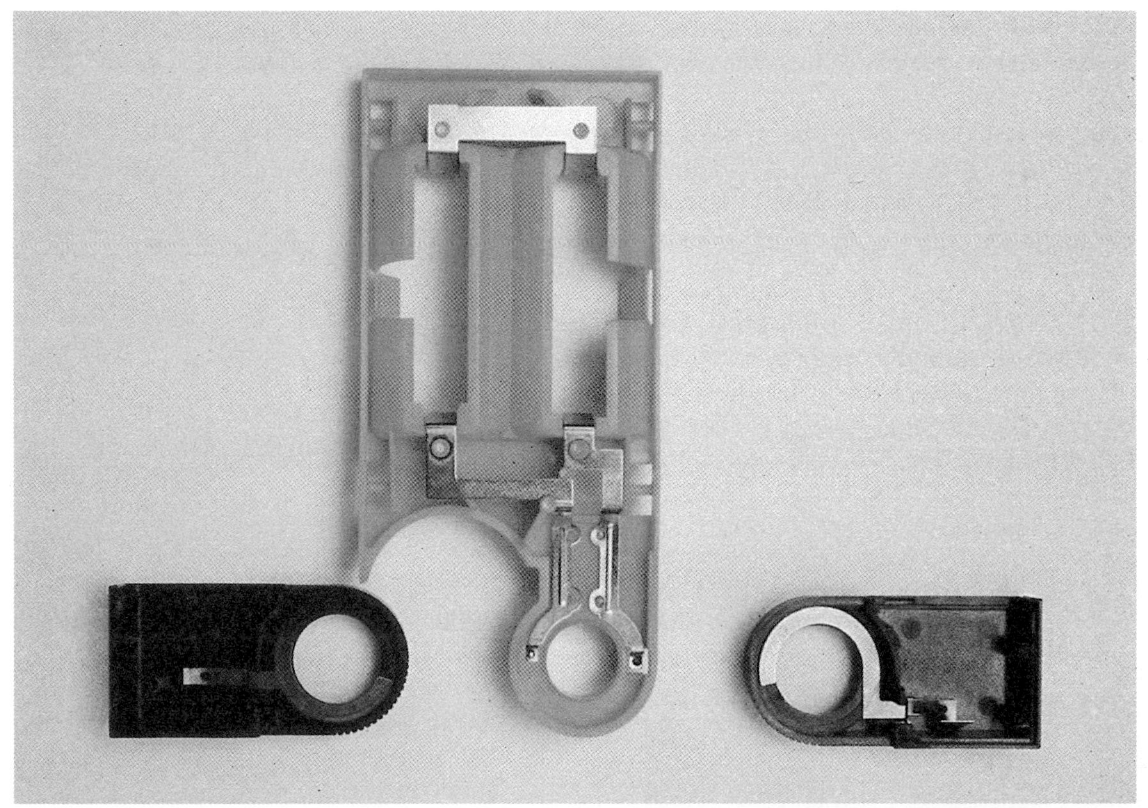

Electrical layout.

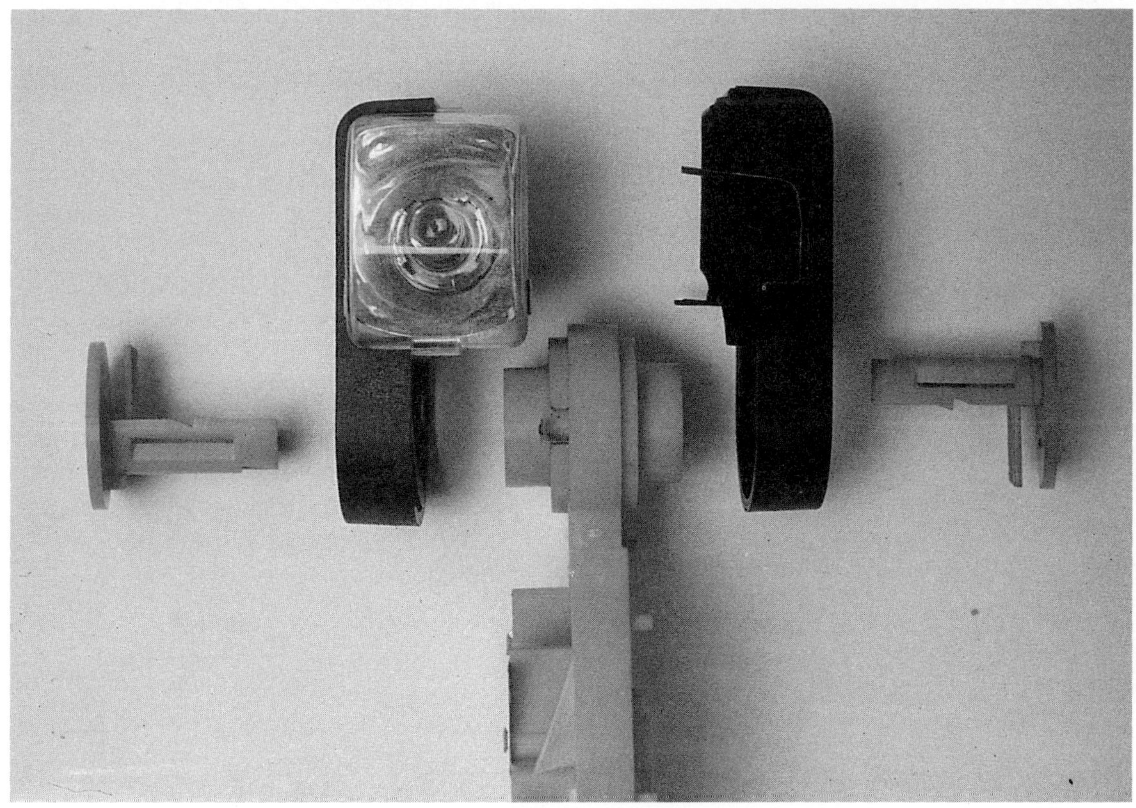

Injection moulded components.

How perfect is design?

David Pye writes about Design and in his book *The Nature of Design*, he states:

> 'Nothing we design or make ever really works. We can always say what it ought to do, but that it never does. The aircraft falls out of the sky or rams the earth full tilt and kills the people. It has to be tended like a new born babe. It drinks like a fish. Its life is measured in hours.'

We often take the designed world about us for granted; we may even assume that everything around us has been well designed, or reasonably so. If something goes wrong – a chair tips over when we sit on it, a zip in clothing jams – we all too often blame ourselves and put the mishap down to clumsiness or carelessness.

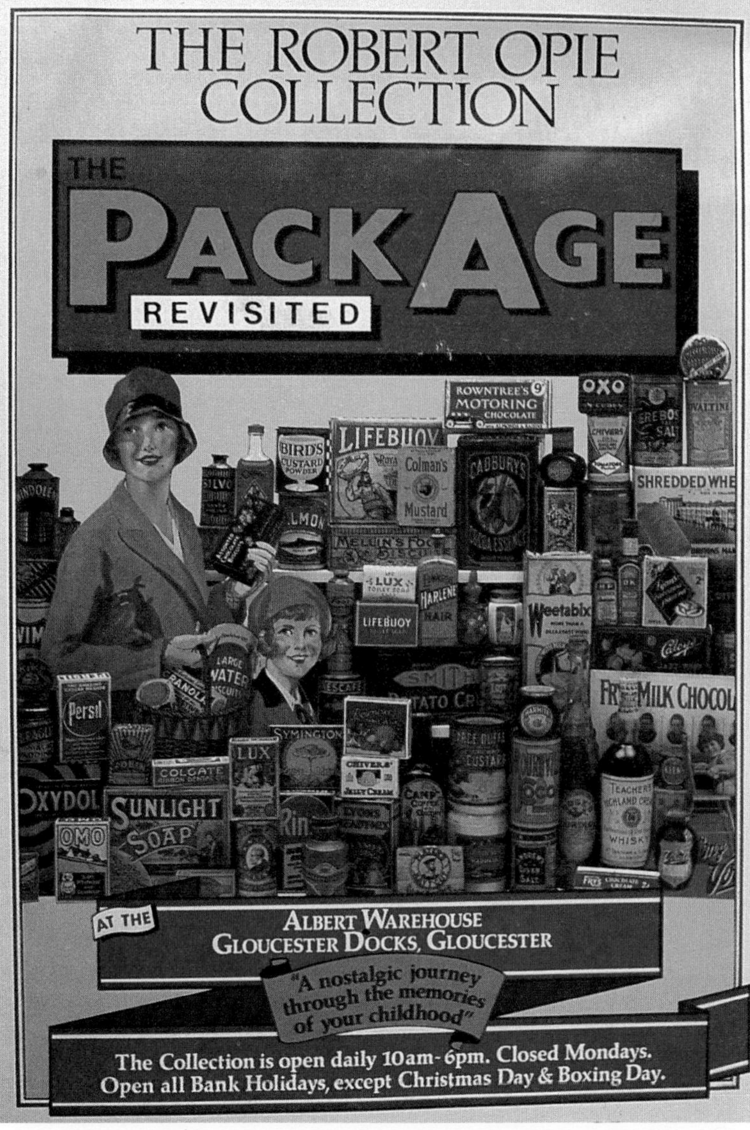

Take the example of packaging. Recent developments in packaging manufacturing techniques and particularly new plastic materials and methods of forming them, have created all sorts of new packaging forms. More than £4,000 million is spent annually on packaging in Britain alone.

But have you:

- had difficulty in opening a carton of milk or fruit juice?
- spilled yoghurt when peeling off a foil lid?
- had difficulty in opening the inner bag of a breakfast cereal packet?
- found it difficult to get into a packet of biscuits?
- struggled to strip a segment of cheese spread of its foil wrapper?

Think of other packaging that you have found unsatisfactory to the user.

Being critical is important to design as it influences its continuing improvement. Designers continually analyse and criticise their work so that first ideas can be modified and improved.

Things are not always what they seem. . .

As our experience grows we are able to make instant judgements about what we see. But without proper investigation, even the most experienced person can be wrong.

E Type Jaguar

The car in the picture above – the Jaguar E Type – was designed with a streamlined look; in fact the form of the motor car dictated the rest of the design. It had a long empty nose, a tiny luggage compartment and an interior too cramped for passenger comfort.

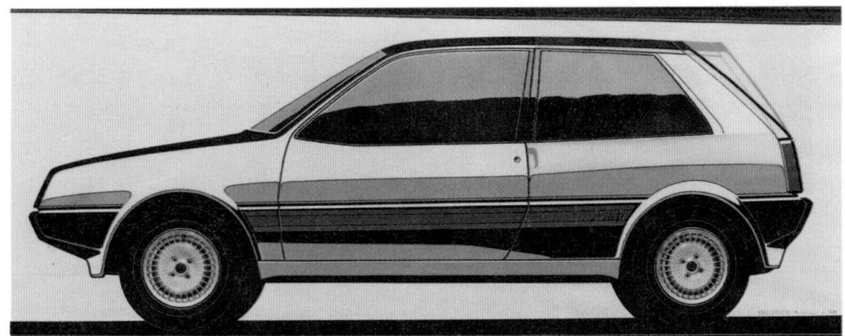

VW Polo

However, you might be forgiven if you said, 'Well, the car was obviously built to be aerodynamically efficient; sleek, long lines to cut through the air with the least drag.' But in reality, it has more drag than most cars built today – the VW Polo, for example. As well as having a lower coefficient of drag (Cd), the Polo has an engine compartment no longer than the power unit beneath, it has an interior as large as possible and a correspondingly sized luggage space.

What do you suppose the design on the right is for?

It is obviously not intended to be elegant, but has been designed to be functional. It's purpose is retrieving corks that have dropped fully inside a bottle of wine – a not too uncommon event. You may think by looking at it that it is a yet another gadget that does not work. In fact it does work, and very efficiently.

Clearly, to judge the worth of designs we need to be wary of first impressions and to carry out further evaluation before coming to any conclusion.

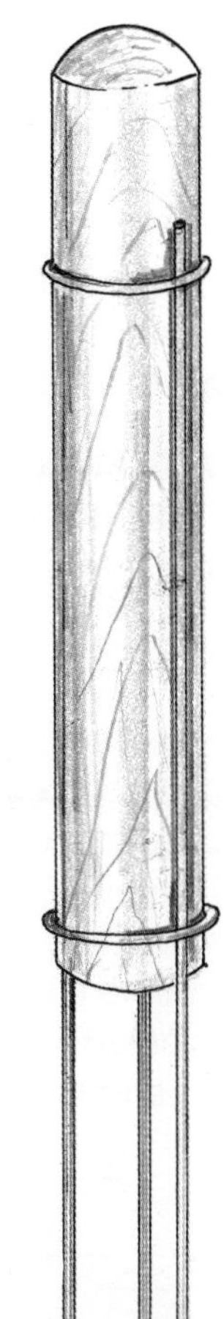

3 Expressing thoughts and feelings about design

You will need your skills of:
Observation
Analysis Criticism
Judgement
Imagination Description
Communication
Aesthetics Design
Presentation

Having found and discussed some of the ways in which designers influence you, how best can you comment on your experience? The aim of this topic is for you to develop ways of making informed judgement and criticism about how designers work and how their designs affect your way of life. You can begin to understand design by appreciating that it involves 'imagination' as well as 'technical expertise'.

Your studies may be written, illustrated, filmed, slide/taped, modelled or you may use any other suitable method of presenting your ideas, feelings and findings. The skills of *observation, description, analysis, criticism* and *presentation* will be required throughout any study of design.

Personal judgement and feelings are good starting points, especially since there is no one way to appreciate design. A successful study should be supported with clear examples of design. Personal likes and dislikes may be the basis of your study. They should be defended, but also tempered by examples of other people's ideas and feelings. This is important so that your study is balanced, interesting and original. Try to explore why there are different opinions about particular designs.

A study of design should include a title, a clear statement about its subject matter and why it has been chosen. You should use suitable sources of information, a reasoned argument which describes and explains what you have found out about the design, a clearly justified conclusion and an appropriate style of presentation.

The following questions, tasks and ideas illustrate some of the different ways in which you may evaluate and understand design. They are not intended to tell you how you should appreciate design, but they do indicate how people often react to design. Your notes and comments should consider:

1 the identification of reactions to designs, your own and other people's;
2 the particular aspect of design which is being observed used or described;
3 the selection of who might need, or be influenced by, the information revealed.

It will be useful to collect examples of designs so that you can have first-hand experience of them. Photographs, drawings and pictures will be helpful, and personal sketches and notes will make a study more interesting to read, as well as original. A study of design should, itself, be designed.

When studying design are you looking at the:
- *designer at work;*
- *something man-made; or*
- *the consequences of design?*

What does design mean?

Words like design and designing are used in many ways. If you look up 'design' in a dictionary it will reveal a number of meanings. It is important that these various definitions are made clear, and that design is not restricted to one meaning. The most practical way to understand the meaning of a word is to consider how it is used, by whom, and in what context. When we design we are 'thinking' and 'creating' ideas about, and images of, the things which we need to make or use. We are all designers in one way or another.

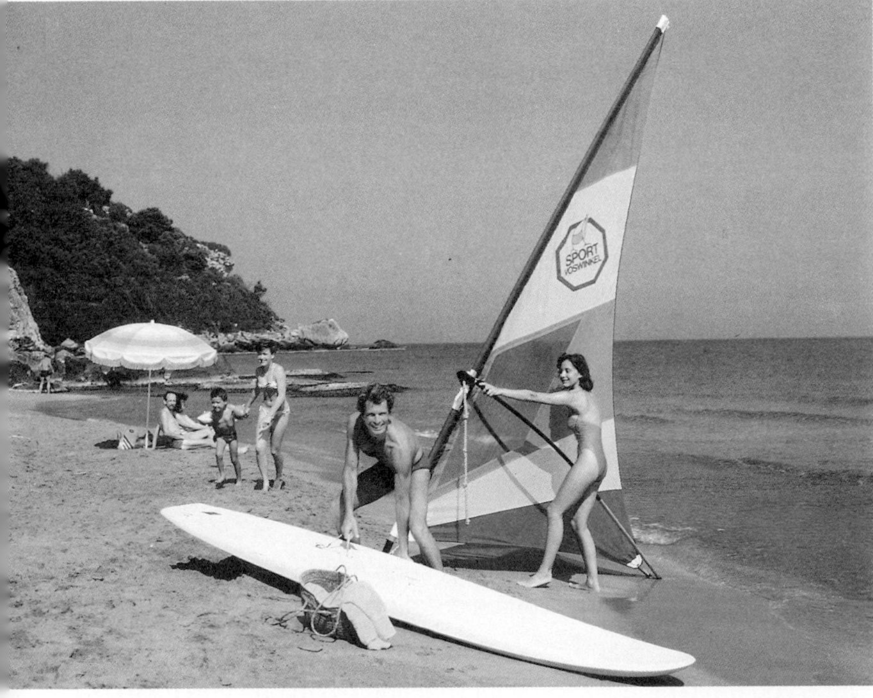

How many examples of design can you find in these pictures?

What does design mean in these quotations?

"Better by design" (Vauxhall)

"She has designs on him" (Common usage)

"Do you wear designer clothes?" (Contemporary usage)

"Designer stubble" (Wogan)

"We are all designers" (Papanek)

"Design is good for business" (Bayley)

"Design is the animating principle of all creative processes" (Vasari)

"He treasures up his bright designs, And works his sovereign will." (Hymn)

"...good design starts from the premise that living is more than just a matter of existing and that everyday things which are both effective and attractive can raise the quality of life ..." (Conran)

"A good basic design is timeless universally relevant more respectful of function and true to material" (Anonymous)

First-hand experience of design

What is your first-hand experience of design? One of the best ways to study design is to consider your natural reactions to man-made things. Look at any design, for example, a sports shoe. If your first reaction is to pick it up, then you are using your senses of sight and touch, including your past experience, to recognise and explain the object. You react to things when they are hot, sharp, delicate or rough, and your memory helps you to cope with such experiences. When you recognise things you name them and know something about what they do and why they have been made. You may take for granted these experiences because they are part of everyday life. However, suppose that you see an unfamiliar object, how do you react then? How do you begin to understand this experience, and what do you say and do? A new design may be in this category.

Your experience of design is not just that of man-made artefacts, from the past or present. It may also involve you in the use of 'systems' which have been devised for you to take action in. A good example of this is a 'fast-service restaurant', which has been designed for anyone to take clear and efficient action to buy and obtain a meal.

Designers also create 'ideas' and 'fashions' for you to use and be part of. An example of this may be found in the idea of a 'holiday in the sun' which has been carefully packaged and promoted by travel agencies.

You may not have been aware that such things have been designed, and that design involves creating not only 'objects', but 'actions' and 'ideas'.

Once you have established your reactions to things you may then begin to appreciate their design, if you have not done so already. All man-made things have been designed in one way or another. By understanding your direct experience of things, new or old, fantastic or familiar, you can increase your knowledge of design. This will help you when you create your own designs.

Seeing is believing! Look at and collect examples of design.

Which senses do you use to understand your examples of design?

Which experiences did you recall?

Do you like or dislike the design?

Do you react to its 'appearance', 'function' or 'value'?

Is it an 'object', 'action' or 'idea' or all three?

Identifying what things do

What is it that you see in examples of design? What do they look like? What do they do? You should aim to be critical of the designs which you see and use. How you express your ideas and feelings about design will depend on how well you question and think about your experiences and opinions.

You should aim to distinguish between facts about a design and your views about its appearance and use for and by people. Can you directly identify a design's function and usefulness to people?

One special feature of the electric carving knife is that it has 'unity'. Its internal, moving parts have been covered, as far as possible, to create unity for the whole product. How important is this for the user? How difficult was it for the designer to bring about in the finished design? Find other examples of such designing and consider what it is that you should question in any design so as to 'identify what things do'.

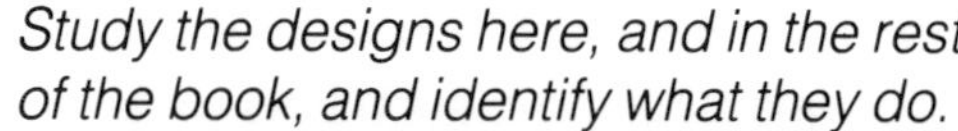

Study the designs here, and in the rest of the book, and identify what they do.

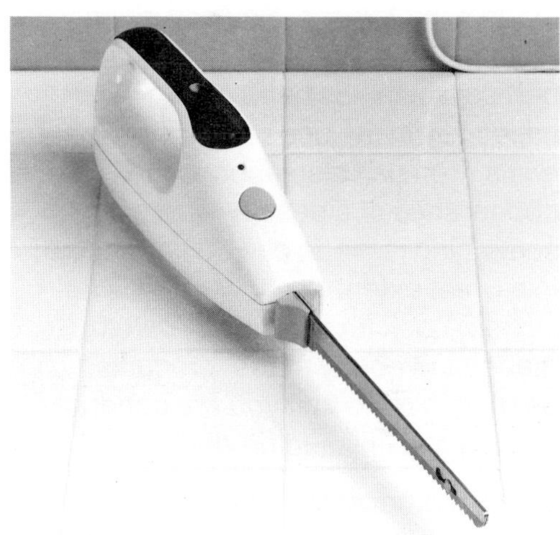

Skyship – The multi-role aircraft described by its manufacturer, British Airship Industries:

> 'The Skyship is uniquely capable of combining the abilities of V-TOL, hover and loiter, with a very high endurance. It can fly in weather which would ground many heavier-than-air aircraft, can undertake a variety of tasks in a highly cost effective manner and is therefore ideally suited for a number of quite different roles.'

The civil applications for the airship are 'promotional', 'passenger' and 'scientific'. Its paramilitary roles involve surveillance, detection of oil pollution and illegal transit, and search and rescue. There are many more uses for this flexible aircraft, can you think of them? Why is it better than a conventional aircraft?

What is 'fitness for purpose'?

Does the function of a design determine its appearance?

How important are appearance and function when you buy something?

What makes a design 'good' or 'bad'?

Can you always know what a design does?

Appreciating a well-made design

You may often find yourselves reacting to designs by appreciating how well-made something is. You can identify the craftsmanship, skill and technical expertise which has been employed, especially in the use of tools and materials. You can also appraise the final appearance of a design. How well something is made can be dependent, to a great extent, on how well it is designed. Look for examples of well made, and poorly made, products, bearing in mind that you are generally looking at a finished product.

Think of other studies which highlight how well made something is. Consider the 'evolution' of a hand tool's design, including the use of the chosen materials for its manufacture and why it came into being.

An example of a written study about how well made a design is, for example a 'hand-made carpenter's plane'. The hand plane, illustrated below, was made by the author's grandfather, circa 1900. He was a highly skilled carpenter-joiner in Camberwell, London. The plane was handcrafted for a specific job, involving mahogany mouldings for an Edwardian bank. He earned less than £2 per week and made most of his own tools, usually without the aid of drawings, but always to a high standard of accuracy and finish. The material for this plane is beech, but very often boxwood was used because of its hardness and closeness of grain. The steel blade was formed and ground from an old chisel. The plane's base is slightly curved so that the inside curve of a particular moulding could be shaped and smoothed. Notice the artistry used by the craftsman to give the tool an aesthetic finish in the style of tools of that time. His name was stamped on all his tools.

This plane is essentially an example of hand-crafted design and you may react to and acknowledge the materials used, its style and function, how well it is made and its history. On witnessing a mortise and tenon machine at a Crystal Palace exhibition, he said that such machines were the end of his craftsmanship and the need for his experience, skills and labour.

Collect examples of designs, for example, tools or household goods, and write a description and history for them, with special regard to how well made they are.

What techniques are used to make the design?

Do designers demonstrate their 'skills' for their own sake or for a purpose?

Appreciating the purpose and function of a design

You often react to how well a design suits its purpose and function. Most designs, whether hand-crafted or mass produced, are the results of the continual development of ideas about the best structure and form which a product may take. If a design is successful, especially if it is liked and needed, then it will be reviewed and developed over the years.

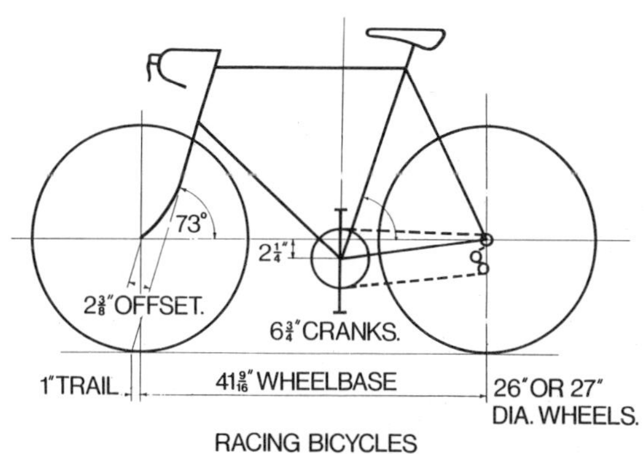

RACING BICYCLES

A racing bicycle is the result of an evolutionary process of manufacture and design. The conventional diamond frame bicycle has remained in its current form for many years and virtually every material and manufacturing route has been utilised.

Technically a racing bike is designed to perform in a certain way, but it will also function in a particular way because of its specific design. 'Modern cycles for racing purposes must now be of upright design, short in wheelbase and are generally used with 27' diameter wheels.' (T.I. Raleigh)

Generally the frame and fork designs for racing cycles require a short wheelbase, essential in a fast racing model. The actual length of the wheelbase is determined by the general design of the frame and forks. Have you enough technical information to understand fully how a racing bike works? Was the specially designed racing bike for the Olympic Games a winner? Is there such a thing as an ideal racing bike for any racer, or even a particular racer?

Look at your own bike, if you have one, and analyse exactly what it is as a machine, what it does and how it functions. Produce a series of sketches and notes to describe the functions of all the parts of a bike, how they fit together and so on.

Who needs a racing bike?

What scale of production is there for such bikes?

How many components does the bike have?

Designs which present information

Many designs are created to find and present information, in one form or another. You can make decisions from the information which certain devices give you, for example 'a light meter'. You can also follow instructions from, and make your own judgements about, the information portrayed in signs and images. An example of this can be seen in the schematic diagram which depicts a famous cricket innings.

Designers may use drawings to explore and contain information about their designs. They may also use images and diagrams to communicate specific information. These designs are only fully effective if they communicate their information clearly. A cartoon can do this very effectively, as in the Punch cartoon below which uses humour and exaggeration to convey its message.

In order to appraise certain designs you will need information about them. You can find this information by studying design briefs, by using the actual design or by canvassing people's views. You can research a design's history and significance to you and other people. You can also draw and represent a design so as to explore what it is. Your personal reactions and feelings, your likes and dislikes, are also valuable aspects of the information which you can find in and about a design.

IAN BOTHAM'S 149 NOT OUT AT HEADINGLEY

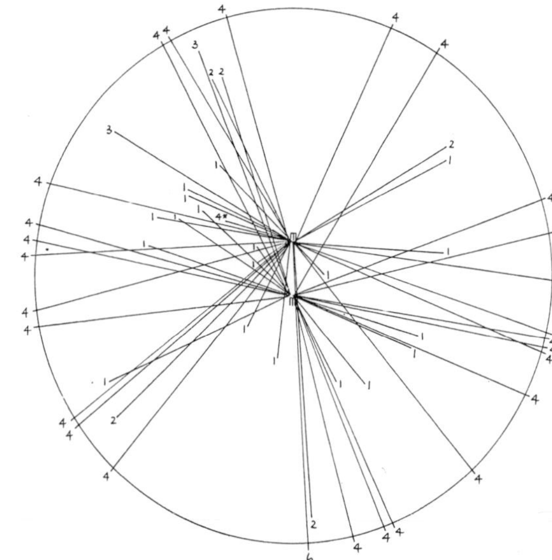

Runs	Balls	Minutes	6s	4s
50	57	110	-	8
100	87	155	1	19
149	148	219	1	27

Bowler	Balls	Runs	6s	4s
ALDERMAN	62	68	1	11
BRIGHT	21	15	-	3
LAWSON	44	44	-	8
LILLEE	21	22	-	5

BOTHAM'S SCORING SEQUENCE
000204200004010000100041000000031 0013014204*0010004040000040404400 4441040000006401000404†400010201 000100010001004000100040104204100 40100044100040000000. * 4 overthrows to the mid-wicket boundary † off a no-ball

NEW CRICKETING DRESSES, TO PROTECT ALL ENGLAND AGAINST THE PRESENT SWIFT BOWLING

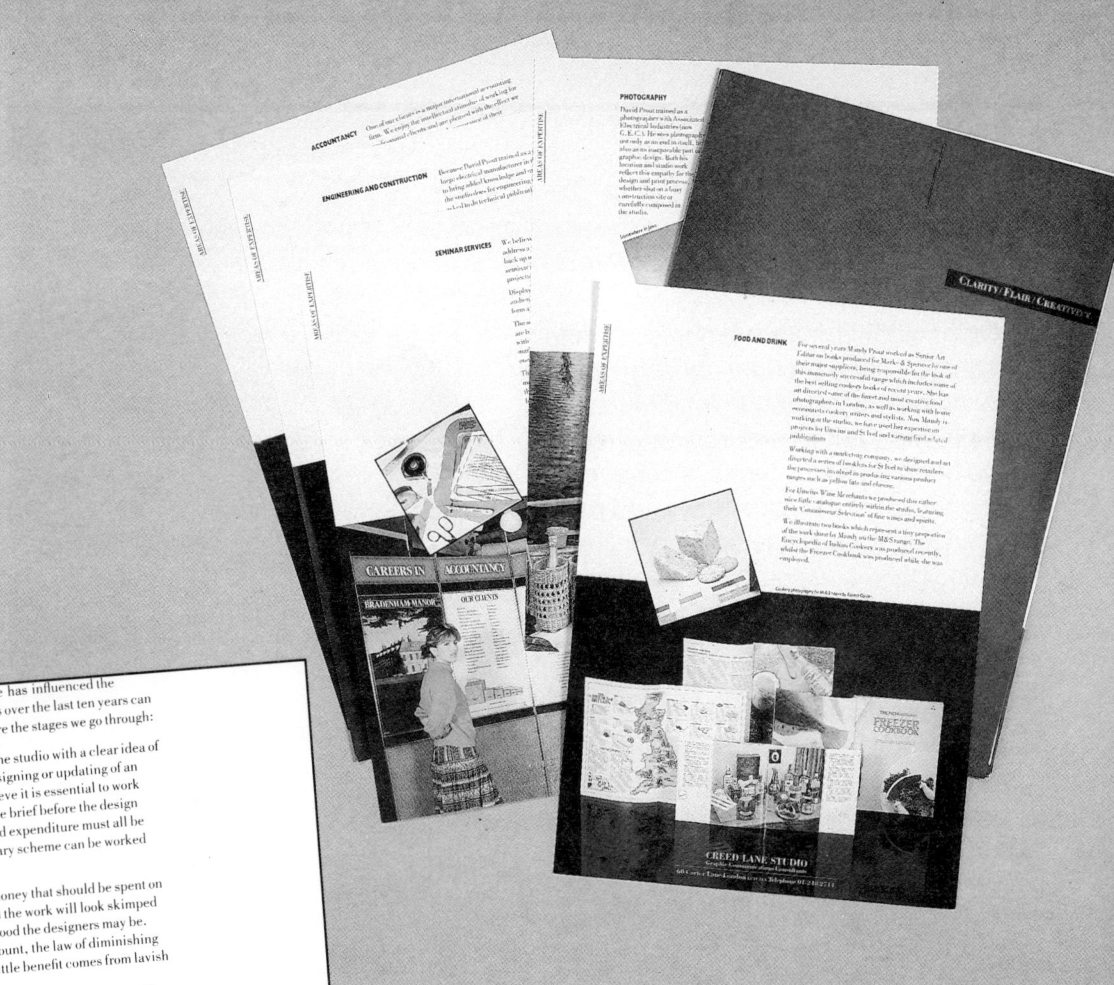

The ways in which our practice has influenced the communications of companies over the last ten years can be seen in our folder. These are the stages we go through:

Researching the brief Except when they approach the studio with a clear idea of their needs, such as the redesigning or updating of an existing publication, we believe it is essential to work with our clients to develop the brief before the design stage. The audience, aim and expenditure must all be evaluated before a preliminary scheme can be worked out.

Budget control There is a right amount of money that should be spent on any project. Too little – and the work will look skimped and inadequate, however good the designers may be. However over a certain amount, the law of diminishing returns comes into play. Little benefit comes from lavish budgets.

Over the time we have been practising, members of the studio have constantly been aware of the financial control needed on projects, and have gained a firm insight into the cost effectiveness of printed media.

Writing the words At Creed Lane Studio the quality of the copy is very important. If the client does not supply a setting script, we can commission an outside writer with specialised knowledge of the subject. Alternatively, draft copy can be ghosted and edited within the studio. Throughout any job we make sure that the copy works with the concept.

Words into print Typography establishes the tone in which the copy will be set and is an integral part of the design. The studio adds flair to copy specification.

Pictures on the page The choice of using photographs or illustrations, or a mixture of both is a subtle one, and a decision which must be taken at the beginning of a job. In most of the examples shown the photographs and illustrations were done by ourselves. Photographs taken in Java or Ryadh can be seen in the Schlumberger and Alfadl work whilst the Unwins photographs were carefully composed in the studio. We drew the diagrams to show oil field activities, but have commissioned work from many fine illustrators.

Hands across the seas We'll never call ourselves Creed Lane Studio International but last year alone we worked in Arabic, Indonesian and French and sent work to Jakarta, Jeddah and Houston. We enjoy arranging translation and travelling abroad to take photographs for our clients. We|are international in outlook and maintain clients and contacts thoughout the world.

Print The studio handles print for the majority of its clients – thereby offering a complete service from brief to delivery. It gives us the opportunity to recommend the best way of producing your job and to monitor the quality throughout.

Delivery We hate to think of our work locked away in a warehouse, and so we frequently undertake our clients' distribution. This may involve sending recruitment brochures to universities in Great Britain or house magazines throughout the world.

The work of a design studio

Design itself can be purchased from design studios and agencies. A well designed 'image', 'product' or 'service' is successful. Many enterprises acknowledge that it pays to advertise and that it is crucial to design well. Study the service which the example of a design studio offers.

What type of designs are shown here?

Do they require specialised information to understand or use them?

Collect examples of designs which find and give information.

What does a designer service offer and who might benefit from it?

Design and new technology

Technological improvements in manufacturing have brought about mass production and consumerism. They have improved living standards and created the need for many types of consumer products. New technologies and rapidly changing knowledge are very influential in design. Many companies and services invest in design and use design departments within their organisations. Research and development agencies are other ways of using design and technology to bring about modified or new products. Can design bring about new knowledge? Is design essential to the improvement of our lives?

In 1919 new technologies involving aircraft brought about a novel idea for landing aircraft in cities. Would this scheme work? If it could work, who would benefit from it?

Design affects the quality of our lives. Does the use of robots rather than people represent the use of new knowledge; and what are the consequences of such a decision? We are surrounded by 'man-made' products, environments and systems. Good design will meet the need for things to be well made, to work well, to be reliable, safe and pleasing and comfortable to use, as well as to be easily maintained and economical to make. Good design will use appropriate materials, tools and manufacturing skills, as well as all forms of knowledge.

What are the motives for these designs?

Do people think highly of them?

Are designers responsible in any way?

How has design and technology improved your living standards?

THE PROBLEM OF LANDING AEROPLANES ON BUILDINGS: THE HANSON SCHEME.

The picture is given under the following title: "Would this circular track solve the landing problem?—The problem of providing a suitable landing-platform for flying-machines in our large cities has always puzzled engineers. This is Mr. H. T. Hanson's interesting solution. A banked track of open grating (its construction is shown by the detail drawing on the left) is carried on latticed towers over a group of buildings. On such a track the pilot can start and alight dead against the wind, as he always must. At one point of the track he runs off upon an elevator platform flush with the roof of a convenient building. By means of the elevator he descends to the garage below."

Do you know how to cope with highly complex and technologically advanced designs? How can you make sensible decisions about them? As a member of the general public how should you be kept informed about them? How much can be taken on trust? What do you need to know? If you are interested to understand advanced knowledge and also wish to somehow become involved in complex projects or issues, how can you be successful in this aim? A study of examples of where new knowledge in design is used or sought may be a good place to start.

'Steam or petrol': if steam had been developed instead of petrol would there be the same transportation that is available today? General Motors concluded that 'whether a practical steam engine automobile can be reliable in the future is still an unanswered question. However, new engineering materials and technology, along with the possibility of new fluids replacing water as the working medium in the cycle, make the steam engine a contender among proposed low emission power plants.'

Once an idea has been tried and tested, people then have the confidence to consider further designs. This may be as much to do with making new things as in using them. Do you really know how a television works; could you redesign one? Would it be worthwhile designing a robot which could carry out design work? Is it possible to design a nuclear power station to outlast radioactive substances? Can a complex system be designed to 'self-regulate' itself and to maintain its own safety standards? Is it possible for designers to ignore the excitement of finding and using new knowledge?

Why are things designed in the way they are?

Who decides how different technologies are adopted?

Do these designs use new knowledge?

When did they come about?

Should a design last forever?

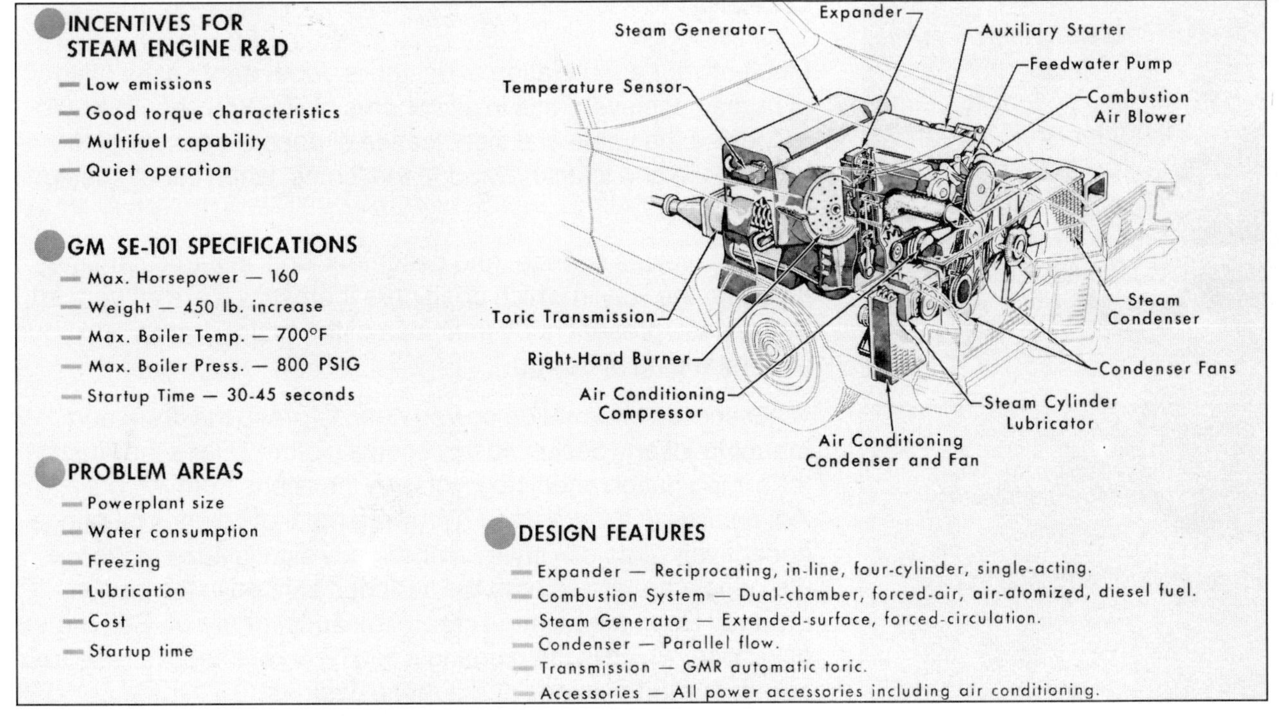

INCENTIVES FOR STEAM ENGINE R&D
— Low emissions
— Good torque characteristics
— Multifuel capability
— Quiet operation
GM SE-101 SPECIFICATIONS
— Max. Horsepower — 160
— Weight — 450 lb. increase
— Max. Boiler Temp. — 700°F
— Max. Boiler Press. — 800 PSIG
— Startup Time — 30-45 seconds
PROBLEM AREAS
— Powerplant size
— Water consumption
— Freezing
— Lubrication
— Cost
— Startup time
Expander
Steam Generator
Auxiliary Starter
Feedwater Pump
Temperature Sensor
Combustion Air Blower
Steam Condenser
Toric Transmission
Right-Hand Burner
Condenser Fans
Air Conditioning Compressor
Steam Cylinder Lubricator
Air Conditioning Condenser and Fan
DESIGN FEATURES
— Expander — Reciprocating, in-line, four-cylinder, single-acting.
— Combustion System — Dual-chamber, forced-air, air-atomized, diesel fuel.
— Steam Generator — Extended-surface, forced-circulation.
— Condenser — Parallel flow.
— Transmission — GMR automatic toric.
— Accessories — All power accessories including air conditioning.

Identifying the background to design

Much of your appreciation of design is dependent on the history of human achievements in all spheres of life. You should aim to recognise the value and significance of people's accumulated experience and to acknowledge the 'times' when certain designs came about.

Design involves change, and designers work in particular times. Knowing the way in which designers themselves are influenced, by the past, present or by their idea of the future is crucial to your understanding of design.

What special information do you need to grasp the 'form and meaning' of any design, in this case a picture? Does the illustrator's imagination affect how you see the scene from *Alice's Adventures in Wonderland*? Why are most of Lowry's paintings deceptively simple in style? Is there any significance to the way the people are drawn or to the factories painted in the background? Does the painting create the atmosphere of 'Coming out of school', which is the painting's title? You will need to research both facts and opinions about these designs.

In what way is a painting an example of design?

How do these designs compare with mass produced designs?

Are these designs unique?

What were the influences on the artists and designers who created these designs?

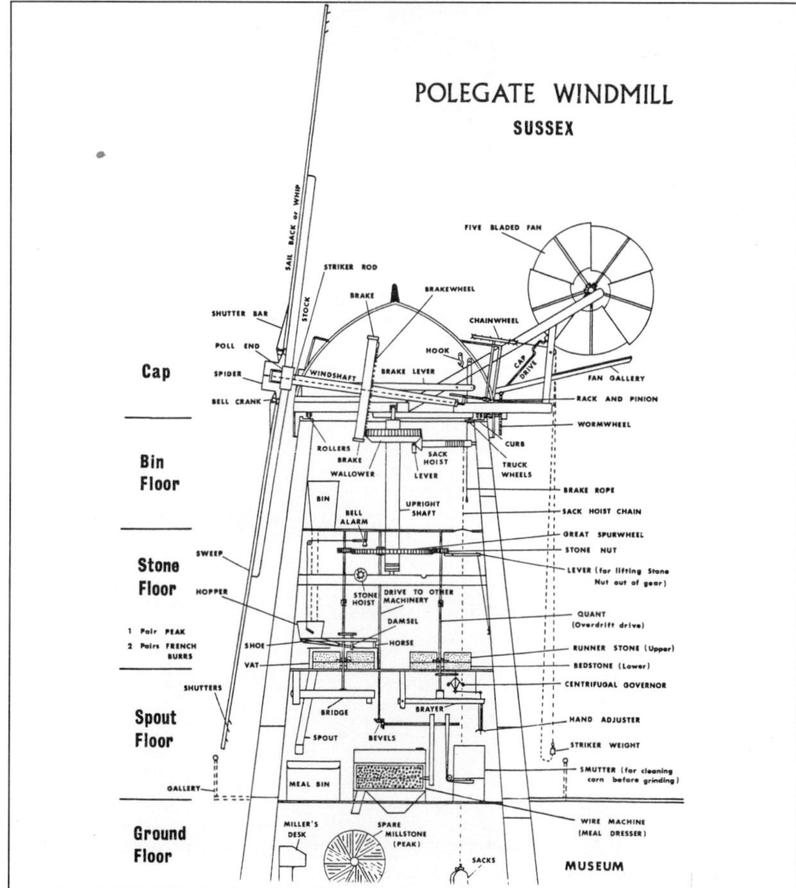

Can you identify the background to the design, development and decline of 'windmills'. Are they considered to be in any way a blot on the landscape? Compare their aesthetic value to the future development of satellite television. For example, how might the commercial development of satellite television affect your way of life and environment? Will city skylines and suburban gardens feature large parabolic dishes as a matter of course? Consider the way in which television aerials have been accepted in recent times.

The history of a design: the Ford Oval

The Ford script-in-oval trademark is one of the best known corporate symbols in the world. It has been in regular use for over half a century, although the script lettering dates back to the very beginning of the company.

When Ford Motor Company was founded in the summer of 1903, Henry Ford's principle engineering assistant, Childe Harold Wills, who had trained as a commercial artist developed a stylised version of the words 'Ford Motor Company'.

This lettering was first used on company communications in 1903 and on a car in 1904 when it was used on some examples of the Model C. The words 'Ford Motor Company' in script lettering were used on a brass plate forming part of the starting handle aperture.

The script with the oval was first used for dealer identification in 1912, but the car identification was still the script: actually a winged triangle in orange, which carried the words 'Ford' (in script) 'The Universal Car'.

The Ford oval is displayed on the front and rear of each vehicle and on the centre of the steering wheel. At the front it is positioned centrally on the radiator grille and at the rear on the boot-lid or tailgate.

The purpose of this programme is to provide an easily recognisable and consistent form of identification for all the Company's European plants, facilities and products.

(Ford Motor Company)

What has been designed in these examples

What influences their use and development?

Design and different cultures

Different people and different lifestyles, from all over the world, have contributed to a myriad of designs. Is there something 'universal' about people's powers to design and make things, or do different cultures produce distinct designs of their own? You should aim to see how various lifestyles are reflected in the things which are designed and made. You should aim to know about, and enjoy, these differences, especially since they can add to the richness of your life. You can begin this design study by thinking of the objects and images which depict your way of life. Can you see them or do you need someone else to show you? In what way are the designs you see and know about part of your way of life, especially since you live in a multicultural society?

Which of the following list of designed objects are part of your way of life, part of someone else's way of life or would be known to anyone in the world: a knife, a potato peeler, a bus timetable, The Louvre, designer jeans, an 11th century Anasazi temple called Casa Rincanada, a sextant, a coin, a dam, an anchor, a Maserati, Kodak, graffiti outside a railway station, a bikini, a kite.

Islamic jewellery

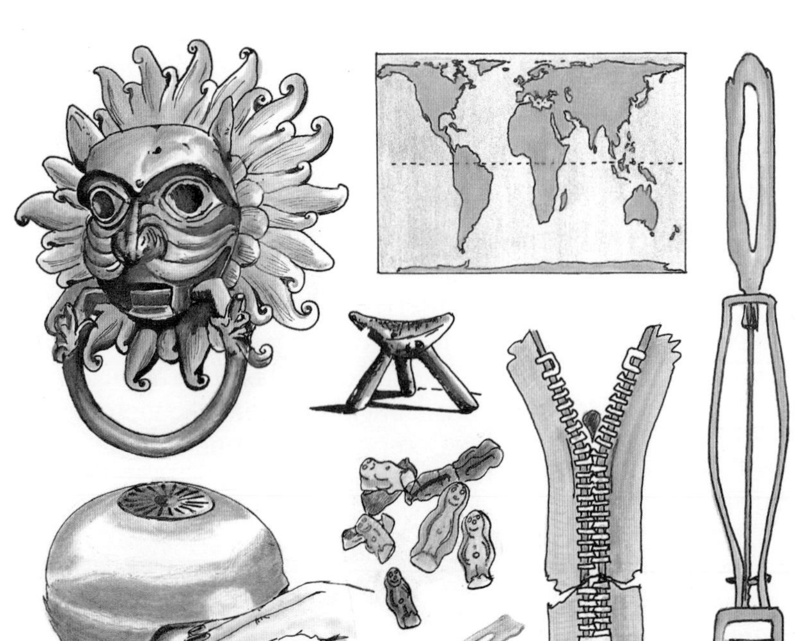

A cornish stone monument

> *Do you know how and why these designs were made?*
>
> *How do people use them?*
>
> *How lasting are they?*
>
> *In what ways are the designs you see and use part of your culture?*
>
> *How do you recognise this?*

What are the different lifestyles or cultures depicted in these examples of design?

Is a television programme an example of design? How does it show different lifestyles? Is entertainment designed? How is design used to make a television programme successful?

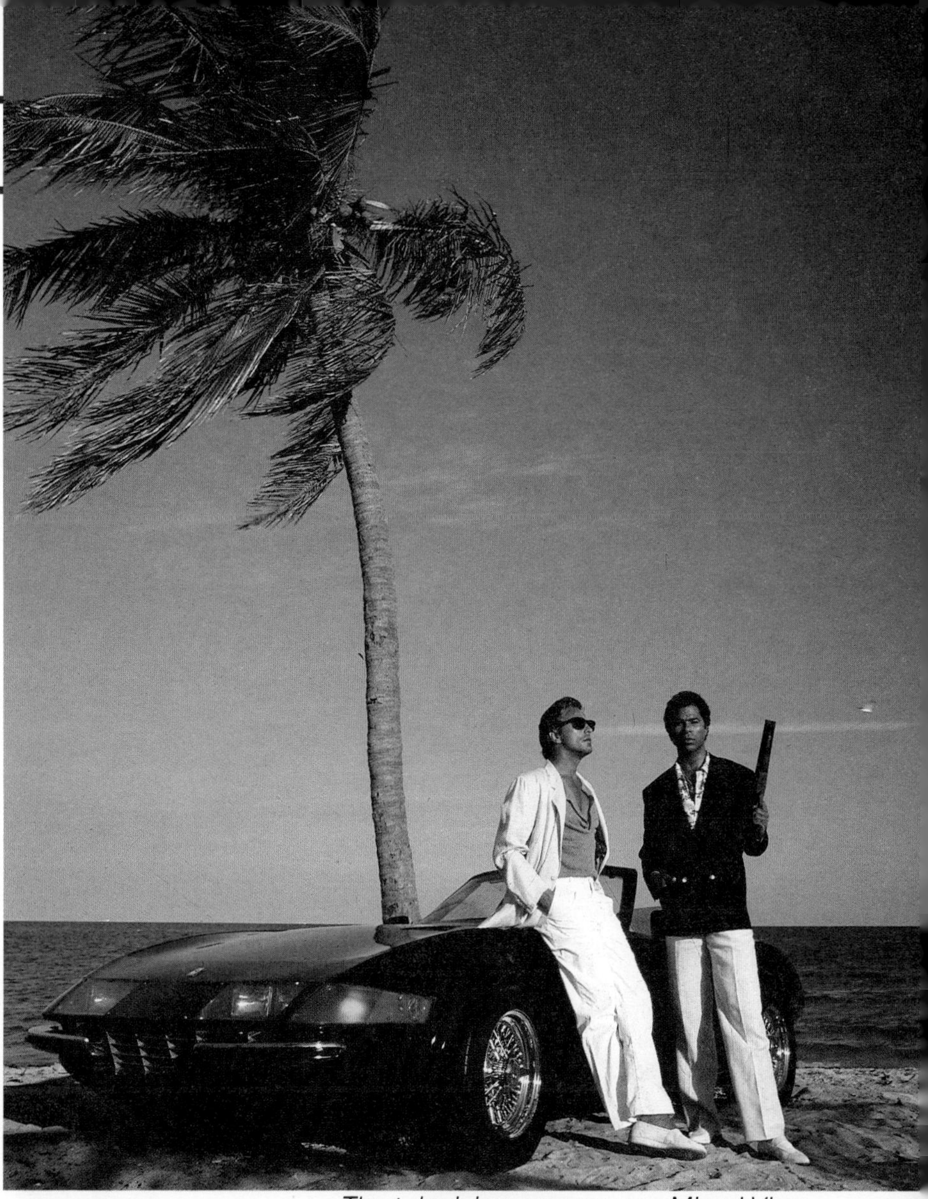

The television programme Miami Vice

A Sioux Indian carving of a horse

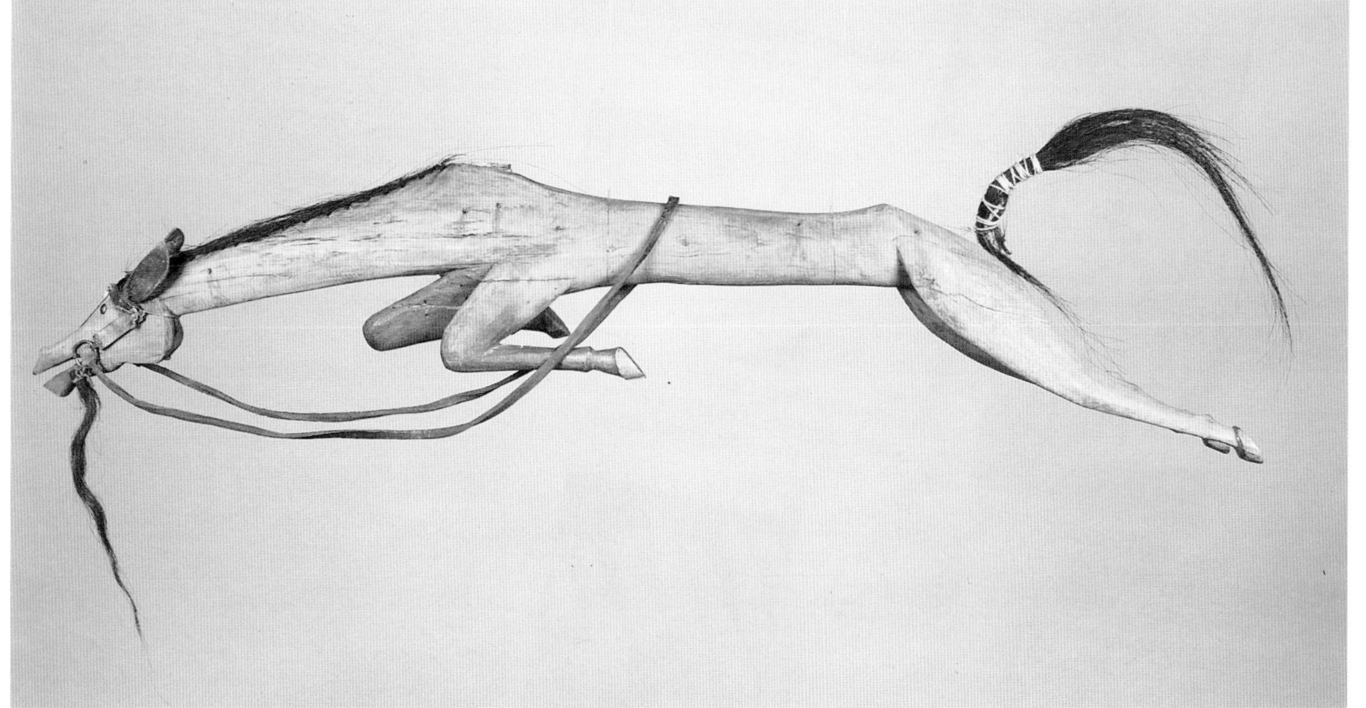

Is it design at all?

All things made by people have been designed in one way or another. Is there such a thing as 'undesign'? Is design the only way in which things change, improve or come into being?

Over the years vegetables have been cultivated, and by processes of selective breeding from plants originally found in the wild there are now many varieties of vegetables. For example, there are seven basic types of carrot used in the United Kingdom.

> 'The recent introduction of F.I. Hybrid varieties has not in any way altered the shape of the roots. Emphasis has been directed to the improvement in uniformity thereby increasing marketable yield and the elimination of discolouration in the crown both externally and internally. Further work is progressing in Hybrids but, again, this will be concentrating on disease resistance . . . rather than the alteration in shape.'
>
> (Asmer Seeds)

Thus, through the process of hybridisation we use nature to create the food we need.

Would anyone in the world know what these things are? Is there anybody in the world who would not understand these pictures?

Autumn King. The latest maturing of all and used for late autumn and winter production.

New Red Intermediate or **St Valery.** Never used commercially but as roots are long with an even taper from shoulder to tip, coupled with a very deep colour, this variety makes an excellent carrot for the show bench.

Early French Frame. Almost globular root used only by the amateur gardener.

Chantenay Red Cored. Wedge shaped carrots used now almost exclusively by the canning industry.

Berlicum. Almost cylindrical but with slight taper towards root end.

Amsterdam Forcing. 'Finger' carrots, cylindrical in shape for very early crops under glass or outside.

Early Nantes. Again cylindrical but heavier roots and later maturing than Amsterdams.

Is man the only designer?

Is design the only way in which things come into being?

What evidence do you need to be convinced that designing has happened?

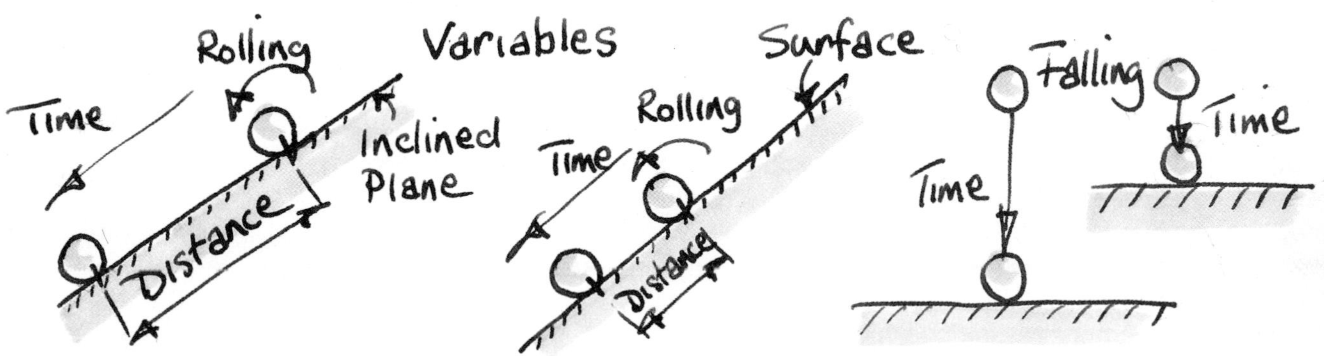

What can you observe when a ball is rolled down an inclined plane?

Scientific experiments may also require designing. A famous example can be seen in the inclined experiment devised by Galileo. This experiment observed '. . . that the distance travelled by a descending body increases in proportion to the square of the time that has elapsed'. The experiment does not need a hypothesis for its design and no theory for its interpretation. How is this so? What can you observe when a ball is rolled down an inclined plane? What are all the variables involved in this experiment? What value does an experiment like this have?

Beavers are capable of constructing distinctive homes, called lodges, using their teeth and feet. They also build dams and canals, living their lives entirely surrounded by trees, rivers and lakes. Does a beaver look at the design and construction of the lodge in which it is born and then build its own lodge by trial and error? It seems that beavers have an innate sense of how things ought to be for themselves. But they do not cut trees to fall in the right position to build from. When building their lodges they react by instinct to stimuli in their environment and not through learned behaviour. Natural selection over millions of years has contributed to any improvements which might have been made by beavers to the design of their lodges. It seems that the more complex a task for an animal the more likely it is to be innate behaviour. Could these ideas be applied to humans? Are we born with an ability to design or do we learn how to design during our lives?

A beaver's lodge

Are carrots designed?

Is a pattern a design? Does its creation require designing?

Is a scientist a designer? Does an experiment involve design?

Is a child's game designed?

Were ancient monuments designed?

Is a beaver a designer?

The influence of designers

You may react to a design because of the designer. You may like certain designers because you admire their work, or because it is fashionable to own an example of their design. You may also react to the ideas and products of companies by identifying with the style and status which these may bring. Generally you acknowledge designers' skills and ingenuity by saying things like 'This is a good idea. . . .', 'Isn't it simple . . . ?', 'I'd like to own one of those . . .', and 'Why didn't I think of that . . . ?'

How designers are influenced, as well as how and why they generate new trends, are yet other ways by which you can understand what designers do. You can admire how they overcome problems. You may appreciate a designer's ability to design something which works well, which looks good and is a pleasure to use.

Designers can inspire artistry and craftsmanship, as well as economic and technical innovation. They can be entrepreneurs and technical experts as members of design teams.

Does a designer create real things?

How do designers use their imaginations?

What does a designer do to influence people?

What is 'style'?

Do we buy things because they are well designed?

How many people were involved in these car designs?

How much research went into these designs?

Did the research find anything new?

Do designers change their minds as they work?

'Using only his imagination and his drawing pencil the stylist designs cars of unsurpassed beauty . . . Dream cars serve a genuine purpose in the world of the automobile designer by stimulating their creativity. Styling is never used entirely for its own sake, but must harmonize with function. The final model of each component is used by the design department as a basis for manufacturing drawings and for production tooling. Any error now can cost millions later.'
(A car is born, Report 6, Volkswagen)

Design on a grand scale . . .

Large scale projects involve many skills and talents in their design and manufacture, including a designer's vision of the totality of a scheme. You react directly with a sense of wonder and fascination for such mammoth designs. You may, of course reject such feelings, but the success or failure of large scale projects affects us all in one way or another. At times you may also react to the sheer simplicity of a design, large or small.

People make designs successful. You either need a design or believe that you want it, and so continue to buy it and use it. Some designs are successful, others are not. Designs can reflect 'popular taste', or change it.

41-Bonboard Scene of EVA . . . The helmet visor of Astronaut Bruce McCandless 11, 41-B mission specialist reflects the outside of the forward bulk head (cabin area) of the Earth orbiting Space Shuttle Challenger. Because of the nitrogen-propelled manned manoeuvering unit (MMU) the astronaut is wearing, he was able to become independent of the mothership, marking the first time in history that a crew member had such freedom. (NASA)

. . . and in the future

There are still unsolved problems and many more worthwhile designs to be created and used. It is not in the nature of designers to ignore the possibilities which the future holds. One generation's fantasies may be another's reality . . .

Preliminary designs for a space station called 'power-tower'. This conception, produced by Martin Marietta of Denver, shows a space station utilising a solar dynamic power generation system. (NASA)

Hidden design

Things are not always what they seem to be. Designs are created not only for their appearance and function but also for their value as status symbols. You may attach meanings and significances to certain designs. This is because many products are designed to have an 'image' or 'hidden message'.

The status which owning certain products gives is a continuing feature of design. Mass consumption has brought about the design for a variety of consumer products. You may have been encouraged, whether you know it or not, to buy things because of their style and fashionable status. Many designs are the product of the notions of built-in obsolescence and planned strategies for selling goods to targeted markets. Advertising uses hidden messages to attract your attention to buy things. Are you aware of the hidden messages in the designs which you know about and buy?

Design can be employed to add certain qualities to products or to mask the effects of their use. The following examples represent some of the different aspects of 'hidden design'. A power station built into a mountain uses natural forces to generate electricity without possibly harmful effects to the external environment. Film and television effects are designed for you to see but not for you to be aware of when they are part of a programme, because this would spoil their impact. Final artwork and instructions for printers represent a design in action, and would ruin the quality of the finished design if they were shown. Often sexuality or family relationships are used as means by which you might be influenced to buy things. They represent our preoccupations with certain ways of life or approaches to life. Would you buy a car which can travel on a ceiling . . . ?

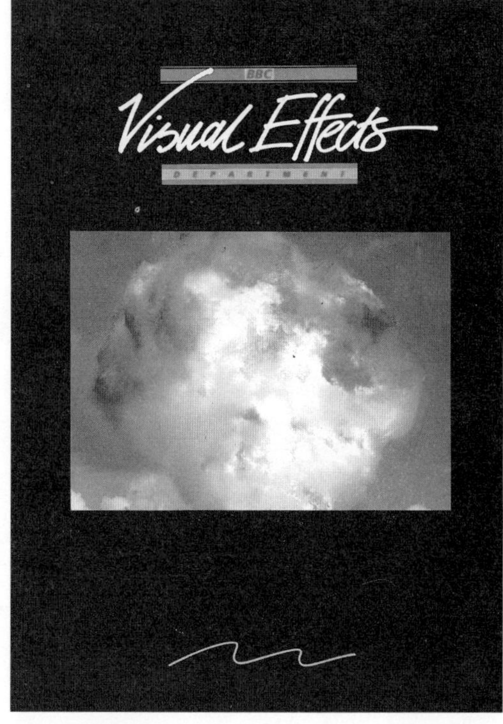

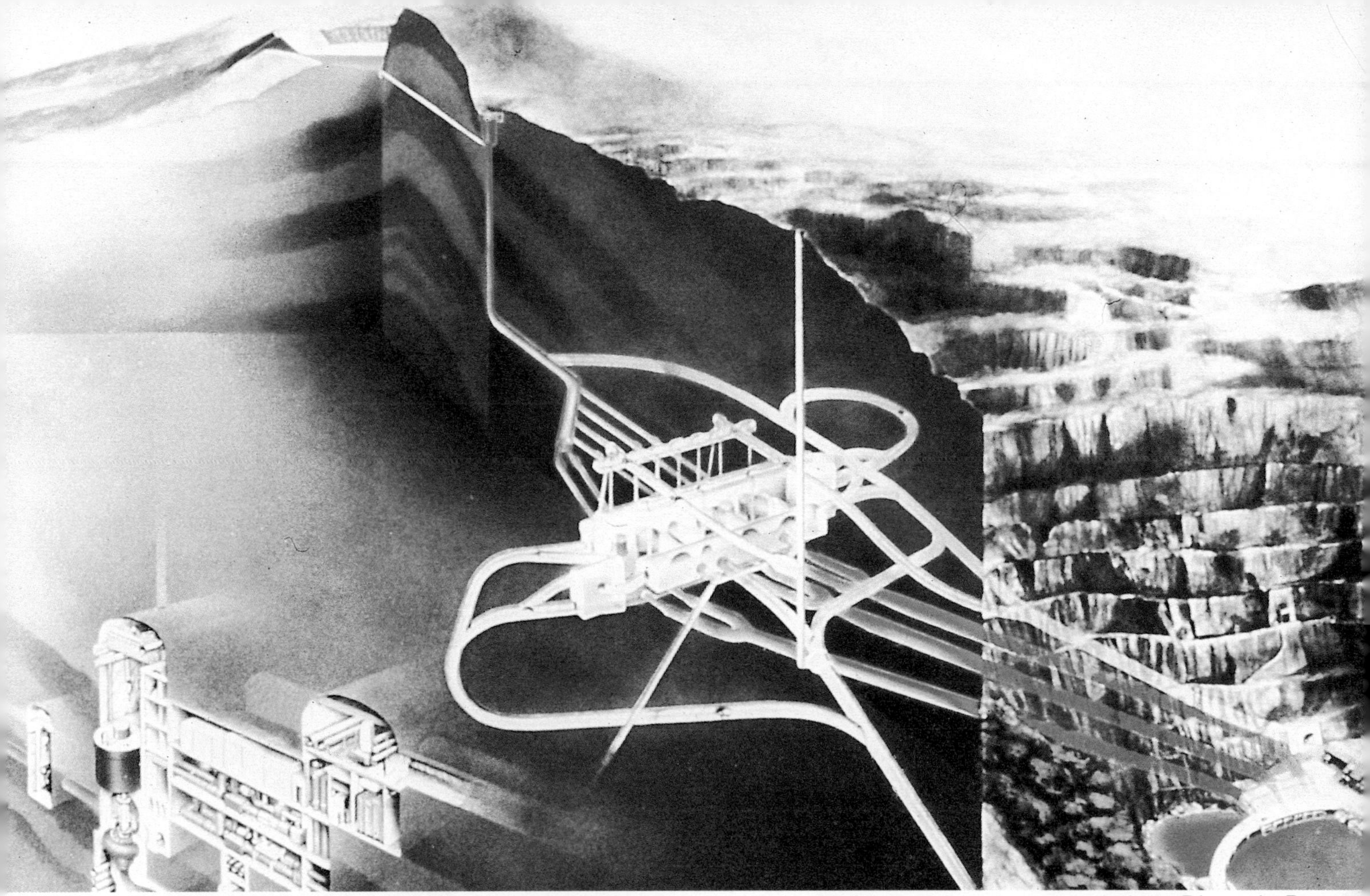

Dinorwig the underground giant. Dinorwig Pumpe Storage Hydropower System, Wales. (CEGB) Six MW generator/motor units operating under 536m head.

Like father, like son.
Little boys can't wait to grow up like their dads. While dads, of course, are just little boys at heart.
With their dad's example–and a little encouragement from you–boys grow up enjoying the healthier ways of life.
They get to know about Flora margarine, too.
Flora's made with pure sunflower oil, so it's high in polyunsaturates.
The taste is one that men – and boys – seem to like. Light and delicate.
How soon will all your men be Flora men?

What has been designed in these examples?

What are the hidden meanings behind these designs?

Why is sexuality used in advertising?

Are you intended to respond to 'hidden design'?

In what ways are 'hidden design' beneficial or harmful?

Variety in design

Designs evolve and change as ideas, experience, technologies and commercial needs vary. This may or may not be deliberate. How far designers pursue alternative designs and bring about your need for new products and services is a continual process. Also, things are not always designed to their full potential.

The restlessness for change and variety, from individually designed, highly specialised luxury goods to the mass production of everyday products, comes from a designer's need to be successful. It may also come from the type of financial support the designer can command. Variations in the quality of designs as well as the multiplicity of choice for consumer products are also reasons for the different varieties of design available to you. Do you choose the designs you want?

Personal stereos

On test: 35 personal stereo cassette players (14 have radio, too). Results, and our price-banded pick of the bunch, overleaf

There are literally dozens of personal stereos on the market, from the simplest that will only play cassettes, to those which will also record on cassette and include a radio. There are special ones which are water resistant, extra-small ones little bigger than the cassette itself, radio-only ones a bit thicker than a credit card but otherwise no bigger, and even one that costs over £200.

We've tested 35, costing from £14 to £75. All can play cassettes, and 14 have built-in radios.

Our tests – see Table

There were three main parts to our tests: we started with a series of lab tests on each set's cassette mechanism, amplifier, headphones, and, if it had one, radio; then five expert listeners assessed sound quality from cassette and on radio; finally, the sets were shared between a panel of 48 users to see how they did in ordinary use. The results appear as ratings in the Table overleaf.

Accessories

In the Table we list the accessories that came with the sets. The Tandy models were the only ones for which headphones were not included – they had to be bought as extras. There are other accessories available as extras (not listed): mains adapter and external loudspeakers, for instance.

Weight and size

Generally, the smaller and lighter, the easier a set will be to carry around, particularly if you want to keep it in your pocket. There are ratings for size and weight (including batteries) in the Table; the Keys tell you the range of sizes and weights that each rating covers.

Running costs

We measured the amount of current each set used when playing a music cassette at a comfortable listening volume. From this figure and the size, number, and cost of alkaline batteries, we rated running costs according to the Key shown under the Table. It would cost a few pence a year to run the set off the mains via an adapter, but, of course, you can do this only when close to a mains socket.

If you're listening to the radio, you won't run the batteries down as quickly as when you're listening to a cassette.

Features

All the sets had volume controls and buttons for play and fast forward wind of cassettes, so we haven't put these in the list of features in the Table; but we have told you which sets have a **fast forward wind button which locks down** (feature d) so you don't have to keep your finger on the button. If you want to go back through a tape, a **rewind** (b) button

Which? December 1985 Personal stereo cassette players 549

VACUUM CLEANERS

A clean sweep of the market

If nearly all your vacuuming is done on fitted carpets, you could go for this upright Electrolux 560 (£90); it did well in our tests

Electrolux 350E

But if you want just one vacuum cleaner to clean stairs, skirting boards, upholstery, hard floors, curtains, and under beds as well, you'd be better off with a cylinder or canister type, and its attachments. You could go for the best in our tests – the pricey Miele S234i (£120, or £164 with its power nozzle), or the cheaper Electrolux 350E (£85)

Why is there variety in design?

Why is it important?

Why do styles change over the years?

How valuable is individual design?

Things alter over the years as needs change, as materials and information improve with increased knowledge. Study the history of any design to find out about its development. Contrast what you find with modern variations. Topics like 'swimming clothes', 'chairs', 'writing implements', 'anchors' or 'a sport' may be useful starting points. Consider categories like 2-D or 3-D designs, useful or silly, and universal or specialised.

Why are similar designs produced?

How do you make a choice from many alternative designs?

On what do you base your choice?

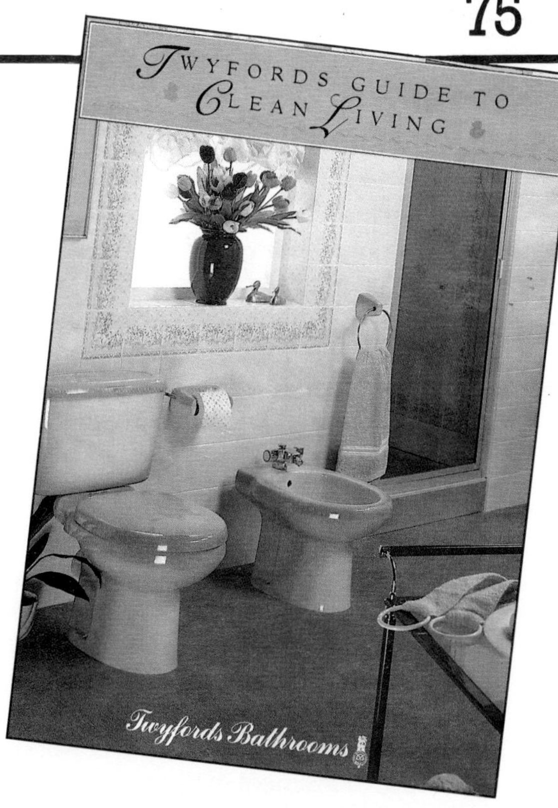

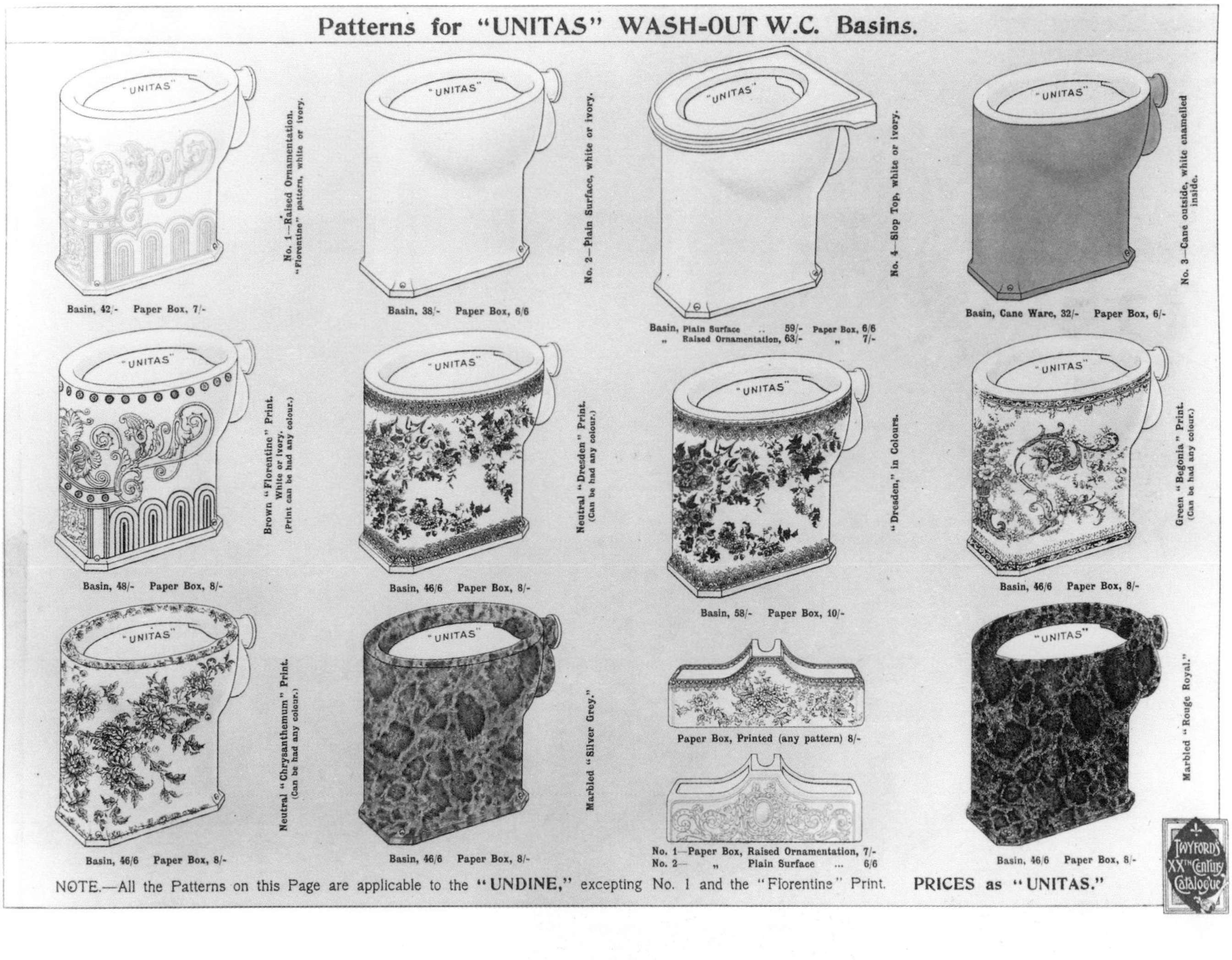

Patterns for "UNITAS" WASH-OUT W.C. Basins.

"UNITAS"
No. 1—Raised Ornamentation. "Florentine" pattern, white or ivory.
Basin, 42/- Paper Box, 7/-

"UNITAS"
No. 2—Plain Surface, white or ivory.
Basin, 38/- Paper Box, 6/6

"UNITAS"
No. 4—Slop Top, white or ivory.
Basin, Plain Surface .. 59/- Paper Box, 6/6
" Raised Ornamentation, 63/- " 7/-

"UNITAS"
No. 3—Cane outside, white enamelled inside.
Basin, Cane Ware, 32/- Paper Box, 6/-

"UNITAS"
Brown "Florentine" Print. White or ivory. (Print can be had any colour.)
Basin, 48/- Paper Box, 8/-

"UNITAS"
Neutral "Dresden" Print. (Can be had any colour.)
Basin, 46/6 Paper Box, 8/-

"UNITAS"
"Dresden," in Colours.
Basin, 58/- Paper Box, 10/-

"UNITAS"
Green "Begonia" Print. (Can be had any colour.)
Basin, 46/6 Paper Box, 8/-

"UNITAS"
Neutral "Chrysanthemum" Print. (Can be had any colour.)
Basin, 46/6 Paper Box, 8/-

"UNITAS"
Marbled "Silver Grey."
Basin, 46/6 Paper Box, 8/-

Paper Box, Printed (any pattern) 8/-

No. 1—Paper Box, Raised Ornamentation, 7/-
No. 2— " Plain Surface ... 6/6

"UNITAS"
Marbled "Rouge Royal."
Basin, 46/6 Paper Box, 8/-

NOTE.—All the Patterns on this Page are applicable to the "**UNDINE,**" excepting No. 1 and the "Florentine" Print. **PRICES as "UNITAS."**

TWYFORDS XXTH Century Catalogue

Design and aesthetics

Your aesthetic judgement depends on how capable you are of appreciating 'beauty'. This is often known as your sense of 'good taste'. You may also have 'ideals' by which you make your judgement of things. Very often designers seek ideal solutions for their design problems. However, they can also produce the minimum required to get a job done especially when working under 'pressure', and when keeping costs low. Any design can be improved upon since improvement and change are the very nature of design.

Your judgement of design is based on your likes and dislikes, your sense of good and bad, your accumulated experience, as well as your own designing. You should aim to make your own judgements about design. Do you know when a design is in good taste or poor taste; pleasant to look at and use, or, by contrast, whether it is objectionable in any way, too costly to make or buy, dangerous to use or incapable of working properly? Your aesthetic judgement of desgin is of great value to your own designing. It is also important that you recognise and feel a sense of beauty in the things which other people create. Why is this valuable?

Can you find one element in these designs which can be criticised?

The need for change

A new design often comes about because a designer becomes dissatisfied with something. In this case he or she might say things like: 'If only I can devise something to stop so and so happening'. This attitude or feeling is very often the starting point for design. But designers are not the only people who may feel this way. Who else may become dissatisfied with things?

From a need for change may emerge new ideas, which can be tested and pondered over; this can be the beginning of designing. Sometimes design comes about because of deliberate planning and thought; in this case you think first, then design. You can analyse your ideas and schemes for a design, or you may be guided by the actual solution for your design and make it as you design it.

Being aware of the need for design and defining who may benefit from it is important for successful designing.

An example of a design which is a response to the need for change is the Mercedes-Benz 'jumping windscreen wiper', described by one expert motoring observer as 'practically a re-invention of the windscreen wiper'. It is a device incorporating a crank mechanism which 'pushes' the single blade wiper up into the corners of the screen. This way it clears 86% of the screen's surface.

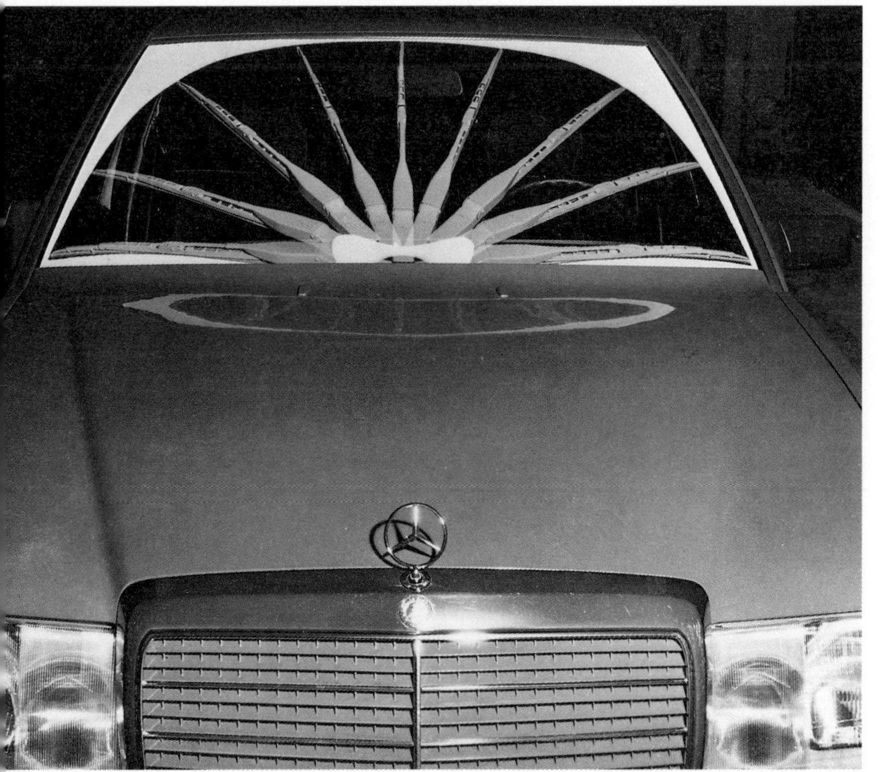

Tiles of the Unexpected

The brilliant vivid mosaics by Eduardo Paolozzi at Tottenham Court Road are the crown jewels of a complete modernization of the station. The mosaics pick up local specialities—music, videos, computers.

Finishing touches are now being put to the Northern Line platforms and subways, together with the escalator shafts and passageways up above.

At street level, we've widened the subway from the Dominion corner, as well as revamping other entrances.

It's been a long job, with inevitable inconvenience. But we hope you'll like the result.

WELCOME TO TWEETER AND WOOFER LAND

SNAP! SNAP! SNAP! SNAP!

When do you know that there is a need for change?

Does the whole design need changing or only part of the design?

How do designs evolve?

Who or what decides on change?

What do we do when we design?

Designing is essentially a matter of thinking about things in the future. Different designers design in different ways. Some design is intuitive and spontaneous, but a great deal of designing involves research and trial and error. You may conceive ideas for designs or they may be given to you in the form of a brief or specification.

Designers create designs, not real things. They design and imagine 'the appearance of things', they draw up 'plans from which things can be made'; they also communicate the possible 'ways in which things can be used by people'. Designers draw, take notes and make models and prototypes; they also analyse their findings and present proposals for the making and realisation of their designs. Designers communicate their ideas, firstly to themselves, then to those who will make the design, and sometimes to those who will use the design. Designers 'change', 'modify' and 'bring about new concepts' for all manner of man-made things, whether two-dimensional or three-dimensional.

An essential 'design process' is to think first, then act. At all times, you should be prepared to 'go back to the drawing board' whenever you realise that you can do better. Good designing comes from continual research and the pleasure of creating new ideas. It also may come from ingenuity and inspiration.

Did this designer work to a plan and sequence of events?

Did the designer explore different possibilities; if so, how and why?

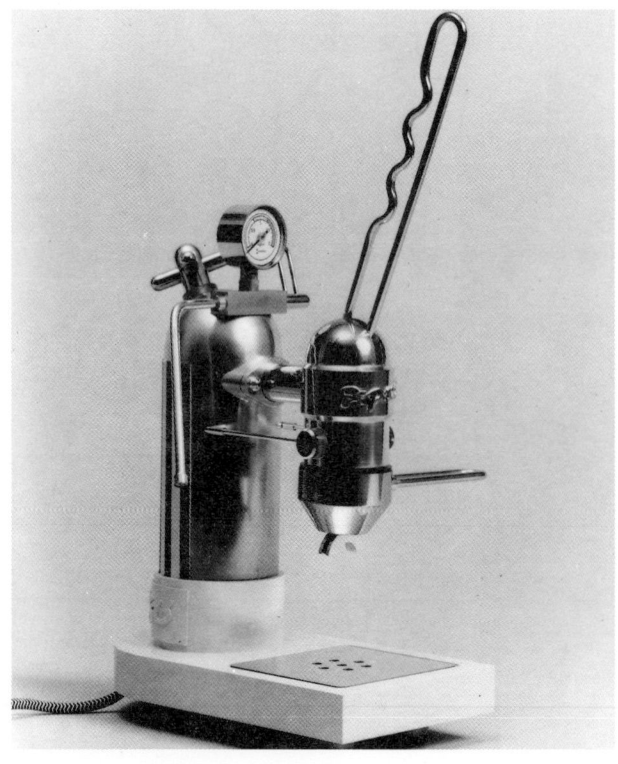

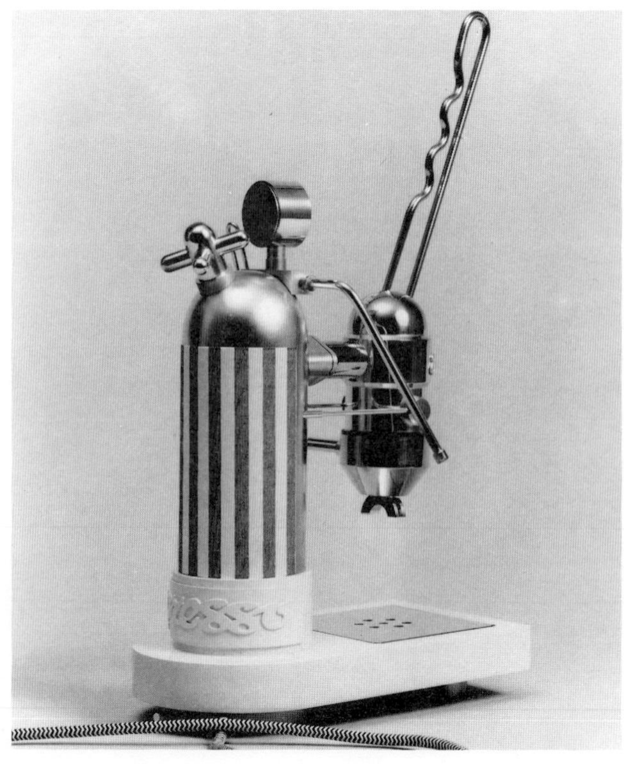

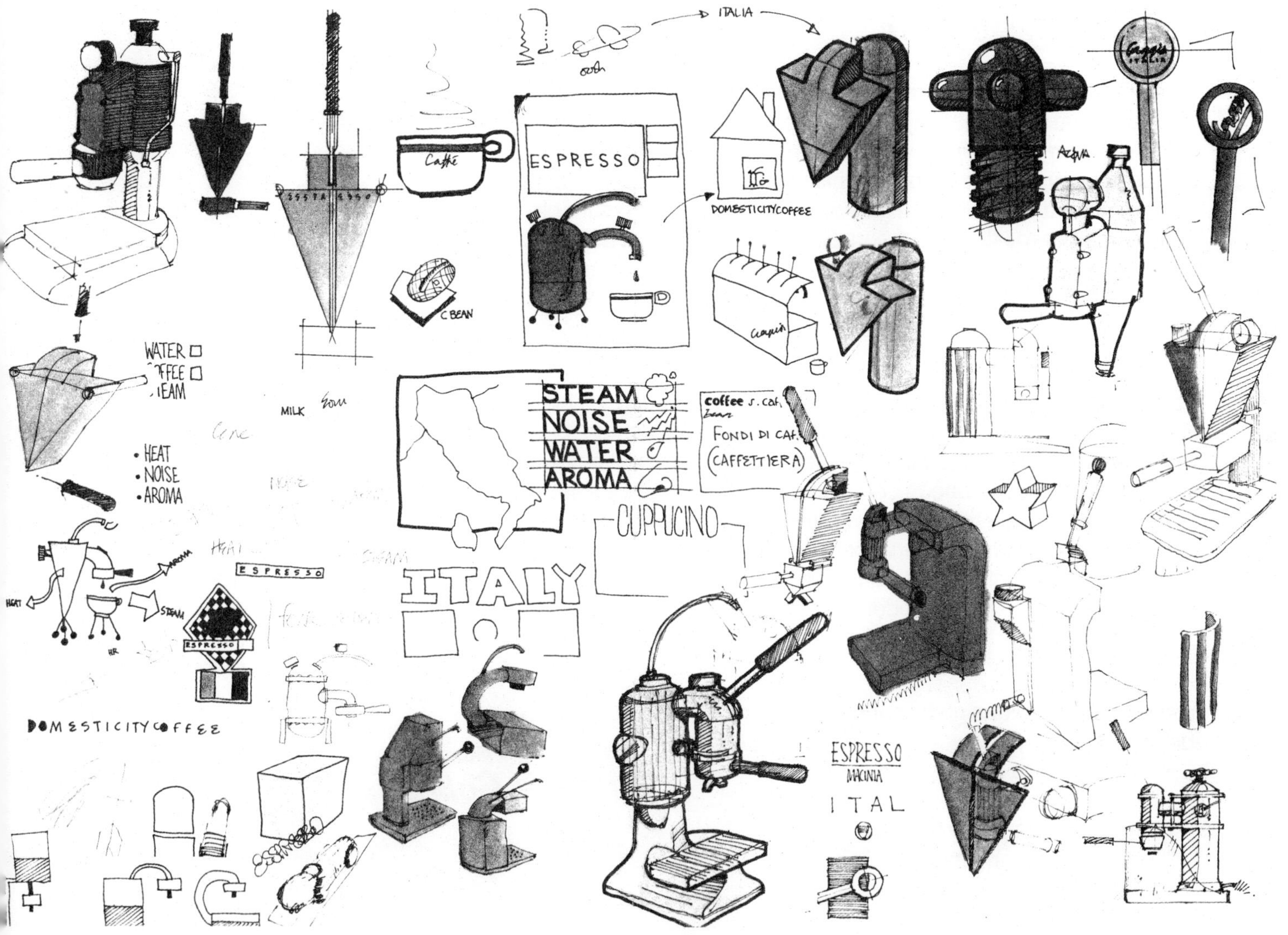

'While working on the design for the machine, I concentrated on the symbolism of the object and selected materials and forms which seemed to suggest themselves through its functional and social roles. The espresso was an exercise in using shapes and finishes that echo the function of the machine, e.g. chrome suggests hot water to me through its use in objects like kettles and taps. A main concern was for the espresso to have a strong visual presence, in and around the kitchen. Coffee drinking is a social pastime and the espresso takes on a central role in that activity. The traditional smell and noise of espresso making are its most striking features and demand a strong visual quality to them. Lots of knobs, dials and levers were used to encourage maximum participation in the preparation of espresso coffee.

My design process included a trip to Italy to look at existing machines, followed by working on preliminary sketches and block models. The prototype which is represented here, developed from this design.'

A.P. Dawey on his design for an espresso coffee machine.

Is a design a whole design or a collection of parts and functions to be designed?

How do the parts of a design relate to the whole design?

How does the inside affect the outside of a design, and vice versa?

Do design problems and issues stay the same or change over the years?

Do designs occur to fulfil certain needs or do designers create these needs?

Evaluating design

To evaluate a design you need to know something about it, to work out what you might say and to whom you might communicate the information. Pick out the essential quality and essence of a design, structure the way in which information about it can be communicated and set down a description and criticism suitable for whoever needs the evaluation. Ensure that plenty of examples are given, including comparisons, to support each element of the appraisal and write a conclusion, summing up the value of the design. You should aim to be as imaginative in your *interpretations* of design as you might be in your own designing.

Ordering
Describing
Designing
Classifying
Comparing
comparing
Positioning
Presenting
inter-relating
Evaluating

You should aim to be the originator of your design studies. Use the ideas, issues and questions outlined here about design for your own studies. Each example of design is unique and has arisen from particular needs or has been chosen to solve a problem. More often than not, you will see or use designs which are modifications of the original concept. You should aim to get behind the 'eye' of the designer to see how and why he or she designs. Establish your confidence to understand and appreciate design by knowing something about it and showing sensitivity to individual choices and styles.

You can evaluate design by considering:

- the influence of design on your way of life;
- your awareness of design and its value to you and everyone else;
- your identification of your reactions to it; as well as
- your understanding of design and designing.

You are all designers, in your own ways, and you are all capable of knowing and saying something about design.

FOOD AND DRINK

Coca-Cola – the real thing?

That J S Pemberton's original formula Coca-Cola had just one year to go to its 100th birthday mattered not one jot. Last year, Coca-Cola company chiefs decided to scrap the formula and replace it with new, 'smoother, rounder' Coke. They hadn't counted on the loyalty of America's Coke fans, who flooded Coca-Cola HQ in Atlanta with demands for the reinstatement of their favourite soft drink. Less than four months after its withdrawal, original Coke was back in the shops as Coca-Cola Classic, alongside the new version.

British Coke lovers will have the chance to try new Coke themselves when it's launched in the UK this year (there'll be Coke Classic, too). But in order to give you up-to-the-minute buying advice, we had cans of new formula Coke sent from America to our labs at Harpenden. There, 50 discriminating cola drinkers compared new and original Coke, and new Coke and its biggest rival, Pepsi. The tests were carefully controlled, and the tasters weren't told what brands they were tasting.

Last time we tasted colas (*Which?* August 1984), our tasters slightly preferred Pepsi to the other brands, which included original Coke. What did they think this time? In these latest tests:

- when given original Coke and new Coke, 14 tasters couldn't tell a difference. Of those that could, 18 preferred new Coke, and 18 preferred the old
- when given new Coke and Pepsi, nine testers couldn't tell a difference. Of those that could, 21 preferred new Coke and 20 preferred Pepsi.

Which only goes to reinforce our conclusion last time round that you might just as well try the cheapest cola of any brand you can buy, and keep on trying till you hit on the one you like best.

New Coke is about to be launched here: we've tasted it in advance – with some interesting results

What may be added or taken away from any design to make it better?

Making a start on your study

You will need to collect and analyse information for your studies. You should aim to use all the resources available to you, including your library, friends and 'contacts' and the subjects which you have studied.

Your research may involve taking photographs. Sometimes you will need 'snaps' to record ideas quickly and sometimes you will need clear, carefully taken pictures. The more you do yourself, the better your study will be, but do not be afraid to ask for advice and help. Letter writing is also an important way to find information. Writing to companies and organisations can be useful. Always write to a person if possible or use a title if you cannot find a name, for example, The Public Affairs Officer.

Your design study will in itself need designing. When you are thinking about the problem of how to put over what you have found, you make notes, diagrams, doodles and drawings. You may produce tables, graphs or diagrams to depict the information you have found. These ways of representing what you understood, need designing. Use all your skills and resources to present your findings well. Use pictures, colour, all your graphic design techniques and drawings and also include titles and written information and their sources.

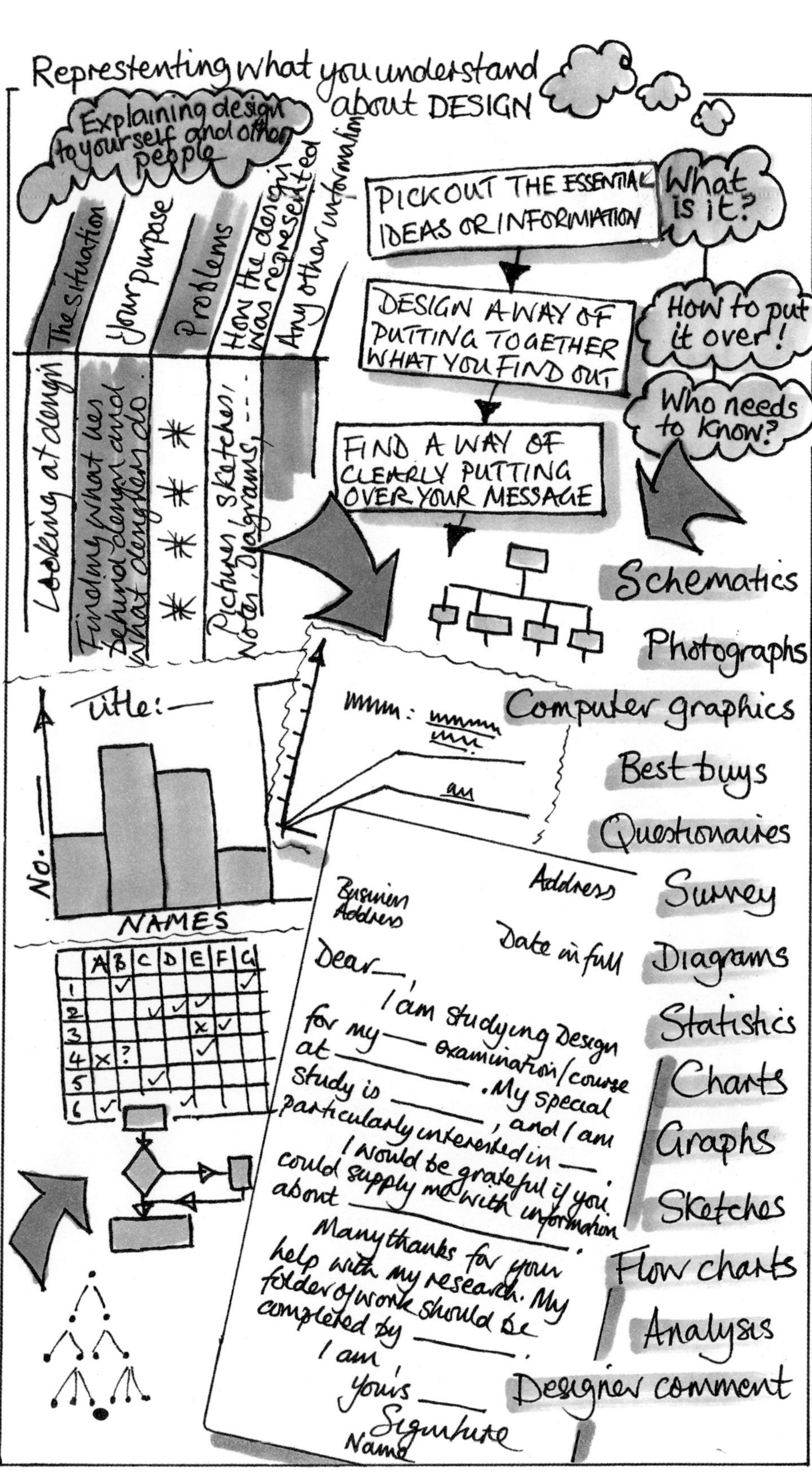

Use the statistical information in the *Which?* article on 'Coca-Cola – the real thing?' for your first representation of information.

What your design study should include

Here are some examples of design studies produced for work in design. Your study should include:

1. a title;
2. a clear statement about the subject matter and why it has been chosen;
3. the use of suitable sources of information related to your topic;
4. a reasoned argument which shows an understanding of the particular design by description and explanation, including other people's views;
5. clearly justified points of view throughout your study;
6. an appropriate style and format of presentation, for example a display or a folder.

You may not always be able to consider these points in the order given here. They will resolve themselves as you become involved in your research. Use the ideas given in this book, as well as your own ideas, for starting points.

An idea for a design study

'Before and after . . . or is it just a facelift?!'
How can manufacturers of very familiar everyday things like cans of beans use design to improve and update their product, rather than invent a new one? In this example, why did the designer keep to the same colours and design?

The aim of a commercial design exercise like this is for the manufacturers to increase their sales and profits. To do this they need to keep their products both in the public's eye and mind. A quick and relatively straight forward way to do this is to restyle the packaging graphics for an item like baked beans. Michael Peters and Partners were commissioned to 'discreetly' update the Heinz Baked Bean product. The 'after' design, shown on the right, has more gold lettering, a white line which is intended to emphasise the labels background and subtle changes in the lettering type. This project took many months but a bolder 'look' to the basic baked bean can label was achieved. Did you notice the change or did you pass it by?

The graphics for packaging is often changed. See if you can find similar examples.

Use this idea for a design study. Can you pick out the different stages of this study from the checklist for forming a study? Be a journalist or an academic, but get involved, be confident and use your ideas.

Section Two: Designing

Designing requires you to think, and to be imaginative in your problem solving and creativity, since you will be dealing with objects, actions and ideas in your mind. This is especially valuable if your work results in the invention or production of an original creative idea, a new machine or device, a fresh image or picture, or a better way of seeing or understanding our way of life. Can you say anything about the difference between a design created from an inspired idea and one produced by long, hard research? Where does our ability to design come from? Are we born with this ability or do we learn how to do it as our lives unfold?

Designing is essentially a matter of thinking about what it is you want to do and how you may achieve your ideas. The subject-matter for a design may be found in many areas of human experience. A design idea may come from the designer or be given as a brief by someone else. Designers think about future object. It is the subject-matter which makes design what it is, when it is completed; they produce a design, and not the final object. It is the subject-matter which makes design what it is, since there is no one process or procedure which is designing.

A designer draws, notes, models and analyses ideas, and simulates possible outcomes. These ideas are communicated to the designer alone or to anyone else working alongside the designer. Designing is exploring, testing and proposing some sort of change or action. Sometimes designing happens as something is being built or made. In this case the designer is being led by their solution for a particular design idea. Sometimes designing only comes about through research, analysis and judgement of alternative proposals. At other times it is intuitive.

Designing can mean many things to different people. Generally it involves creating 'the appearance of things' and 'their function', as well as 'knowing about the consequences which designs bring'. Designing implies that a designer wants something to happen or change. It is what you make of it in your time.

So that your designing has some structure to it your work should include:

1 a design folder which shows the progress of your ideas and the accumulation of information for your designs;
2 set of finished designs;
3 an evaluation report for each of your designs.

Understanding problems, Style, Awareness, Alternatives, Plan. Application of processes, Sensitivity, Media, Materials, Modification, Observation, Appraisal, Compare, State, Criticise, Present.....

Is there only one way to design?

Your folder should have in it design briefs which clearly state what you intend to design. You should show that you understand the design issues which you are studying. Investigate and analyse the information you require for your work. If your design is the result of an analysis, you should show the range of proposals which you have considered. At this stage your thinking may not produce solutions, but proposals for action. If you have formed your design as you have made it you should indicate at a later stage why you did what you did. However, you should explain why you have finally chosen one course of action. Your selection of appropriate techniques, processes and materials to make your design should also be noted. A plan for how you will realise your design will be helpful to you so that you can hold together all the different elements of your work. Your presentation drawings, models and notes should be of a good standard, since it is at this stage that designers convince other people of the value of their ideas.

When you come to realise your design, your work should show that you know how to use materials with skill and sensitivity, and that you know how to use certain tools and techniques for making things. Your realised design should have quality to its finish and presentation.

Your evaluation report should describe and compare what you have made with your original brief. It should be well presented and include comment about modifications and further developments and improvements for your design.

The designing described in this book takes you through various stages of thinking, planning, making and testing. The examples are based on open-ended design briefs which will have many possibilities for your designing. There will be activities which support the generally recognised areas of Design Education: Two-dimensional and Three-dimensional Designing, Technology, Fashion and Fabric, Food and Living Studies and so on.

There are many examples of students' work for you to study and think about. It is important for you to discover why design is a valuable human skill, and for you to produce your own designs.

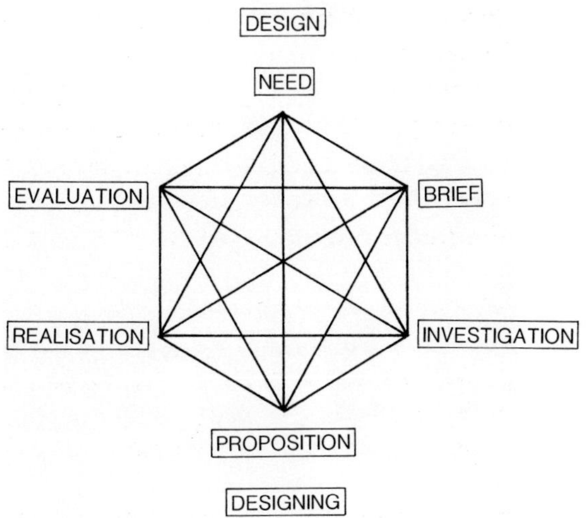

How useful is this set of processes for your designing?

The designer at work

This series of design examples (pages 86–89) demonstrates many of the activities in which a designer engages. Lesley Robson-Foster, graphic designer, works for BBC Television. She has kindly provided her sketches, notes, photographs, drawings and technical data, including a diary, for the design and filming of titles for *The Money Programme*. These examples are given so that you might experience the work of a professional designer. You will see that it is often complex and requires imagination, confidence and skill. Throughout this work, can you find the 'images' used for money, finance and economics? You are invited to produce your own designs as well as to evaluate the folio of designing.

Money Prog Titles

First Week in October.
Suggest having new titles to Editor, and also re design computer graphics to match.
Go away to think of ideas. Doing programme work all the time so only get about 2 hours a week to actually do anything constructive about new titles.

Thinking about making the logo out of a hologram, want something transparent so I can see live action behind.
Go and visit hologram companies - very expensive
Borrow a rainbow transmission hologram on thick acetate - spend a morning at rostrum camera house - BATFILMS with the hologram - trying to film it. Had to build lighting jigs because light has to be at a certain angle. Quite nice results - but very hard to control exact results
Go off that idea!

Last Week in October.
Decide to use 1" thick perspex model, had it made by model makers Alistair Bowtell.
Then had it photographed at 20° intervals see photographs. It had to have a wire through it, that was later retouched out on photographs.

A professional graphic designer's diary

Perspex model

Retouching work on the photograph to remove the supporting wire done by a professional retoucher

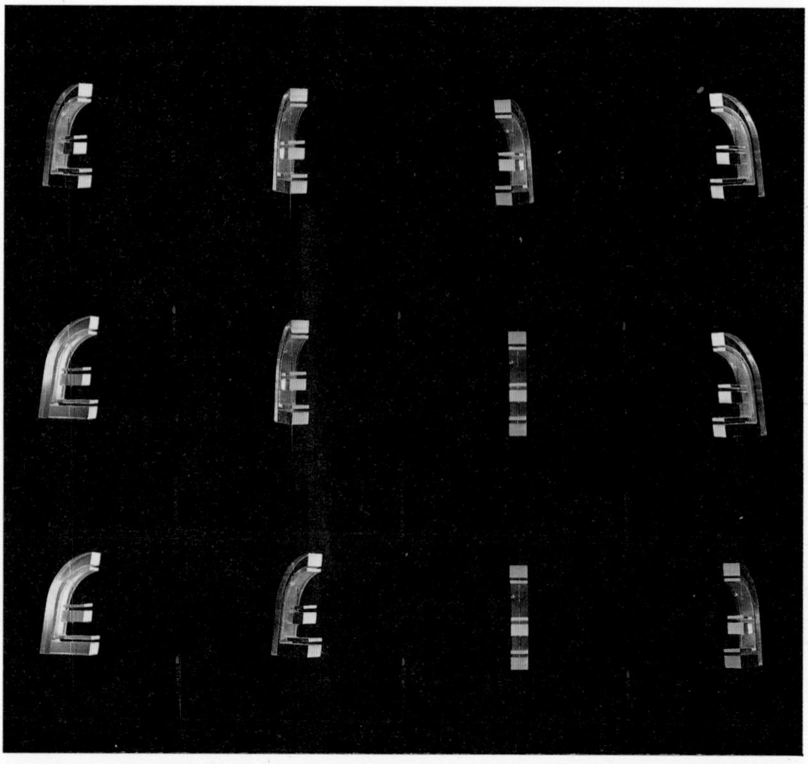

Needed to photographed against black, so
Live action can be superimposed against
black, leaving pound image over Live Action
Peg all pictures in registration to each
other so that when shot in sequence
they appear to animate.
Tests look good - Show Editor.
Have long chats with him and studio
director about subjects ob live action

Last week in November.
Visit Geoff Aptell, a company who specialise
in optical work, to discuss the job.
Take rough storyboard. Get an estimate
Have to Artwork and live action
shoots finished and to Geoff Aptell
by second week in December.

Go out to find locations with Studio
Director of the Money Programme
after much deliberation choose
nine locations. Battersea Heliport,
Nat West Tower, Inside Stock Exchange,
Stephen Bayley's Office in the Boiler House,
Metro in Newcastle, British Aerospace
model plane, British Aerospace milling
metal, Marks & Spencers door in Chiswick
Building Oil Rig in Scott Lithgow Shipyard.

Polaroid snaps taken for research

Set of still frames from the titles using different locations

What is an image in designing?

Are your images based on pictures or are they arbitrary signs?

Which image would you design for money?

Contact prints of locations

Have to arrange all these shoots, take cameraman, so we can discuss lighting. Have to persuade Nat West tower people to turn there lights out, one at a time!

The sequence is supposed to be a little story of the business day, ie. starting the morning, landing at heliport, BMW waiting to take you to work, tube train, lunch, cleaning up at Stock Exchange, lights going off! etc.

Starting shooting December 2

2 solid weeks shooting.

Look at rushes daily (rushes - film shot day before and processed overnight)

Choose one take from each section, only need 48 frames of each one, (2 seconds)

Edit together version of titles to show editor. (without graphic bits on)

Take this and artwork to Geoff Axtell to have all ~~two~~ the interpos work done for the opticals.

Have to go there daily to look at tests.

See final tests on Christmas Eve

Get finished thing back on Jan 10th.

Transfer from 35mm to Videotape to transmit. Lay music on from original 1/4" soundtrack. TRANSMISSION!

Extract from rough storyboard and dope sheets for 'timings'

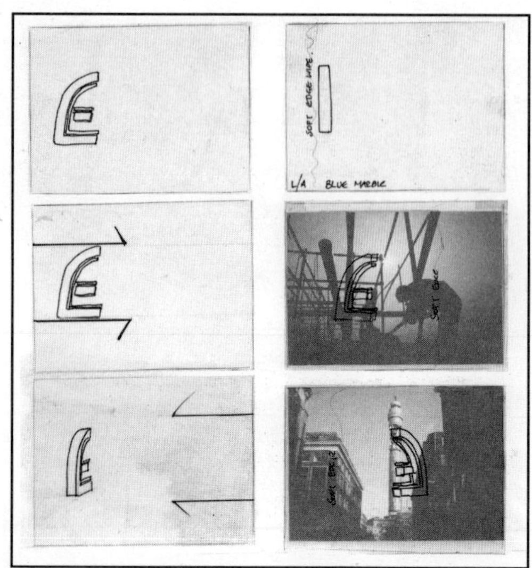

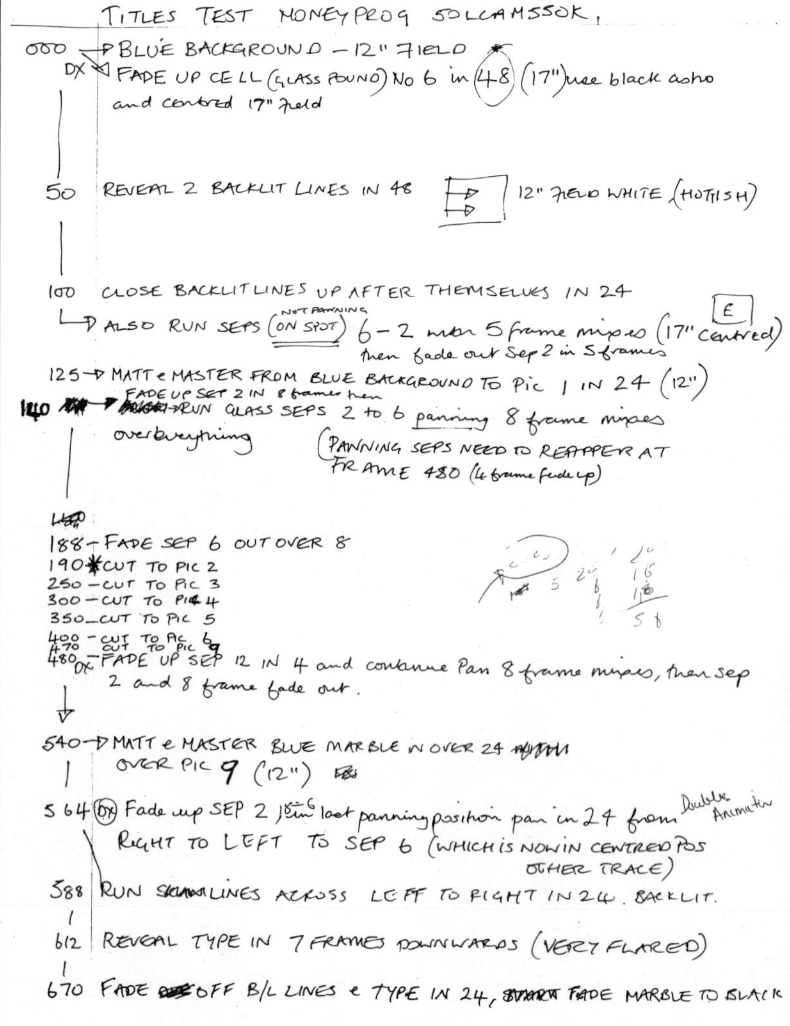

TITLES TEST MONEYPROG 50LCAMSSOK,

000 → BLUE BACKGROUND – 12" FIELD

DX → FADE UP CELL (GLASS ROUND) No 6 in (48) (17") use black asho and centred 17" field

50 REVEAL 2 BACKLIT LINES IN 48 — 12" FIELD WHITE (HOTISH)

100 CLOSE BACKLIT LINES UP AFTER THEMSELVES IN 24 [E]

→ ALSO RUN SEPS (ON SPOT) (NOT PANNING) 6 – 2 with 5 frame mixes (17" centred) then fade out Sep 2 in 5 frames

125 → MATT e MASTER FROM BLUE BACKGROUND TO PIC 1 IN 24 (12")

140 → FADE UP SET 2 IN 8 frames then RUN GLASS SEPS 2 to 6 panning 8 frame mixes over everything (PANNING SEPS NEED TO REAPPEAR AT FRAME 480 (4 frame fade up)

188 – FADE SEP 6 OUT OVER 8

190 * CUT TO PIC 2

250 – CUT TO PIC 3

300 – CUT TO PIC 4

350 – CUT TO PIC 5

400 – CUT TO PIC 6

470 – CUT TO PIC 9

480 DX – FADE UP SEP 12 IN 4 and continue Pan 8 frame mixes, then sep 2 and 8 frame fade out.

540 → MATT e MASTER BLUE MARBLE IN OVER 24 OVER PIC 9 (12")

564 (DX) Fade up SEP 2 18" last panning position pan in 24 from RIGHT TO LEFT TO SEP 6 (WHICH IS NOW IN CENTRED POS OTHER TRACE) Double Animation

588 RUN LINES ACROSS LEFT TO RIGHT IN 24. BACKLIT.

612 REVEAL TYPE IN 7 FRAMES DOWNWARDS (VERY FLARED)

670 FADE OFF B/L LINES e TYPE IN 24, FADE MARBLE TO BLACK

A dope sheet with instructions for the rostrum cameraman from the designer

The more graphic pound logo at start and end of sequence, was done by John Vince at Middlesex Poly using his PICASO programme. 24 frames of spinning pound onto cel. These cels were then painted by hand, by a cel painter, and then also sent to Geoff Axtell.

The type – The Money Programme was shot using SLIT SCAN photography at Geoff Axtell's.

Designer – Lesley Robson-Foster BBC
Assistant – Allison Bryan BBC
Rostrum & Optical & Slit Scanwork, Geoff Axtell Associates Ltd.

Photographer – David Graeme-Baker BBC

Model Maker – Allistair Bowtell Ltd

Photo Retoucher – John Clark

Cameraman – John Howarth BBC
Director – Don Harley.
Computer Animation – Middlesex Polytechnic

Cel Painter – Prish Hackman.

Film Editor – Dave Farley BBC

Labs – Kays SFL and Ranks

Final version of the titles for The Money Programme

What image would you design for:

- *a television documentary programme on graffiti;*
- *a travel book motif about the Isle of Skye;*
- *a cartoon about good taste?*

The electronic graphics area at Lime Grove Studios, BBC Television

Information graphics

Designing diagrams, charts, maps, signs, graphs, scale drawings, computer graphics, and so on is concerned with producing an overall image which communicates a message clearly. You should aim to bring an original insight into your information graphic design.

First, define the problem to yourself, then redefine it linking your thoughts and feelings about the topic with the presentation of a graphic design. From the information about whales and whaling is it true to say that 'nothing is wasted in whaling accept the whale'?

Think about the most important aspect of information to be conveyed in your design. It will include words and pictures, which are important compositional features of the layout of your design. You should choose a letter style suitable for the message being put over. Parts of your design will require research and originality and should include interesting drawings, photographs and other graphic devices. The design should have unity, so don't forget the background and format.

Remember, the images which you design for communicating graphically will have a working context. You are representing something for people to use and understand, including yourself. They are designs which represent information two-dimensionally.

Events Statistics
Problems information
Structures Opinions
Beliefs interpretations
Data Values Facts

Where does the information come from in these design briefs, and how accurate is it?

What other information do you need?

Are you dealing with the whole issue or only part of it?

What type of 'information graphic' have you designed?

What is the context and use of your design?

Which image of the idea, issue or product in your design did you employ?

Ten years ago there were three million African elephants; today, there are one million three hundred thousand elephants in the wild in Africa.

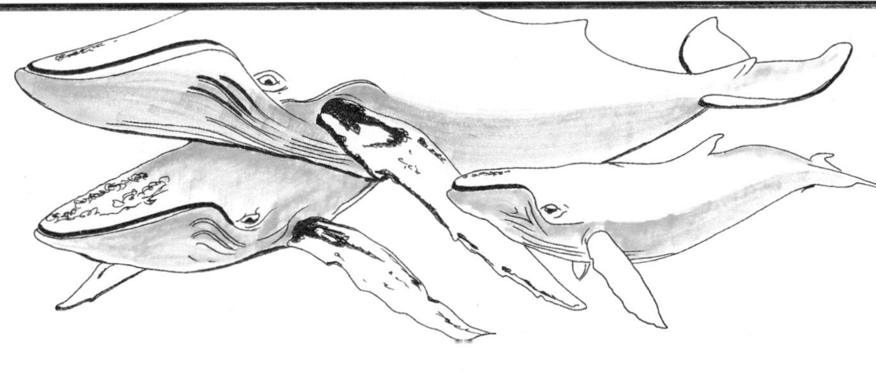

DESIGN BRIEF

Design, lay out and illustrate an information graphic which communicates the significant information to be found in the following sets of data. Select an appropriate context and use for your designs, for example, car stickers or graphics for a television news item.

Whale scale		*Maximum length*	*Estimates of total population size*	
			Pre-exploitation	*Present*
	Bryde's whale	16 m	90 000	90 000
	Sei	18 m	256 000	54 000
	Humpback	16 m	115 000	10 000
	Right whale	18 m	100 000	4 000
	Sperm whale	18 m	2 400 000	1 950 000
	Fin whale	25 m	548 000	120 000
	Blue whale	30 m	228 000	14 000
	Double decker bus to same scale			

'If we can't save the whale we can't save humankind.'

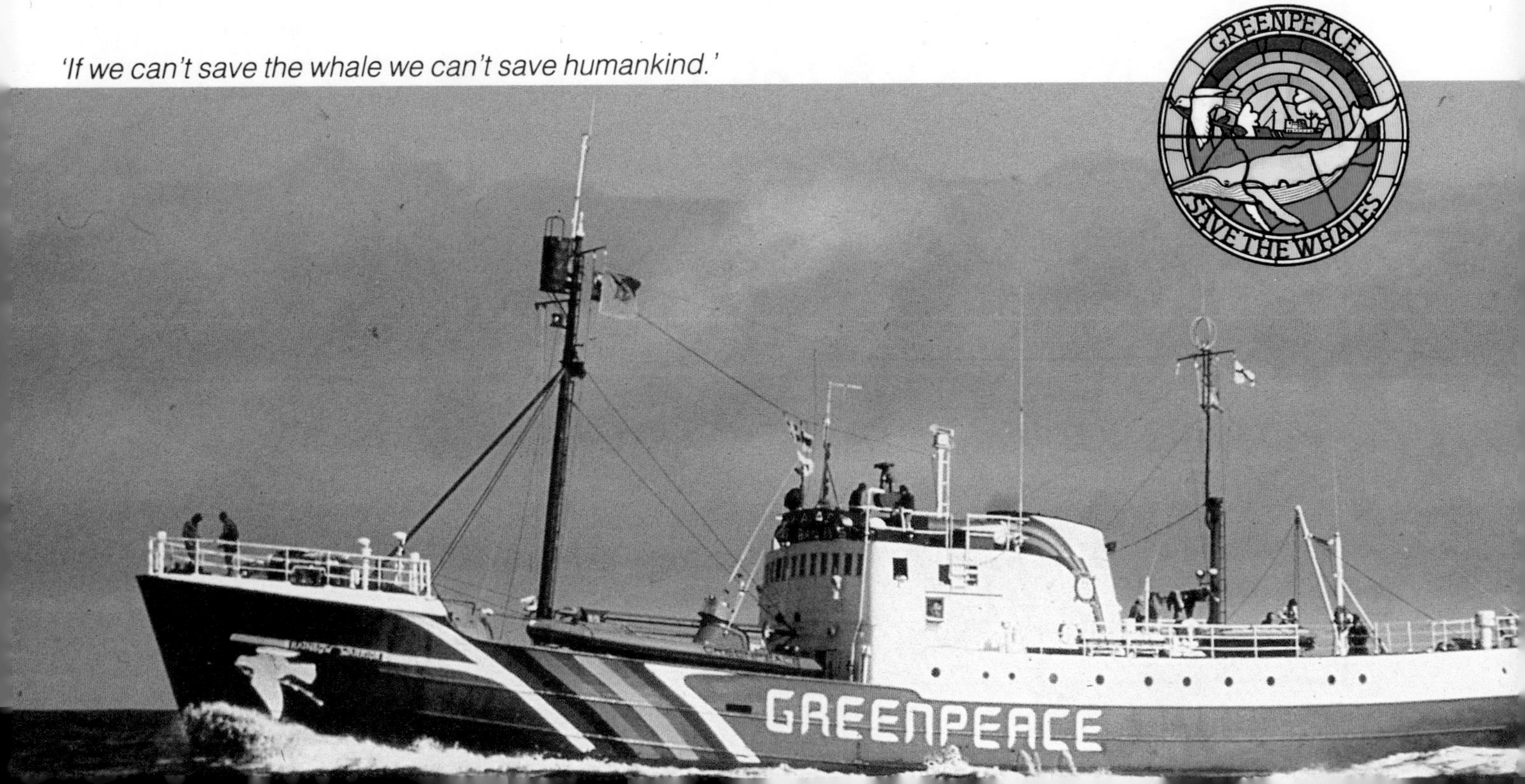

Designing with colour

Designs have shape and form which may be either two- or three-dimensional. This may be conveyed through the way something is made, through the materials used to structure it, or through the use of colour. These activities aim to concentrate your attention on how and why colour is used in design. This may also enable you to appreciate form and meaning.

Colour may be used to give a design impact: it can create illusions of size, it can make writing more legible, as well as bringing about product identification. It may also suggest feelings and moods for some people. See if you can discover these ideas in the designs you use and create.

Colour is used in advertising to attract your attention to a product, to bring about a desire in you to have the product and then to actually persuade you to buy the item. Can you remember doing this at any time? What other functions does colour have in design? Find examples where colour is *not* used: what impact do these designs have?

Did you work on your first idea or several others?

How is 2-D design different from 3-D designing?

DESIGN BRIEF

Study designing with basic and complex shapes combined. For example create a motif which places an animal shape in a circle. Make the animal fit easily into the shape or burst out of it. Experiment with regular and irregular shapes, for example a shield shape. Interpret your designs in colour.

DESIGN BRIEF

Using an heraldic device design a sign, in colour, for an old inn. Show the name, a heraldic beast and a clear statement about the service offered by the inn. The proprietors are keen to promote the quality of service they offer as well as the age of the inn.

Woodpecker cider is Bulmer's second oldest brand and was launched in 1897; *Strongbow* was launched in 1960.

Labels serve many functions. They have been used to full effect in Bulmer's cider product identification. Before working on your own design, consider the following questions in analysing the success of Bulmer's label:

- How important is colour in label design?
- What has a colourful bird like a woodpecker to do with cider?
- Are there any regional aspects to cider promotion?
- Should a label design be composed of drawings or photographs; should it be a single image or a montage; should it be based on full colour, black and white or a tonal range of colours?
- How important will different styles of lettering be to a label design?
- What style of lettering is suitable for cider?
- What functions do labels serve?
- Do all the above examples have 'labels'?

Think about the obvious images for cider, for example, apples, barrels of cider, apple orchards and so on. Beware of clichés and aim to be original, so that your design will influence people to buy and drink cider.

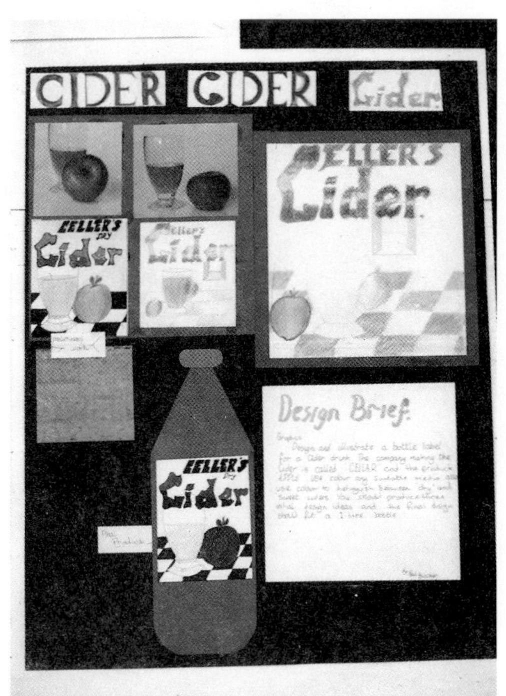

DESIGN BRIEF

Design and illustrate a label for a cider drink; devise a company name, as well as a product name. Use colour and any suitable media for your design. Distinguish between varieties of cider, for example between 'sweet' and 'dry'.

Preserved foods

Originally, the human diet was very simple. It contained only raw, natural foods such as berries, shoots and plants, and later small animals and fish. As man evolved, his foods and their treatment evolved too. Gradually more foods were introduced into the diet and were treated by preparing, mixing and cooking. As industry and technology developed and lifestyles changed, the 'treatment' of foods has largely been taken over by food manufacturers. As a result, food products have become more complex, more refined and more processed. The food industry has now brought us a much wider variety of foodstuffs, but not necessarily a more healthy diet. For various reasons, the manufacturers often 'refine' foods, and add fat, sugar and salt.

Today there is a growing consensus of opinion from scientific, medical and nutritional bodies, that suggests a regular diet of processed, highly refined foods contributes to body diseases and disorders. A diet consisting of more natural wholefoods, with less fat, sugar and salt, and more fibre, is now recommended.

However, manufacturers are faced with strong competition, so their products must appeal to the customer if they are to stay in business.

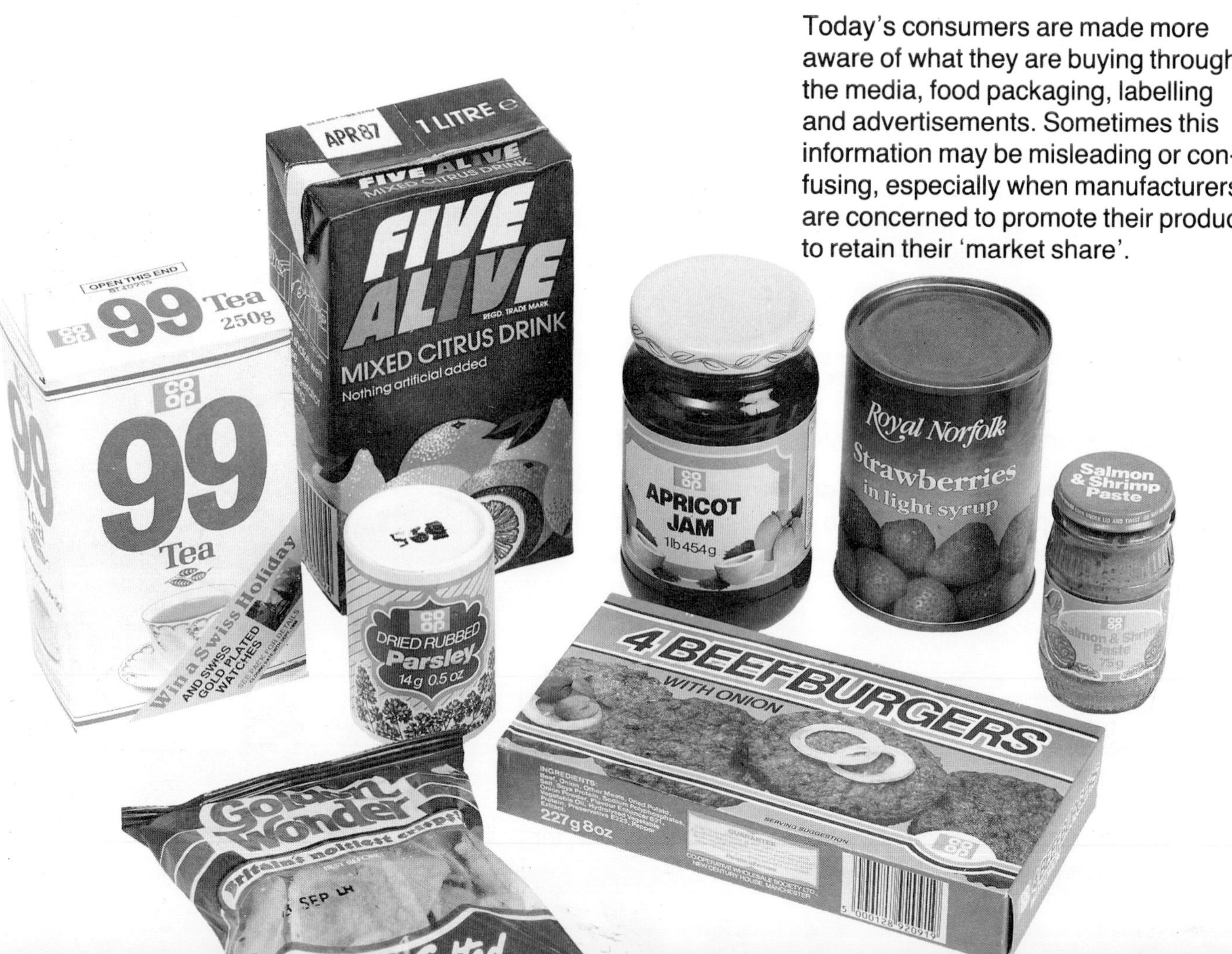

Today's consumers are made more aware of what they are buying through the media, food packaging, labelling and advertisements. Sometimes this information may be misleading or confusing, especially when manufacturers are concerned to promote their product to retain their 'market share'.

DESIGN BRIEF

You are working for a large food company and have been asked to design and promote a healthy range of preserved and/or convenience foods, with a traditional, 'natural', wholesome theme.

The products should be suitably labelled and packaged, and presented as a shop window display. The promotion of your 'product range' should be original, appealing, yet clear and honest. It should aim to inform the consumer accurately, as well as attracting him/her to buy the products.

Initial investigation

Before you can begin to plan your product range of preserved and/or convenience foods, you will need to identify the main problems posed by the design brief. These are:

- Which types of foods are classified as preserved or convenience foods?
- What ranges exist on the market now?
- Which are the most popular products?
- What preserving methods are used commercially?
- What preservation methods are available for domestic use?
- Which foodstuffs are preserved successfully?
- Are these products 'healthy'? If not, can they be adapted to make them so?
- Which food products can be produced to give the customer 'value for money', yet make a profit?
- How can the foods be packaged to appeal to and inform the customer?
- How can the products be attractively displayed and promoted?
- What methods of preservation are available to you in school?

Investigation areas

Listed below are several suggested areas for investigation. Some of these you may want to research in more depth than others.

1. Study the historical and socio-economic trends of preserved and/or convenience foods e.g. the use of ice, spices, salt and the sun; changing lifestyles, developing technologies.
2. Study the reasons for preserving food. Why does food decay, and how can this be prevented? Look at other reasons as well e.g. economy, convenience. Which foods preserve well?
3. Research the commercial methods of food preservation e.g. tunnel, spray and roller drying, AFD, quick freezing, canning, UHT, vacuum packing and so on. Explore the types and use of chemical and other additives, and the effects that these may have.
4. Find out which methods of preservation are available on a domestic scale. What special equipment, if any, is required?
5. Conduct a survey to find out what sort of products consumers want, and how they prefer to see them packaged. What nutritional information do they want on labels?
6. Research the food value of the various foods and products that you intend to make. Are these chosen products 'healthy foods'? If not, can you reduce the fat, sugar and salt and increase the fibre content? Will the food value of the ingredients change when preservation has taken place?
7. Find out the cost of all ingredients used, and the time taken to make the product. Are the products profitable? Are you producing a good variety of products in your range; flavours, textures, sweet, savoury and so on.
8. Investigate the methods of packaging your products. What is the function of the container/packaging? Which materials are suitable? Look at the many types, sizes, shapes and materials used for commercial products. What are single and double packaging?
9. Create an image for your product: a name, logo and slogan. How do food manufacturers do this? Is a colour scheme important? Can you incorporate this theme into your package?
10. Find out what information is printed by law on a food label. Do you wish to include additional information? Design your labels to incorporate your product theme.
11. Investigate the methods used to promote and advertise products. Which methods would you employ? Can you illustrate at least one method, e.g. poster, carrier bag, presentation box, cook's apron, etc?
12. Look at shop windows for display ideas. How will you display your products clearly and attractively? Will you need additional 'props'?

Finding information, inspiration and ideas

The following areas may help you to find information, ideas and answers.

The local shopping centre: Look in shops; observe the types and variety of preserved/convenience foods stocked. Look for 'natural' wholefoods stocked by supermarkets, delicatessen shops and counters; 'wholefood' shops and market stalls.

People: Observe products that people buy. Ask retailers about the most, and least, popular lines sold. Talk to families and friends. Organise a survey or design a questionnaire.

Manufacturing companies: Write to large companies such as Heinz, Birds Eye, Del Monte, Metal Box for information of their products, processing methods and so on.

The media: Look for ideas on product availability and the methods used to advertise these in newspapers, magazines and television commercials.

Products: Collect labels and packets.

Libraries: Look under food, history, agriculture and design sections of school and local libraries.

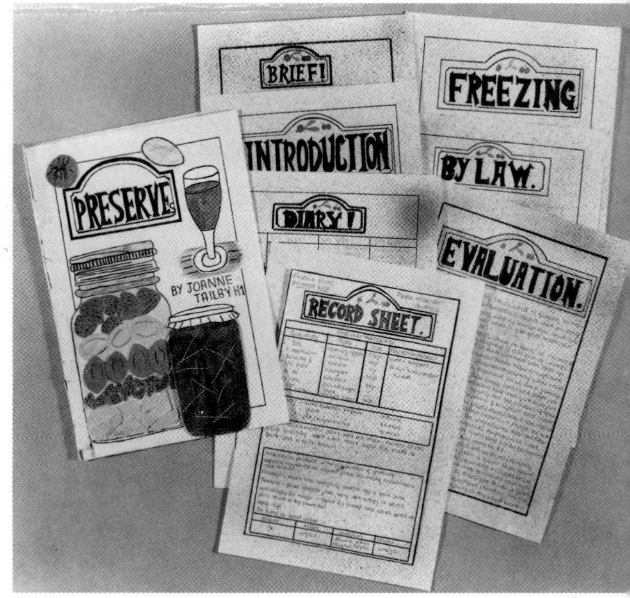

Recording information and ideas

Methods used to record information and ideas may include: writing, charts, graphs (pie, bar, linear, etc), samples, models, tapes, photographs, flow charts, magazine/newspaper cuttings, activity sheets, 'tasting panel' result slips, sketches, diagrams.

Prototypes and solutions

For every 'product' that you decide to make during this design brief, you will need to record your activities, observations, results, and conclusions. This will assist you in making the modifications required for your final 'product range'.

An **activity record sheet**, commonly used throughout your practical investigations, will be useful, and will enable you to make fair comparisons and conclusions.

An example of a practical activity record sheet, designed for this brief, is illustrated here.

Practical activity record sheet – Preserved foods

Dish/product chosen: ____________ Date: ____________

Chosen Materials			
Quantity	*Type*	*Cost*	*Techniques and sequence*

Timing

Time taken to – prepare materials ____________
– cook ____________
– finish/pack/pot/wrap ____________

Evaluation of dish/product

How successful was it in terms of:

General appearance:
Flavour:
Texture:
Shelf life:
Suitability for range:
Food value:

Analysis in terms of health

Does this dish/product contain		
– large amounts of	**SUGAR**	YES / No
– large amounts of	**FAT**	YES / No
–	**SALT**	YES / No
– very little	**FIBRE**	YES / No

If the answer is Yes to any of the above, can you modify the recipe originally used, in order to make the product more 'healthy'?

Marketing

For honest marketing, which category does this dish/product fall into?

A 'healthy' product, perhaps suitable for everyday, general eating ______________________

A 'non-healthy' product, containing foods to 'watch', suitable for celebration or occasional eating ______________________

Costing

How many portions/or what weight yield did you obtain? ______________________
What was the total cost of the material used? ______________________
Calculate the cost per portion/pack/jar/bottle. ______________________
How much would this product sell for? ______________________
What is the margin of profit made from the materials? ______________________

Packaging

What type of packaging is required for this product?
Which materials could be chosen for this packaging?
What type of packaging have you chosen? Why?
Could you improve upon this package if you had more resources/better facilities more time? How?

Labelling

List the ingredients, in quantity order, as they will appear on the ingredients label for this product.
Does this product require instructions e.g. for reheating or serving? If so, what information will you supply?

Realisation

The final realisation of this brief will be in the form of a 'shop window' display. This may include:

- A given number of products, made by you during this project. You should select those which show variety, and demonstrate an understanding of the brief. These products should be clearly and neatly labelled and well packed.
- Clear illustrations, sketches or models of the container types that you would ultimately choose for your products.
- Promotional, advertising and marketing methods designed for your products, in order to inform the consumer clearly and to attract him/her to buy.
- Additional 'props' to enhance your display and project your chosen theme.

A photograph taken of your display will record your realisation of this brief.

A completed display using the theme 'Country Preserves'.

Preserves for the festive season.

Evaluation

This could show evidence of the evaluation that you made while you were working on the brief. The practical activity record sheet will be central to this evaluation. Secondly, the evaluation that you make at the end should be shown, i.e. of your realisation of the whole brief.

The following points may help you to do this. Re-read the design brief set and then look carefully at your display or photograph. Ask yourself the following questions:

1. Have I answered the brief to my own satisfaction? How well did I cope with the ten main problem areas of the brief? Did I find other problems; if so which? Did I encounter difficulties with this brief? How did I overcome these?
2. Have I produced a variety of preserved and/or convenience foods? Have I produced a 'healthy' product range of foods that can be incorporated into everyday meals, or a range that is suitable only for occasional or celebrational eating? Have I made this information clear to the public?
3. Do my chosen containers/packages and labels 'function' as I intended them to do?
4. Have I created a 'wholesome', 'natural' product image? Have I chosen a theme that is clear, attractive and representative of my product range?
5. Are my final ideas commercially viable? Will the content of the products appeal to the public; will the products attract attention away from similar products produced by other companies. Can my products produce realistic profits?
6. What further improvements could I make, e.g. choice of foods, preparation or cooking techniques, types of containers, labels, lettering, overall theme, final display and so on?

A final display with some of the individual items.

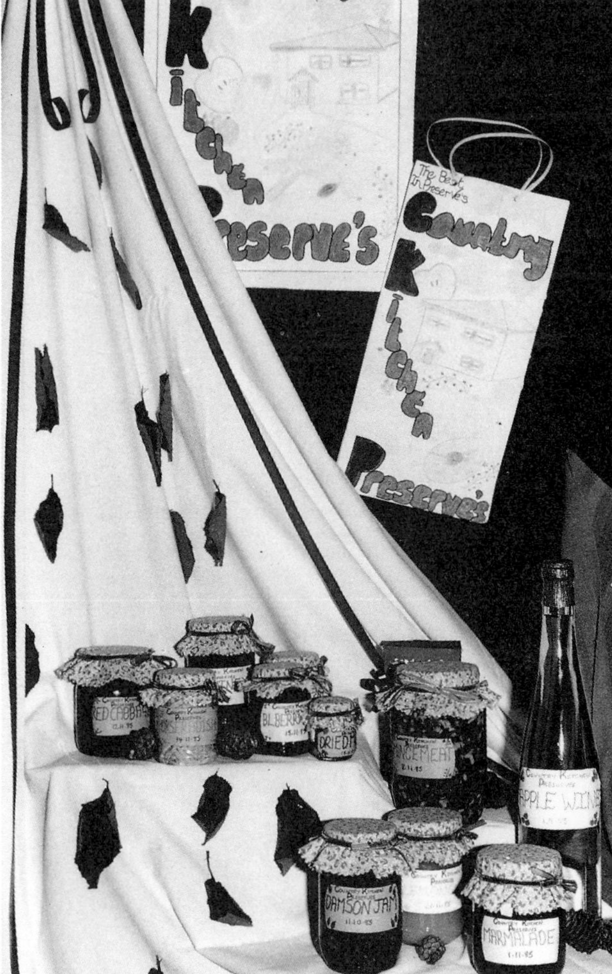

Designing your own clothes

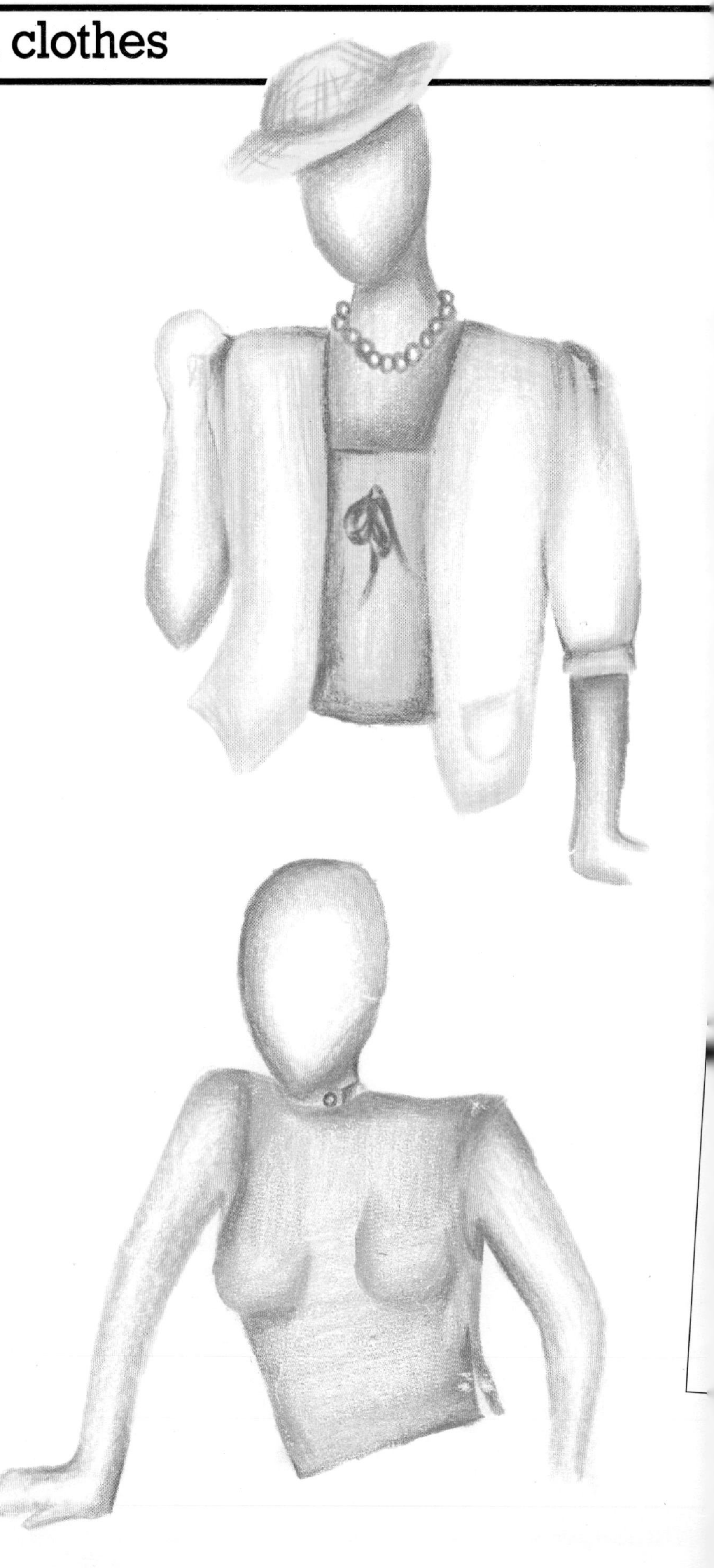

Every day you wear clothes that have been designed by a fashion designer working in the textile and fashion industry. We rarely know the names of these people but their ideas are developed and worn by thousands of people.

Well known designers, like Bruce Oldfield, make 'one-off' garments for individuals like the Princess of Wales. They do not have the problem of making garments as inexpensively as possible. They choose the fabric, colour, style and price! Their name sells the product.

Designers working in the fashion industry do not usually choose the fabric or colour of their creations; they have to work to certain constraints.

Cost

The final cost is already decided. This includes fabric and the time in making it up. What other expenses must a manufacturer consider when deciding upon the final price of a product?

Market research

Most designers have to work for a specified market, e.g. two to five year-olds, fourteen to ninteen year-olds.

Construction

A machinist will have to put the garments together as simply and as quickly as possible.

You might like to try the fashion design brief on these pages or the one later in the book. In both cases, you will have to consider the market requirements, materials, methods of construction and cost of the finished garment – all parts of the designing process.

So have a go – be a fashion designer!

DESIGN BRIEF

Set yourself a theme, such as design an item of clothing for summer wear.

You may wish to put constraints or limits on the design:

- the cost, e.g. £2.50
- the amount of fabric, e.g. 1 metre
- the scope of the design, e.g. a fashion top, or a design for a T-shirt.

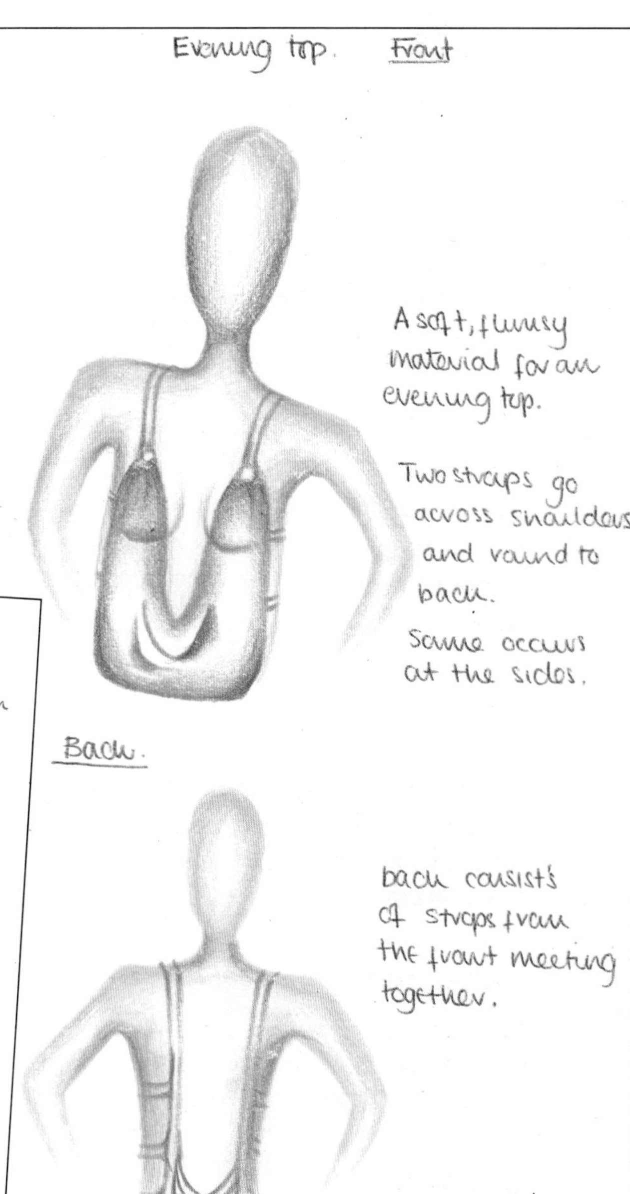

Evening top. Front
A soft, flimsy material for an evening top.
Two straps go across shoulders and round to back.
Same occurs at the sides.
Back.
back consist's of straps from the front meeting together.

Analysis

You will have to consider the 'look' for the season as well as the fabric, colours, fastenings, cost. Also whether the style will suit you!

Research

Look in magazines, shops, the street, and at television programmes. Sometimes films influence fashion: can you think of an example? Pop stars often wear the current 'look'.

Jot down and sketch the trends in style, colour and fabric for the season.

This student's research sheet shows the style for the season but there is no reference to colour and fabrics. Fashion designers usually research fabric and colour trends thoroughly.

Can you think of other ways of collecting research materials?

Ideas

Put down *all* the ideas that occur to you. Remember that these must take into account any limitations you have given yourself. As you sketch your ideas, you might like to consider problems in construction of the garment, suitable fabrics, and appropriate fastenings.

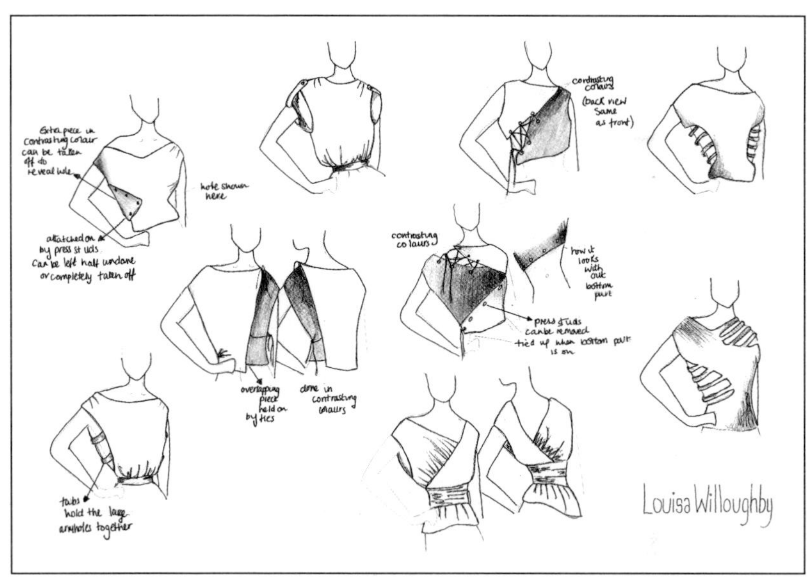

The final proposal

In this design brief you are both the designer and the customer! Before drafting your pattern, ask someone to check your body measurements. When the pattern has been drafted, make it up in calico or old sheeting to check that it is correct and the style suits you. It is often quite easy to draw an exciting fashion idea on paper. By making a mockup, you can experiment with suitable seams, facings, fastenings and wearability, establishing, for example, whether you can move about in the design, and how it looks from every angle.

How will you evaluate your work?
– By photographs?
– Asking the opinion of friends?

Remember to look back at the analysis of the problem you set yourself. Have you really solved the problem?

Computer aided jewellery design

There are many starting points which you may use to develop your imagination and ideas for jewellery designs. These may include:

- Shapes and forms in nature.
- Exploring the properties of materials such as *acrylics* and *polyester resins*.
- Designing a range of jewellery to be worn with a particular range of clothes.

In this particular project you can use a computer to help you generate shapes which you can then develop into design ideas.

As you might expect the designer has not escaped the influence of the micro-electronics revolution, though the full impact of computer power in the world of design has been slower than many other applications. This is due to the fact that effective Computer Aided Design (CAD) requires extremely large memory capacities, and fast processing of large graphics. This type of computing power involves the investment of large sums of money, but once installed it offers many advantages to the user, including fast and compact electronic storage of drawings, and recall of drawings which can be easily reproduced and modified.

Renault Cars have installed a sophisticated computer controlled robot operating on a CAD system. Stylist's drawings are interpreted by the computer into plan form on a screen and a tracing console. Once the plans have been prepared, the life size model can be constructed by the 'sculptor robot'!

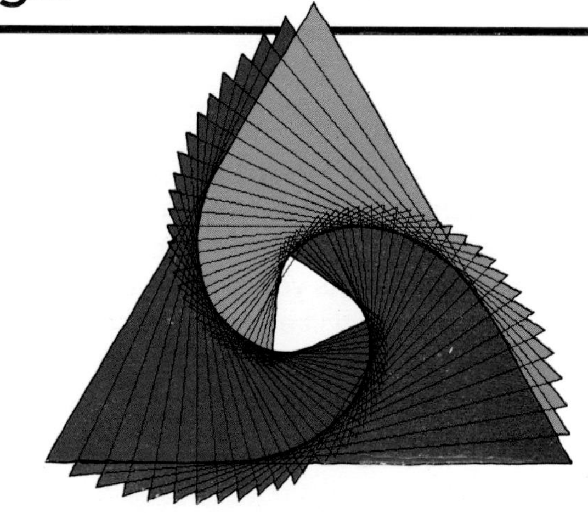

Wire?

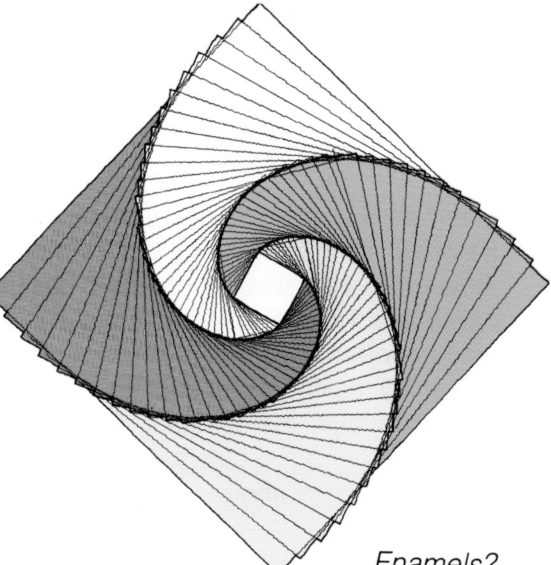

Enamels?

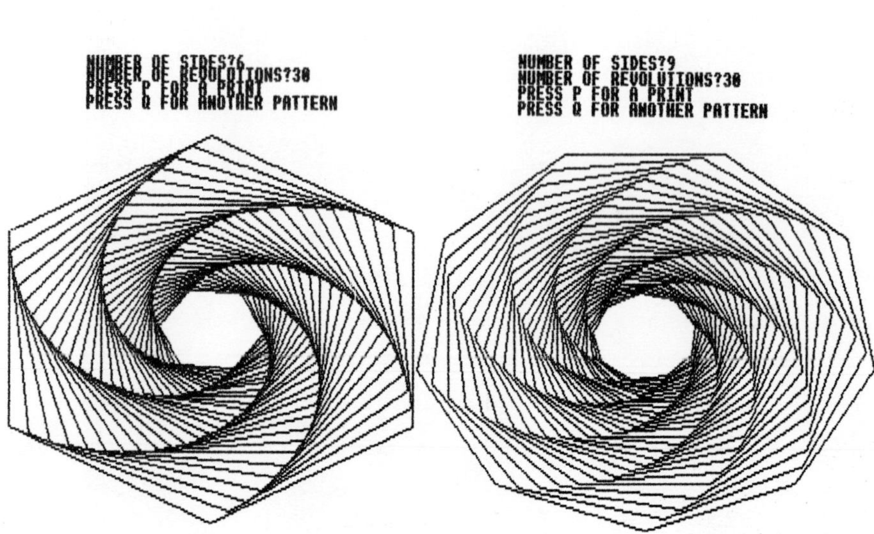

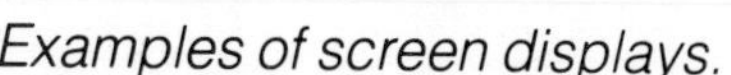

Examples of screen displays.

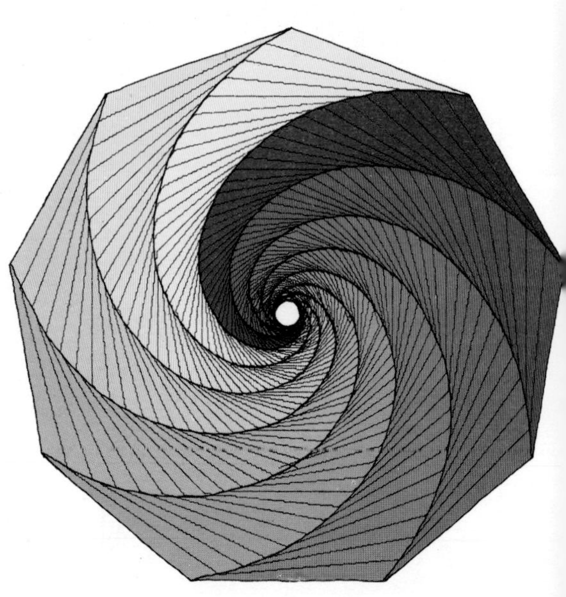

Sheet, engraved, etched?

Using the computer in design projects

The following program is written for the BBC micro-computer and is short and relatively simple so that it may be quickly entered into the computer. The program makes use of the ease with which the computer can generate a variety of geometric patterns. These could then be utilised in design projects or kept in a design resource sketch book as an additional source of inspiration for later design work.

Two program listings are given. The first gives the basic program in its simplest form. The second brings in an interactive facility which enables the user to input information to control the type of pattern being generated. The second program also contains a dump for a plotter of the MCP40 type. These plotters provide an economic way of producing hard copies of the patterns. Other routines can be written to suite other plotters if they are available. If an Epson type dot matrix printer is available then a screen dump ROM such as WATFORD ELECTRONICS DUMPOUT 3 can be used to obtain a hard copy of the screen images. If this ROM can be used then program 2 should be modified by changing commands as follows:

The command in line 310 will produce a dot-matrix print-out of the screen image on an Epson type printer when REM is removed at both lines 300 and 310. At 300 the command *GIMAGE ESP will provide you with a print out of your design.

Program 1

```
10MODE0
20D=30:R=500
30FOR V=1 TO 35
40PROCFIGURE(640,512,R,R,6,D)
50D=D+5:R=R*0.95
60NEXT V
70END
80DEFPROCFIGURE(XC,YC,XR,YR,N,D)
90PROCORIGIN(XC,YC)
100A=2*PI/N:DR-D*PI/180
110MOVE XR*COS(DR),YR*SIN(DR)
120FOR P=1 TO N
130X=XR*COS(P*A+DR)
140Y=YR*SIN(P*A+DR)
150DRAW X,Y
160NEXT P
170ENDPROC
180DEFPROCORIGIN(XC,YC)
190VDU29,XC;YC;
200ENDPROC
```

Program 2

```
10 MODE0
20 D=30:R=400
30 INPUT"NUMBER OF SIDES",N
40 INPUT"NUMBER OF REVOLUTIONS",T
50 FOR K=1 TO T
60 PROCpoly(640,430,R,R,N,D)
70 D=D+5:R=R*0.95
80 NEXT K
90 PRINT"PRESS P FOR A PRINT"
100 PRINT"PRESS Q FOR ANOTHER PATTERN"
110 command$=GET$
120 IF command$="P" THEN PROCprint
130 IF command$="Q" THEN 10
140 GOTO 110
150 END
160 DEF PROCpoly(XC,YC,XR,YR,N,D)
170 PROCorigin(XC,YC)
180 A=2*PI/N:DR=D*PI/180
190 MOVE XR*COS(DR),YR*SIN(DR)
200 FOR P=1 TO N
210 X=XR*COS(P*A+DR)
220 Y=YR*SIN(P*A+DR)
230 DRAW X,Y
240 NEXT P
250 ENDPROC
260 DEFPROCorigin(XC,YC)
270 VDU 29,XC;YC;
280 ENDPROC
290 DEF PROCprint
300 REM *GIMAGE EPS
310 REM END
320 VDU1,18
330 D=30:R=225
340 PRINT"M240,0":PRINT"I"
350 FOR K=1 TO T
360 A=2*PI/N:DR=D*PI/180
370 PRINT"M"+STR$(R*COS(DR))+","+STR$(R*SIN(DR))
380 GOSUB440
390 D=D+5:R=R*0.95
400 NEXT K
410 PRINT"A"
420 VDU3
430 CLS:GOTO20
440  FOR P=1 TO N
450 X=R*COS(P*A+DR)
460 Y=R*SIN(P*A+DR)
470 PRINT"D"+STR$(X)+","+STR$(Y)
480 NEXT P
490 RETURN
```

Ergonomic problems

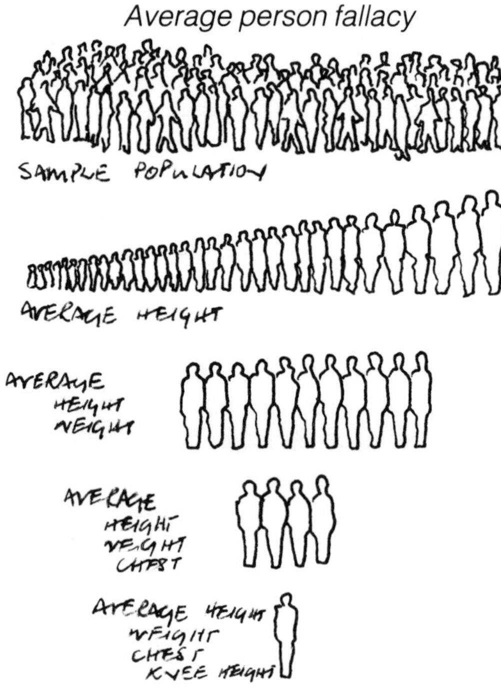

Ergonomics is concerned with the relationship between designed products or systems and the people who use them. Knowledge of anatomy, physiology and psychology is of enormous help to the designer; for some designs it is essential.

If you are working on a design problem that is related to a human need, you will be more successful in your work if you are aware of the human factors relevant to the problem.

Anthropometrics

Anthropometrics deals with the relationship between the dimensions of people and the designs they use.

How does a designer tackle the problem of designing for people of different heights, reach, hand sizes, etc.? Should he or she design for the 'average' person?

In reality the average person does not actually exist. Even where a situation needs to account for just one human dimension, the average – or mean-dimension is not usually suitable. If a doorway, for example, was designed to enable the person of average height to pass through, then clearly half the population would have lumpy heads! It would be equally unrealistic to design the doorway to clear the tallest person. Designers usually compromise by ignoring the 5% smallest and the 5% largest dimensions in people. In ergonomists' language, the dimensions between the 5th and 95th percentile are considered.

On pages 136–143 there is information on designing a kitchen. Clearly, ergonomic factors here are very important, and a well designed kitchen will suit a large proportion of the population. The design illustrated opposite is for an adjustable kitchen.

Consider the feasibility of this and other adjustable designs.

The cost of ignoring ergonomics

Identify a design that has failed to meet a human need.

*What is the **cost** to you as the user of that poor design?*

Consider the cost in terms of:

- *the design failing to complete a task;*
- *frustration;*
- *discomfort.*

What other costs can there be?

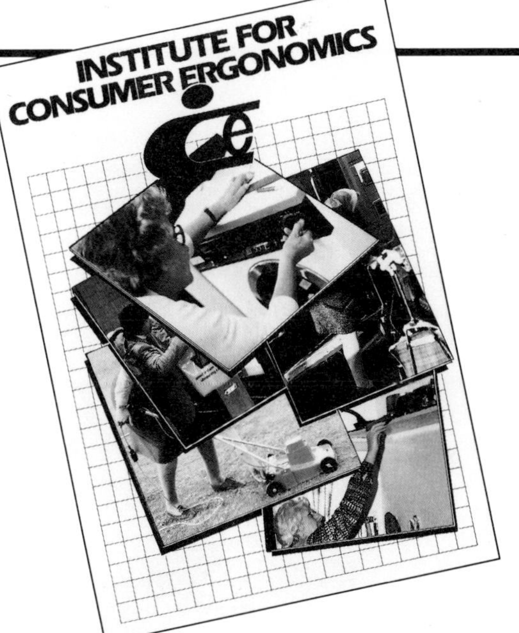

ICE is an independant organisation that carries out ergonomic consultancy work for government, industry and commerce.

An adjustable kitchen – an ideal solution?

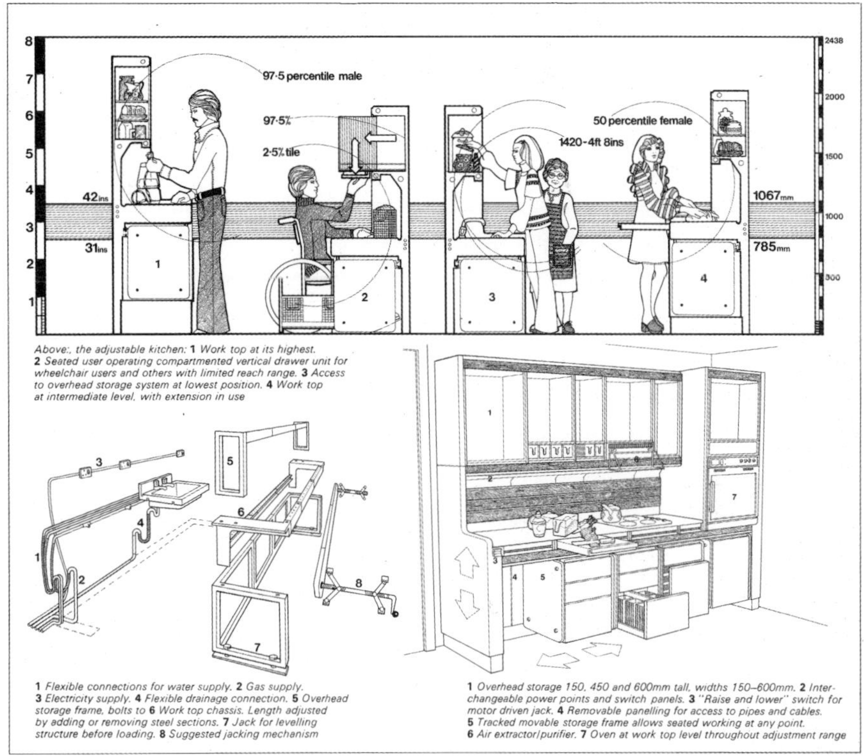

Above:, the adjustable kitchen: **1** *Work top at its highest.* **2** *Seated user operating compartmented vertical drawer unit for wheelchair users and others with limited reach range.* **3** *Access to overhead storage system at lowest position.* **4** *Work top at intermediate level, with extension in use*

1 *Flexible connections for water supply.* **2** *Gas supply.* **3** *Electricity supply.* **4** *Flexible drainage connection.* **5** *Overhead storage frame, bolts to* **6** *Work top chassis. Length adjusted by adding or removing steel sections.* **7** *Jack for levelling structure before loading.* **8** *Suggested jacking mechanism*

1 *Overhead storage 150, 450 and 600mm tall, widths 150–600mm.* **2** *Interchangeable power points and switch panels.* **3** *"Raise and lower" switch for motor driven jack.* **4** *Removable panelling for access to pipes and cables.* **5** *Tracked movable storage frame allows seated working at any point.* **6** *Air extractor/purifier.* **7** *Oven at work top level throughout adjustment range*

Identifying a problem

Ergonomics is important to many design activities as many products and systems are planned to be used by people.

Some problems that you as a designer may wish to investigate will demand ergonomic research. The following situations are examples:

- using keyboards on a calculator, remote control or telephone
- using telephones
- handling and using tools and instruments
- sitting
- carrying loads in outdoor pursuits
- drying hair
- noise nuisance.

Can you think of more situations?

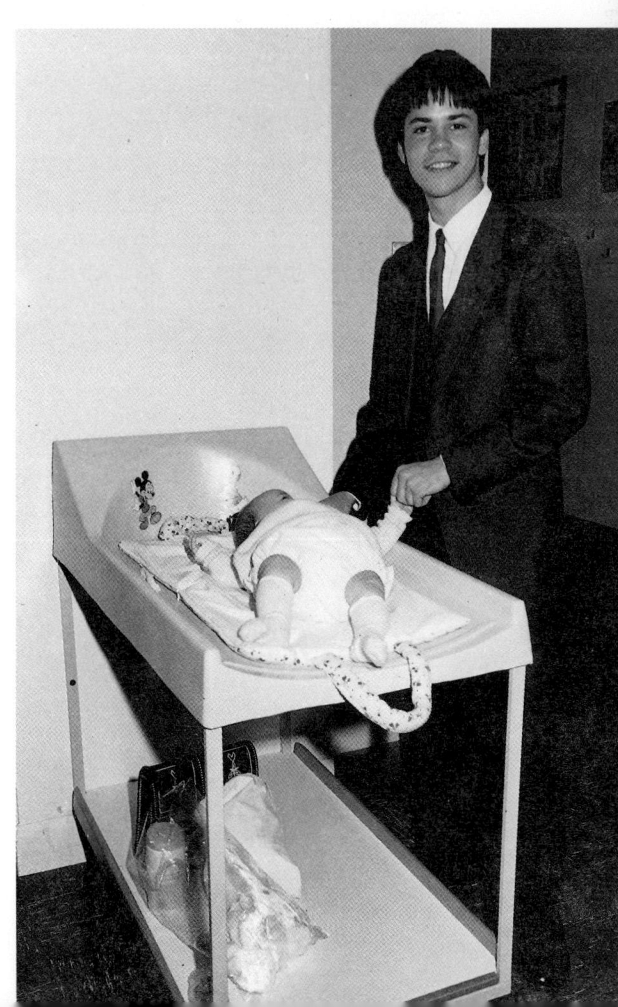

Trying to change a baby's nappy in a public place can be a difficult task if special facilities are not available. A prizewinner in the Design Council's 'Schools Design Prize', Julian Webster designed a nappy changing unit which could be installed in any public place – lavatory, aircraft, train etc. Julian researched the problem and explored several solutions before deciding on a GRP unit, moulded in relation to babies' size and shape.

The following example is related to the problem of carrying awkward loads:

DESIGN BRIEF

Design a means of carrying in comfort a shopping bag and/or a cardboard box tied up with string and/or a sheet of glass 500mm × 500mm.

This design problem clearly requires consideration for the people who will use the device. Ian, aged 14, decided to work on the problem of carrying the sheet of glass and conducted his work in the following manner:

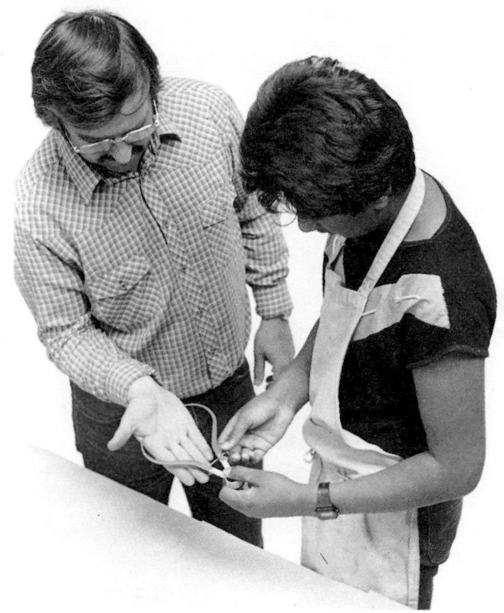

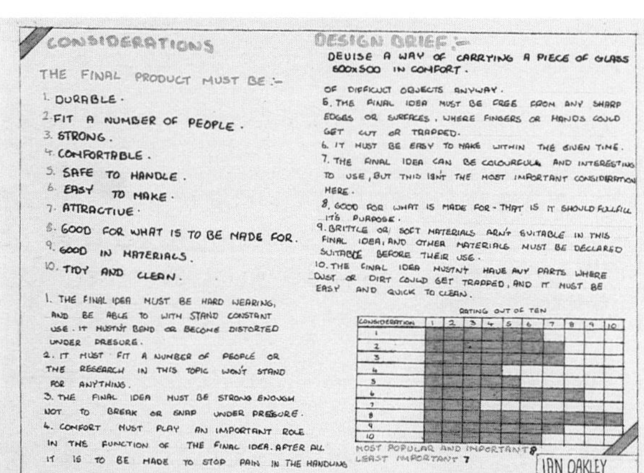

CONSIDERATIONS

THE FINAL PRODUCT MUST BE :-

1. DURABLE.
2. FIT A NUMBER OF PEOPLE.
3. STRONG.
4. COMFORTABLE.
5. SAFE TO HANDLE.
6. EASY TO MAKE.
7. ATTRACTIVE.
8. GOOD FOR WHAT IS TO BE MADE FOR.
9. GOOD IN MATERIALS.
10. TIDY AND CLEAN.

1. THE FINAL IDEA MUST BE HARD WEARING, AND BE ABLE TO WITH STAND CONSTANT USE. IT MUSTN'T BEND OR BECOME DISTORTED UNDER PRESURE.
2. IT MUST FIT A NUMBER OF PEOPLE OR THE RESEARCH IN THIS TOPIC WON'T STAND FOR ANYTHING.
3. THE FINAL IDEA MUST BE STRONG ENOUGH NOT TO BREAK OR SNAP UNDER PRESSURE.
4. COMFORT MUST PLAY AN IMPORTANT ROLE IN THE FUNCTION OF THE FINAL IDEA. AFTER ALL IT IS TO BE MADE TO STOP PAIN IN THE HANDLING OF DIFFICULT OBJECTS ANYWAY.
5. THE FINAL IDEA MUST BE FREE FROM ANY SHARP EDGES OR SURFACES, WHERE FINGERS OR HANDS COULD GET CUT OR TRAPPED.
6. IT MUST BE EASY TO MAKE WITHIN THE GIVEN TIME.
7. THE FINAL IDEA CAN BE COLOURFUL AND INTERESTING TO USE, BUT THIS ISN'T THE MOST IMPORTANT CONSIDERATION HERE.
8. GOOD FOR WHAT IS MADE FOR - THAT IS IT SHOULD FULLFILL IT'S PURPOSE.
9. BRITTLE OR SOFT MATERIALS AREN'T SUITABLE IN THIS FINAL IDEA, AND OTHER MATERIALS MUST BE DECLARED SUITABLE BEFORE THEIR USE.
10. THE FINAL IDEA MUSTN'T HAVE ANY PARTS WHERE DUST OR DIRT COULD GET TRAPPED, AND IT MUST BE EASY AND QUICK TO CLEAN.

DESIGN BRIEF :-

DEVISE A WAY OF CARRYING A PIECE OF GLASS 500x500 IN COMFORT.

RATING OUT OF TEN

CONSIDERATION | 1 | 2 | 3 | 4 | 5 | 6 | 7 | 8 | 9 | 10

MOST POPULAR AND IMPORTANT 8

LEAST IMPORTANT 7

IAN OAKLEY

1 *Recording relevant ergonomic data*

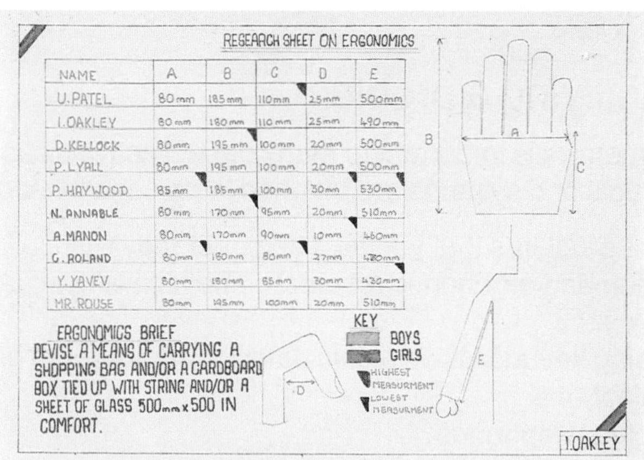

RESEARCH SHEET ON ERGONOMICS

NAME	A	B	C	D	E
U.PATEL	80mm	185mm	110mm	25mm	500mm
I.OAKLEY	80mm	180mm	110mm	25mm	490mm
D.KELLOCK	80mm	195mm	100mm	20mm	500mm
P.LYALL	80mm	195mm	100mm	20mm	500mm
P.HAYWOOD	85mm	185mm	100mm	30mm	530mm
N.ANNABLE	80mm	170mm	95mm	20mm	510mm
A.MANON	80mm	170mm	90mm	10mm	460mm
G.ROLAND	80mm	180mm	80mm	27mm	470mm
Y.YAVEV	80mm	180mm	65mm	30mm	430mm
MR.ROUSE	80mm	195mm	100mm	20mm	510mm

ERGONOMICS BRIEF

DEVISE A MEANS OF CARRYING A SHOPPING BAG AND/OR A CARDBOARD BOX TIED UP WITH STRING AND/OR A SHEET OF GLASS 500mm x 500 IN COMFORT.

KEY

BOYS

GIRLS

HIGHEST MEASURMENT

LOWEST MEASURMENT

I.OAKLEY

2 *Analysing the problem*

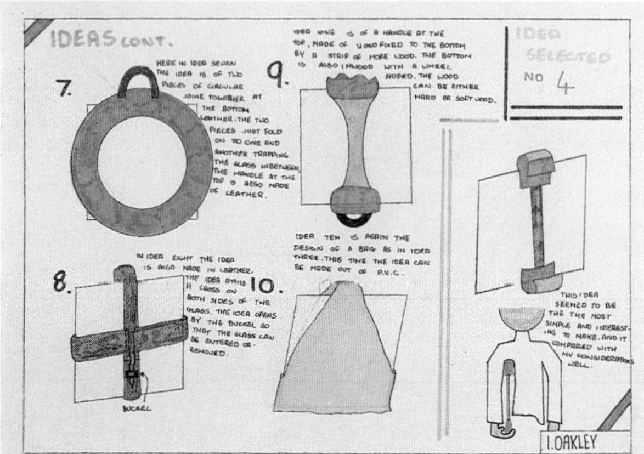

3 *Exploring ideas for realisation*

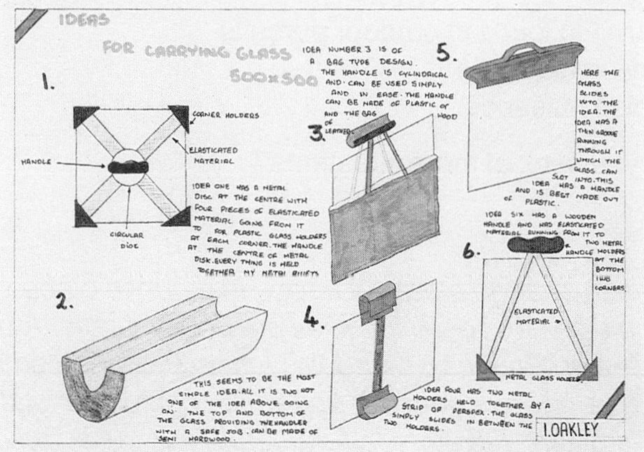

4 *More ideas*

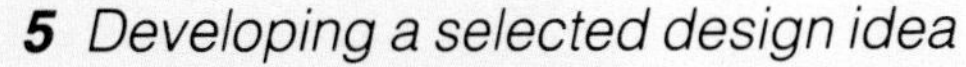

5 *Developing a selected design idea*

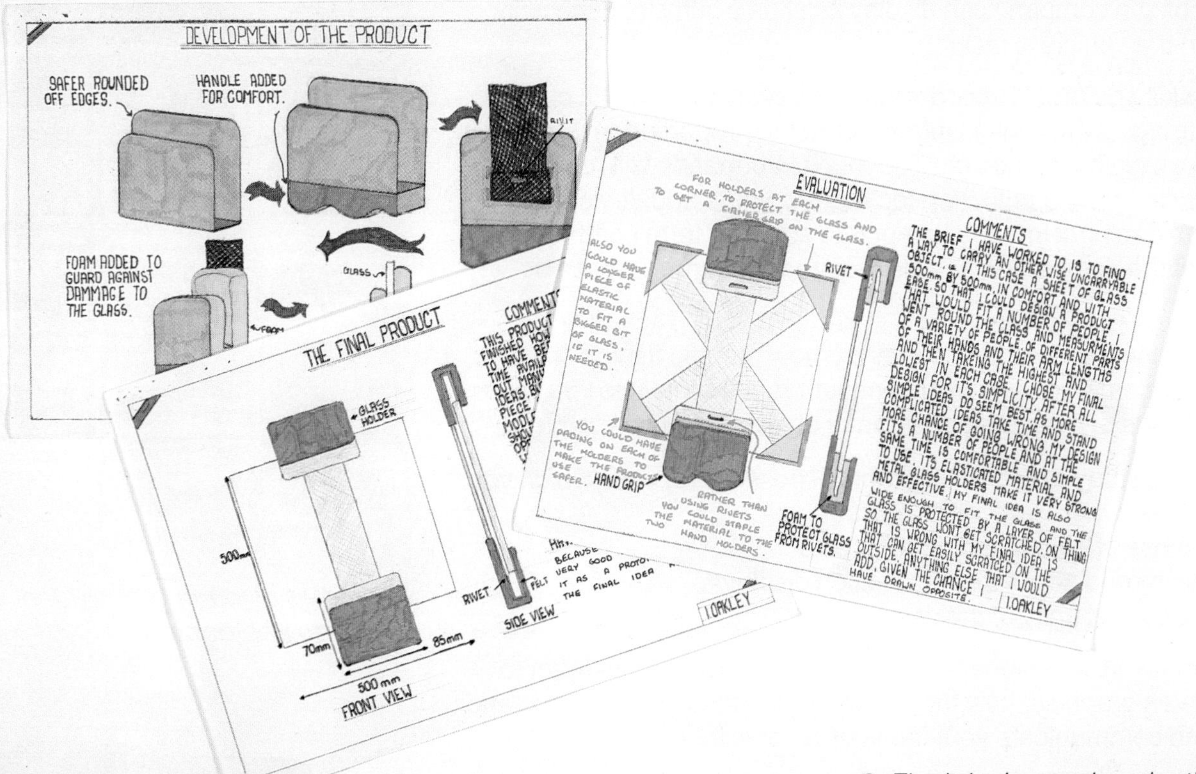

6 *Final design and evaluation*

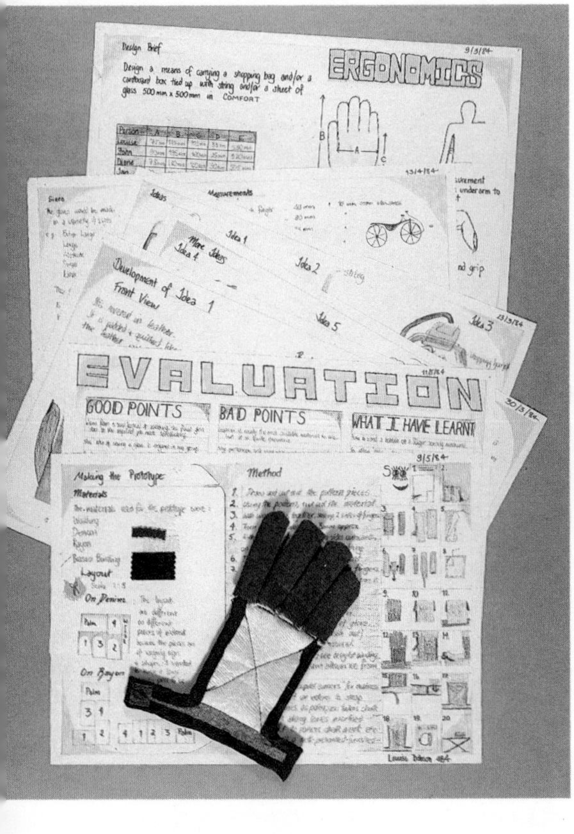

Louise decided from the outset to design a device that would meet all three requirements. She considered several methods and materials for construction, finally selecting and making up a padded glove.

Designing for the diabled

Real problems such as those experienced by many disabled people provide a worthwhile starting point for designing. Ergonomic research can be critical to successful design.

Can you identify some of the situations that create a need for good design for the disabled? For example, arthritis makes it difficult for some people to open jars and bottles.

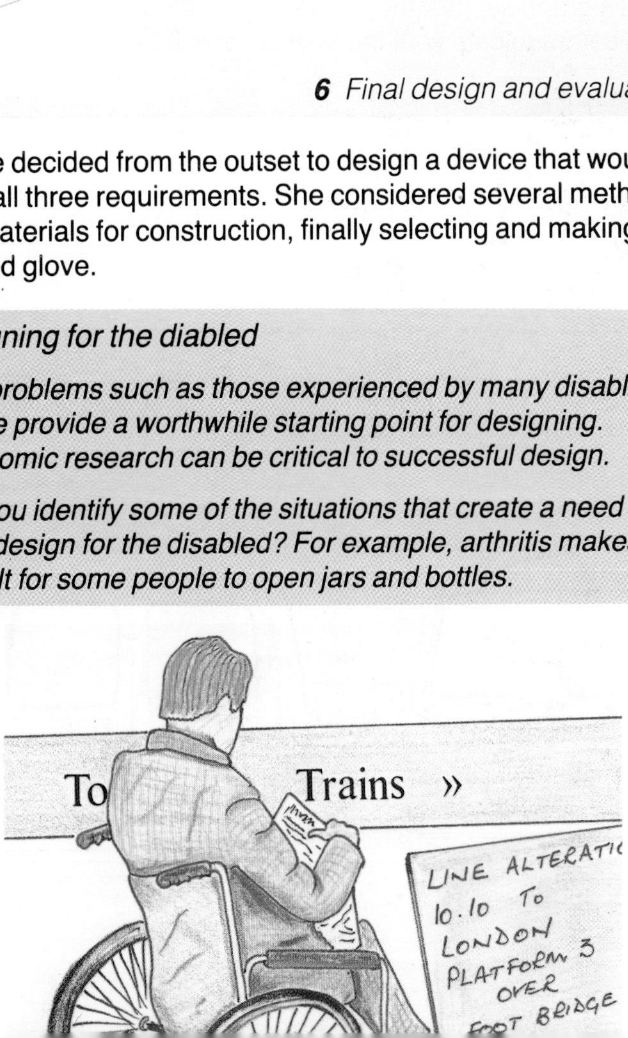

Vehicle graphics

Vehicle livery uses design to promote and advertise a company's 'message'. The design of 'van graphics' is a problem involving how best a company can display itself on a vehicle, especially when the vehicle is moving.

The skill and art of livery design is the presentation of a consistent image, which takes into account the proportion of the area to be covered by the design. Too much information will result in confusion for the onlooker; too many colours and devices will not create the 'right image'. Immediate and long term communication of the company is what is required; its name, service or product.

This activity invities you to analyse how graphic design is used on vehicles which you might encounter. It also invites you to design the styling and appearance of a commercial vehicle.

Set up a study, using photographs if possible, of vans which you might see where you live. Consider:

- the use of colour and other effects
- the immediacy of the information displayed
- the overall unity of the designs.

Your task as a designer is to bear in mind how people react to your van graphics, how they might understand your designs and how to communicate your ideas on a vehicle.

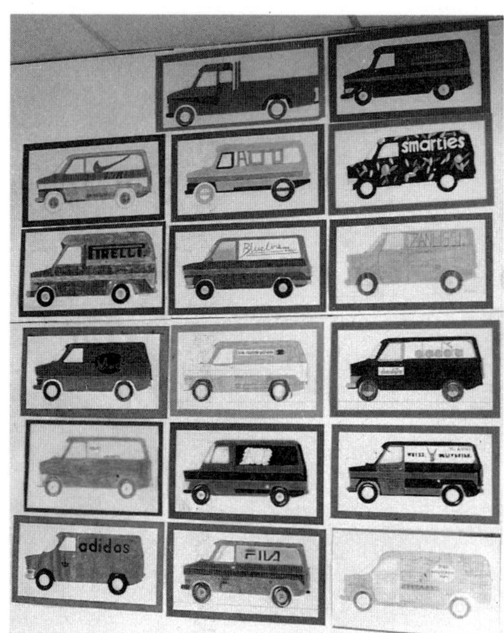

Examples of fourth year student van graphics photographs

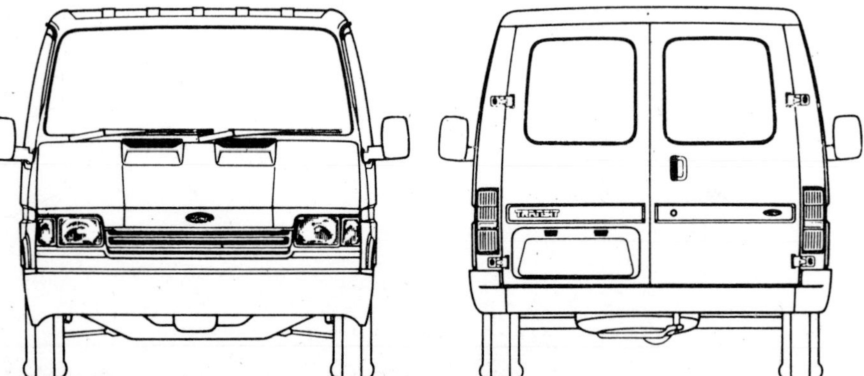

What should vehicle livery display?

What is the message in your design?

Why should 'communication' be both immediate and long term?

What is the 'right image'?

Should a name always be bold?

A complete study involving van graphics

DESIGN BRIEF

Design and illustrate the livery for a company known to you, or invented by you. The following information is given as a starting point for your designs. Your design should show:

- A bold name and the use of clear lettering and letter styles.
- An overall colour scheme suitable for the promotion of your organisation.
- The use of a logogram if required.
- Any other graphic device e.g. flash lines, background shapes.

Illustration design

The purpose of this activity is for you to consider the research needed to produce illustrations. This will include the development of precise and complex drawings, as well as your consideration of where technical illustration may be used. Use pencils, technical pens and/ or poster paint for your designs. Aim to produce a technically 'correct' drawing for a realistic situation. Use all your drawing skills to create shadows and reflections, using multi-media effects and techniques. Both freehand and mechanical drawing will be useful in these activities.

A technical illustration using sectioning and ghosting.

A freehand illustration of a curlew drawn in ink with a technical pen for high contrast when being printed.

DESIGN BRIEF

Select a view of the 1957 Cadillac. Illustrate it in full colour and establish a context in which it can be used. The research is started for you so that you can begin an illustration. Your presentation of your work will also be an important factor in the success of this activity.

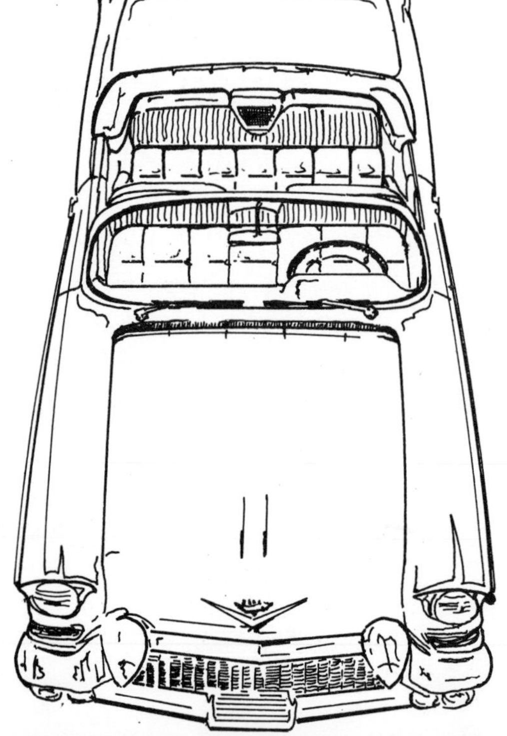

1957 CADILLAC FLEETWOOD SERIES 60

Specifications:

Wheelbase	*133.0″*	*Engine*	*OHV V-8*
Height	*59.1″*	*HP*	*300*
Length	*224.4″*	*Comp. Ratio*	*10:1*
Width	*80.0″*	*Speed*	*4800RPM*
Min. Road Clearance	*6.2″*		

The General Motors' designer for the 1950s' Cadillacs was Harley Earl. His designs were influenced by his interest in jet aircraft and flight, the Lockheed Lightning P-38 was particularly influential. Can you see this influence in the 1950s' Cadillacs? The 1959 'Eldorado' is another example for you to study and illustrate.

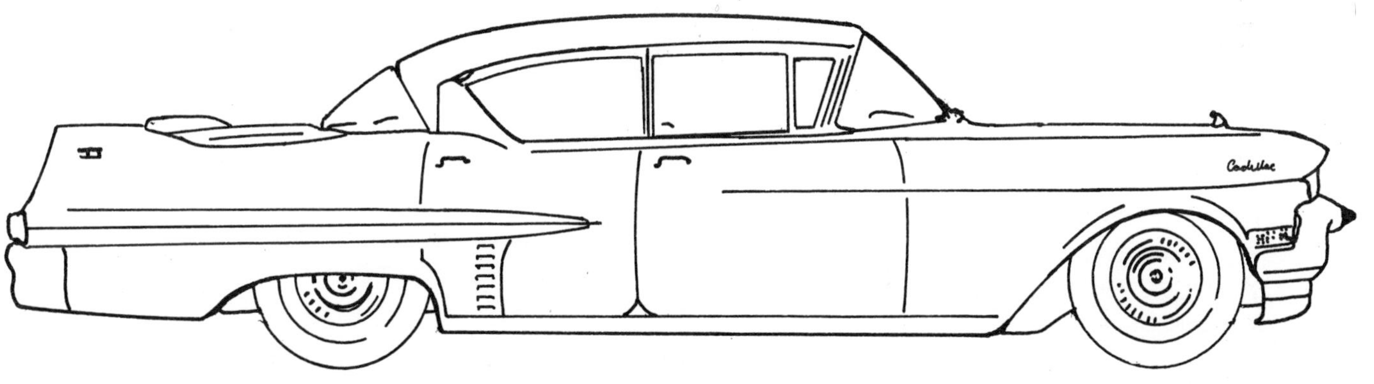

How would you set up a technical illustration? For example for a jukebox.

Where would you use it?

Collect examples of both technical and natural history illustrations, and select your own topic for illustration.

Are illustrations designed?

Are they produced 'before', 'during' or 'after' something is made?

Ceramic design

Sometimes a designer, or a designer/craftsperson, intends from the outset to use a particular medium to realise a design. As a student of design you too may be asked to work in this way. It may be that your design work is conducted in a specialist area with appropriate facilities and materials, and you may have a teacher with specialist knowledge and experience to advise you. You may be working in a workshop for wood or metal, for example.

Here is an example of a design assignment given to a student who worked in a pottery studio:

> Design and produce a piece, or number of pieces, of pottery based on your study of architecture

The way the student approached his work is best illustrated by looking at aspects of his folio.

Rajesh first considered his approach to the design brief. It is a good idea to do this as it helps to order your work, and check your progress.

Rajesh wrote on his design sheets:

> 'I intend to tackle this project by firstly looking at the different architectural styles; for example, types of churches, hotels, statues, bridges etc. Each of these types will be studied and pictures and drawings arranged on my design sheets. The pictures will come from several sources: magazines, brochures, books, postcards, photographs, newspapers, for example. Some ideas will be gained by researching books on architecture.
>
> After I have completed these sheets, I shall select the ideas that interest me the most and develop them into ideas for pottery. From these I shall develop one or two into realised forms.

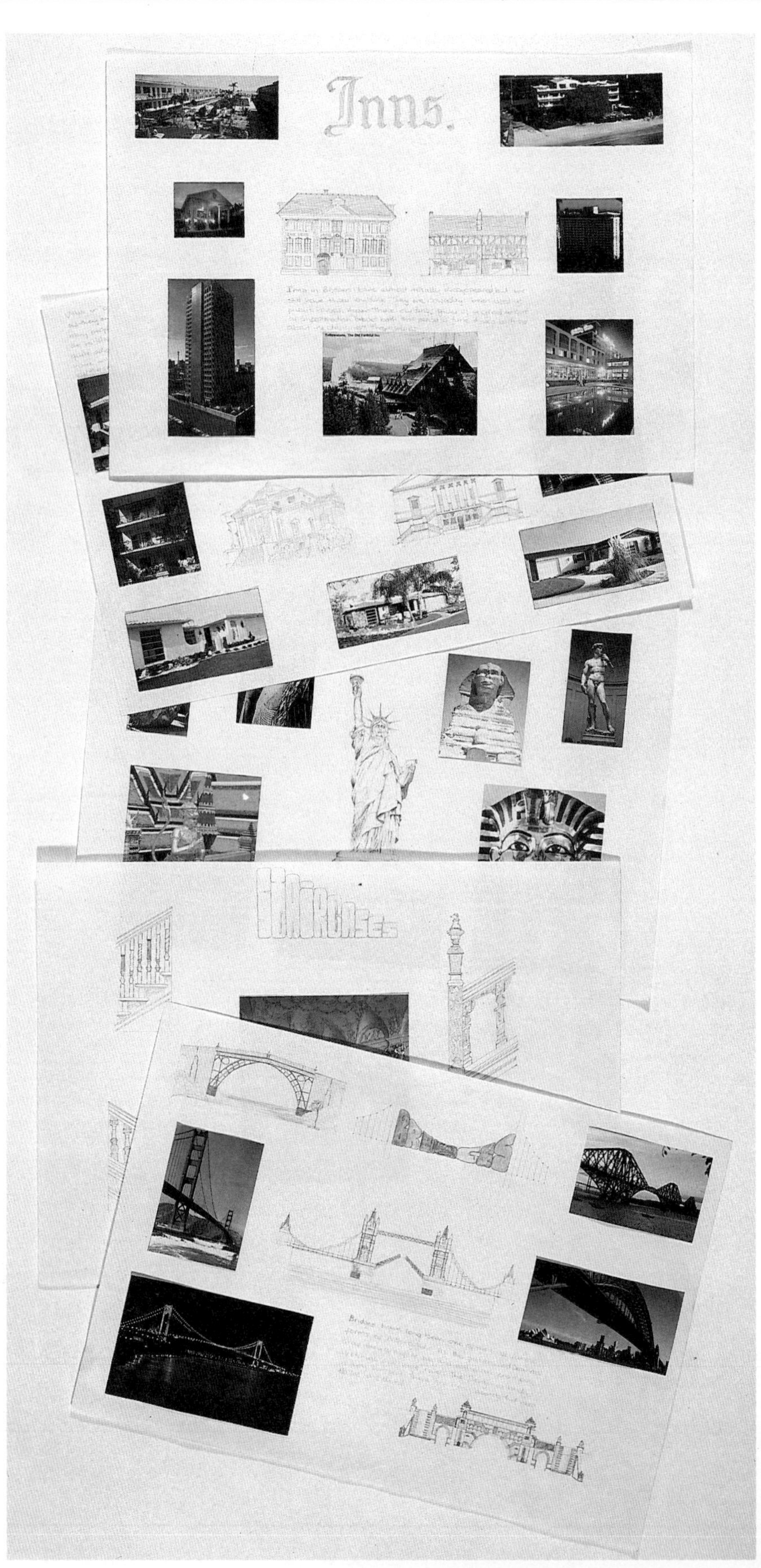

Rajesh studied: civic buildings, statues, great houses, city skylines, gateways and gatehouses, temples, architecture at night, ancient architecture, staircases, villas, inns and bridges. A sample of his design sheets is on the opposite page.

Following his research, Rajesh considered forms a finished piece might take, including a pencil holder based on ancient columns, a money box from ideas he had after studying staircases, and various ideas for decorated plates.

Following some intensive work on these ideas – including recording his own views and comments on ideas – he decided to plan:

- A plate with an applied design based on the Statue of Liberty.
- A plantpot holder the design of which was based on stairs and pillars.

Rajesh carefully planned, step by step, the procedure for making each.

In evaluating his work, he compared the result with the original brief, he recognised problems encountered and suggested modifications in both design and technique.

'The Ancient Architecture research sheet shows a lot of buildings that have pillars; from this I have had the idea of a pencil holder. The Roman numerals underneath are there to give the impression of age.'

'During the time the pot was in the kiln, the pillars began to float on the molten glaze and moved out of the original position. If I make a similar pot again, I shall make sure that no glaze comes between the pillars and the base.'

'. . . I feel that the engraving needs to be larger. The brownish background probably is not ideal – I would have preferred a blue background (sky and sea) and a grey statue. It would also be appropriate to include an engraved background, maybe of skyscrapers.'

Designing murals

At first glance your design brief looks simple.

DESIGN BRIEF

Make a design for a mural for a public place in your local community.

A lot of understanding, research and thought will have to go into this project to make it successful. It will require co-operation with all sorts of people.

Create a painting based on an enlarged design from your initial sketches. Use natural objects, but exaggerate colours and shapes, as well as your interpretation of what you see.

What did you design?

Is art part of design or design part of art?

How useful is design when you have to manage and organise things?

Understanding . . . what is a mural . . . ?
A mural is more than just a painting on a wall. It can fulfil many functions.

Understanding . . . what is a public place . . . ?
A public place is any area, inside or outside, that is used by members of the public – such as a school, community centre, youth club, swimming pool, concert hall, hotel, theatre, club, shopping centre, etc.

Understanding . . . what is your local community . . . ?
Your local community is the area where you live. You, as part of that community, will have special insight into the needs of the community that no outsiders can have and, therefore, you are in a good position to design a mural that members of your community can enjoy.

Research . . . what is research . . . ?
Research is the gathering together of all relevant information and facts that are needed to complete the design as efficiently and as effectively as possible.

Research . . . where is the mural to be situated?
You may know just the place. If not, ask local people and officials of organisations if they can suggest a site.

Research . . . whose wall is it . . . ?
Having chosen a site, remember that it belongs to somebody and permission to use the site will have to obtained.

Research . . . who can stop you . . . ?
Local council planning permission may be needed for a mural on an external wall that is overlooked by residents or passers-by, even though it is not council property.

Research . . . materials.
What is the wall made of? What type of primers and paints are the most suitable? How can you find out? How much will the materials cost? Who is paying? What effect will wear and weather have on your design?

Research . . . equipment.
What is the best way of applying the paint? Will scaffolding be needed and for how long? What about insurance?

Research . . . convenience
Will the painting of the mural affect the use of the building or obstruct corridors, doorways, pavements, etc? How can this be avoided?

Research . . . what is to be painted?
Involve the community if you can. What sort of mural do people want to look at? Can people suggest ideas? Does the use of the building provide an obvious theme? Does the shape of the site provide or suggest a starting point for ideas? Does the building or the locality have any historical connections or geographical features which you can use?

Research . . . who can help you to do the job . . . ?
Would members of the community feel involved if they could take part in the painting? How can you organise this so that people are a genuine help and not a hindrance? A lot of 'helpers' can be difficult to control and the work may be spoiled. Helpers' enthusiasm could be greater than their skill.

As you see, designing a mural is not as simple as you may have thought. There are lots of possible problems. A good designer will have anticipated most of them before work on the actual mural is started.

Remember the design brief only requires you to **design** the mural and that is what your efforts should be directed towards. You are **not** required to paint the actual mural on to a wall, although some may be taken that far, if suitable.

However, your design **must** be for a **real place** and must show evidence of **real research** involving **real people**.

Produce lots of drawings. Keep copies of letters or specialist information which you receive. Show the evidence of your research in written, drawn or photographed ways. Make a scale model of the building in or on which your mural would be painted, particularly if it is an awkward space – **all this is design**.

Toy design

Toys are interesting to design: we were all children once (many of us still are, at heart!) and therefore have first hand experience of playing with toys, knowing about their qualities, such as robustness, appeal, cost, and so on. We can all remember some of our favourite toys.

From the designer's point of view, toys are interesting because there are many aspects that need to be considered and incorporated into the finished design. Safety is one example.

Toys complying with the standard

- provide a secure means of protecting a child from all springs, levers or tubes which could cause injury
- have no sharp points or spikes if they are intended for babies
- have firmly fixed attachments e.g. a child should not be able to pull out the eyes on soft toys and dolls
- are not made of celluloid or similarly flammable materials. Pile fabrics will not flare up, even after washing or dry-cleaning
- are made of safe non-toxic materials
- are accompanied by easily understood instructions for use and maintenance
- carry warnings of any inherent dangers, for example, highly flammable adhesives used in construction kits.

All toys sold in the UK must comply with government safety regulations, which refer to a British Standard for the safety of toys.

BS 5665 and BS 3443

DESIGN BRIEF

If you were given the brief simply to make a toy, you would find the possibilities so wide and varied that it might be difficult to know how to begin research. Answers to questions like the following would be needed.

- What age of child is it for?
- Can it be for an adult – an amusing article for a desk top, for example?
- Is there any limit to its size or the material I can use?
- We have a new baby girl in the family – can I design the toy for her?

The possibilities are numerous. Can you think of some more?

The brief needs refining; to be more specific. Most toys are made with a definite group of users in mind, others are designed for a particular purpose – to help children's learning, for example.

To proceed, therefore, identify the limits of the brief from the following, adding your own ideas to the list. These ideas should be recorded on your design sheets to help you clarify your thoughts and make decisions:

The toy design could be:

1. For a baby under 1 year old.
2. To assist a child to learn to walk.
3. For amusement in the garden.
4. For playing in the bath – any age.
5. To assist teaching how to tell the time.
6. A specific design, like a garage for toy cars.
7. A device which flies using a simple power source.
8. A scaled down model.
9. For use by children in a playgroup.
10. A design that costs less than 25p to make.

A toy design which we can follow through on pages 121–129 is:

'Design and make a pull/push-along toy for a pre-school child. The design should incorporate a secondary movement when the toy is pushed or pulled.'

Needs

What are the specific needs of the user for each kind of toy on your list?

Research

It makes good sense for you – the designer – to analyse the question thoroughly in order that you consider every important aspect. These **considerations** will help with the development of your own design ideas and ensure that you design and make a successful toy. They will also make evaluation of the finished product straightforward as you will be able to compare the finished toy with the design qualities you considered to be important in your research.

Research might be made into all or some of the following, depending on the time available:

- Type of toy
- The purpose of a toy
- Types of movement
- Possible noises
- Existing designs
- Safety
- Means of pushing and pulling
- Material selection
- Strength and construction
- Finishes

It is very important that that you annotate your ideas throughout your designing with your own comments. This will help you to make informed design decisions and will be valuable in communicating your skills in evaluation.

The example list above may be more useful to you if presented like this:

Animals

dog – dogs are familiar to many children. Could be well-known cartoon character.
cat – cats are furry and therefore nice to stroke. Could be a stuffed toy – safety.
elephant – perhaps the trunk could move when toy is pulled.
giraffe – height may cause instability.
cow – not usually much movement; realistic noise will be difficult to achieve.
leopard – could be in a leaping position.
snake – wiggling movement or hissing sound.
gorilla – hairy, ugly – might frighten a small child.

The purpose of a toy

Any design that has a purpose should meet that need as efficiently as possible and it is the designer's job to ensure that it does.

Finding out the purpose of a toy can be done in several ways – by reading about children's play, by asking parents and children. Asking your friends about their favourite childhood toys will also be useful in setting the limits for designing and forming your own ideas.

You could arrange to spend some time with children by visiting a playgroup, or by joining in with small children at play. You could ask the children questions about their preferences for colour, sounds, shapes, surfaces to touch, etc.

How safe should a toy design be?

Investigating possible types of movement and noise

Movement in a toy design may well be achieved by the inclusion of a *mechanism*.

Problem-solving with simple mechanisms can be fascinating and may suggest ideas for inclusion in a toy design. The diagrams here show a desired kind of output in movement given a particular mode of input. Your task is to plan a mechanism for each – or more than one mechanism – that will achieve the desired effect.

Construct working models, working with readily available materials, such as card, wood or 'Mecano'. Other materials can be tried and the experience recorded for possible use in your designing.

Possible noises can also be identified by experimenting. It is important to keep your experiments – they are all a part of your design work that is communicated to others, as well as being a reference for later stages in designing.

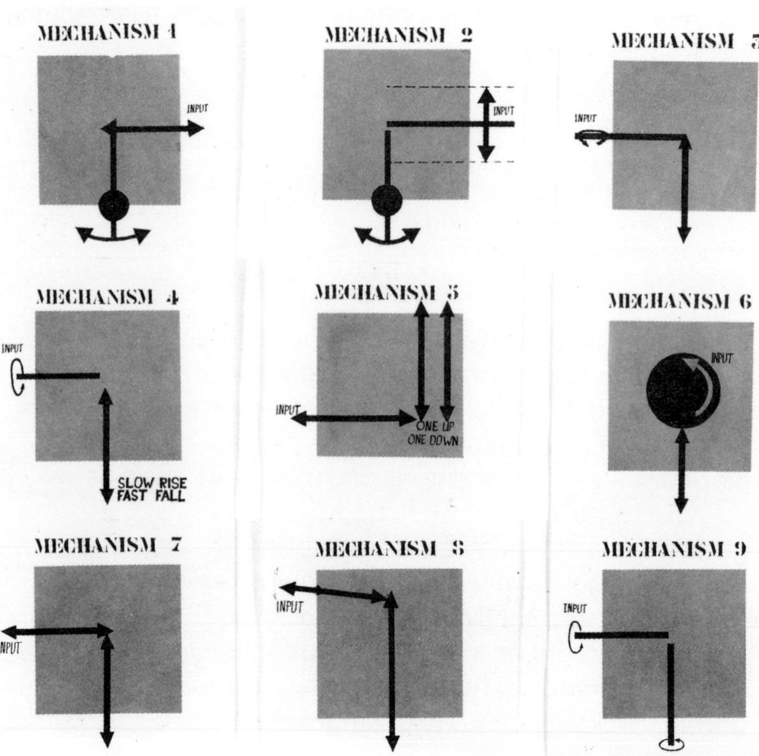

Try making a mechanism.

Existing designs

Designs already in existence are an important resource to you as a designer; many good designs are, in fact, improvements on earlier ideas.

Looking at existing toys can be a very useful exercise. Recording what you observe by drawing, photographing, taking cuttings from magazines and catalogues will help. Recording your own reaction to the toys will help. Where possible evaluate various toys by using them as a child would, and report your findings. Include good aspects as well as making criticisms.

> ***Old hat***
> *Identify other designs which are improvements or variations on a longstanding design or idea.*

Safety

These pictures are all of toys that have been discovered on sale in our shops but which are potentially dangerous to children. It is a good idea to be conscious of the safety features of any design, but especially where children are concerned.

Seeking information from Trading Standards officers and Consumer Safety officers is often revealing. One such person when asked for his views on the need for designers and manufacturers to be mindful of safety, commented:

> 'There is a great need for assessment of products prior to sale including the human element of forseeable misuse particularly with regard to children. Manufacturers and designers should carefully consider what happens when a product such as a toy comes to the end of its useful life – and this should be done at the design stage.'

> ***Unsafe toys***
> *Can you continue this list of hazards in toys:*
>
> *Sharp edges*
> *Flammable materials*
> *Small parts to swallow*
> *. . .*

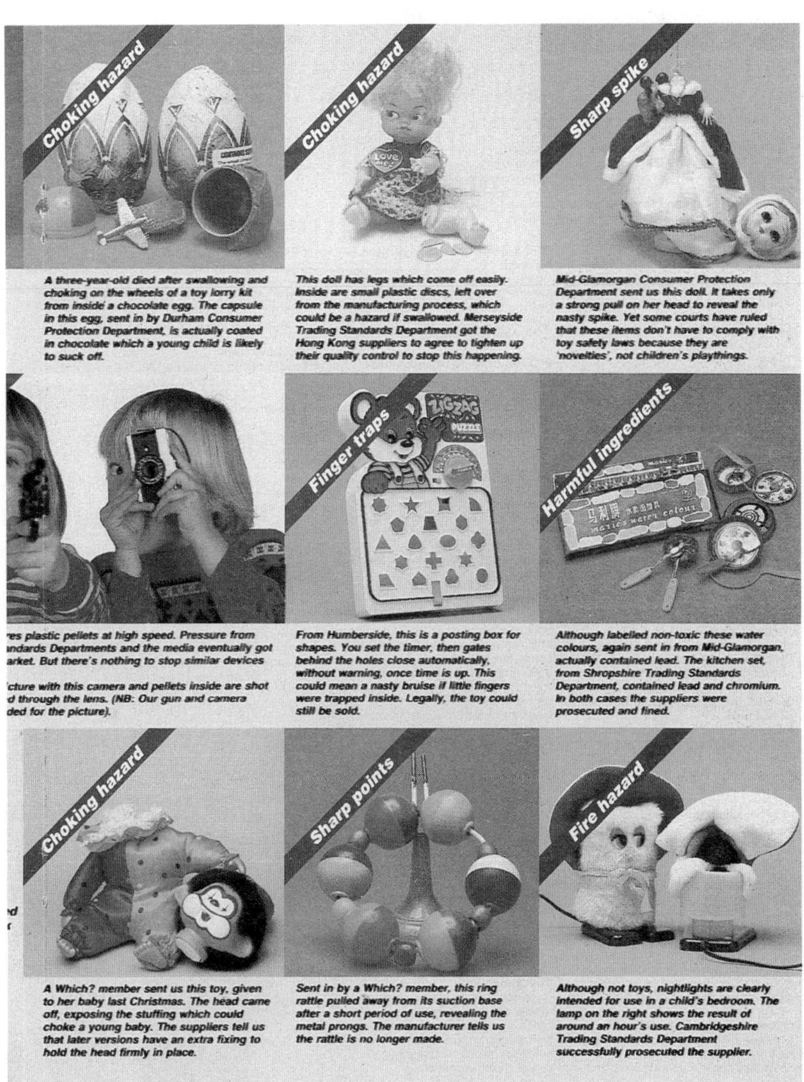

Choking hazard

A three-year-old died after swallowing and choking on the wheels of a toy lorry kit from inside a chocolate egg. The capsule in this egg, sent in by Durham Consumer Protection Department, is actually coated in chocolate which a young child is likely to suck off.

Choking hazard

This doll has legs which come off easily. Inside are small plastic discs, left over from the manufacturing process, which could be a hazard if swallowed. Merseyside Trading Standards Department got the Hong Kong suppliers to agree to tighten up their quality control to stop this happening.

Sharp spike

Mid-Glamorgan Consumer Protection Department sent us this doll. It takes only a strong pull on her head to reveal the nasty spike. Yet some courts have ruled that these items don't have to comply with toy safety laws because they are 'novelties', not children's playthings.

...res plastic pellets at high speed. Pressure from ...ndards Departments and the media eventually got ...arket. But there's nothing to stop similar devices

...cture with this camera and pellets inside are shot ...d through the lens. (NB: Our gun and camera ...ded for the picture).

Finger traps

From Humberside, this is a posting box for shapes. You set the timer, then gates behind the holes close automatically, without warning, once time is up. This could mean a nasty bruise if little fingers were trapped inside. Legally, the toy could still be sold.

Harmful ingredients

Although labelled non-toxic these water colours, again sent in from Mid-Glamorgan, actually contained lead. The kitchen set, from Shropshire Trading Standards Department, contained lead and chromium. In both cases the suppliers were prosecuted and fined.

Choking hazard

A Which? member sent us this toy, given to her baby last Christmas. The head came off, exposing the stuffing which could choke a young baby. The suppliers tell us that later versions have an extra fixing to hold the head firmly in place.

Sharp points

Sent in by a Which? member, this ring rattle pulled away from its suction base after a short period of use, revealing the metal prongs. The manufacturer tells us the rattle is no longer made.

Fire hazard

Although not toys, nightlights are clearly intended for use in a child's bedroom. The lamp on the right shows the result of around an hour's use. Cambridgeshire Trading Standards Department successfully prosecuted the supplier.

*Dangerous toys (*Which? *December 1985).*

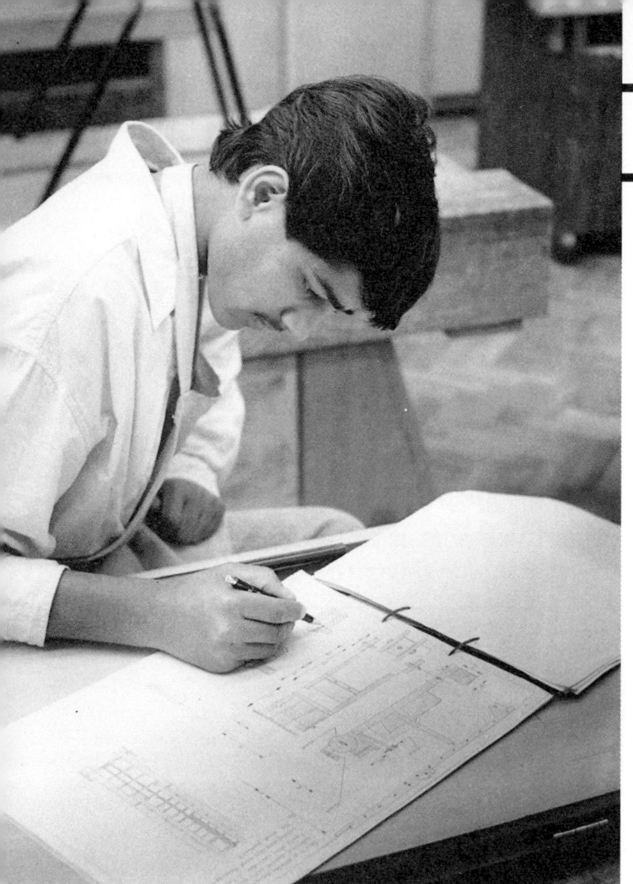

Recording ideas by annotated sketches.

Pushing and pulling

Investigate how toys may be pushed or pulled. Take into account the child's height and hand size – to do this you could gather your own anthropometric data and tabulate the results (see page 108).

Consider the use of a cord for pulling – how might it be attached? Is a handle necessary, what form and which material could be used?

How do children push and pull? Do they always stand, or do they lie and kneel?

You could evaluate ways of pushing and pulling in a practical way and then report your findings.

Tolerances

In your experience, do children always use toys carefully?

How much tolerance do you think should be allowed for in the design of a toy to allow for misuse? How much tolerance should be allowed for in designs generally? Does this vary from one design to another?

Establishing methods of paint finishes to multifibre board (MDF).

Materials and construction

Having given thorough consideration to safety and methods of creating secondary movement in your toy design, you may well have found that ideas on the selection of materials and construction have already suggested themselves to you.

Consider alternative materials for your toy design; be wide-ranging in your selection for consideration. There will be reasons for favouring one against another and you should analyse the reasons for your selection. You might give thought to availability, cost, colour, working characteristics, equipment and tools required for fabrication, visual appeal, personal preference, and so on. (The section on material selection on page 166 may be of help.)

Whichever approach you make in selecting materials you will need to do some research. Use the resources available to you – books and worksheets in your design department, your school and local libraries, the experience of your teacher.

Record your thoughts and the results of your deliberations. Sometimes, when considering a particular material or construction, it is valuable to test the idea. Materials testing often needs to be carefully planned, particularly if comparisons are to be made between the performance of alternative materials. If results are to be valid, there needs to be replication of the test.

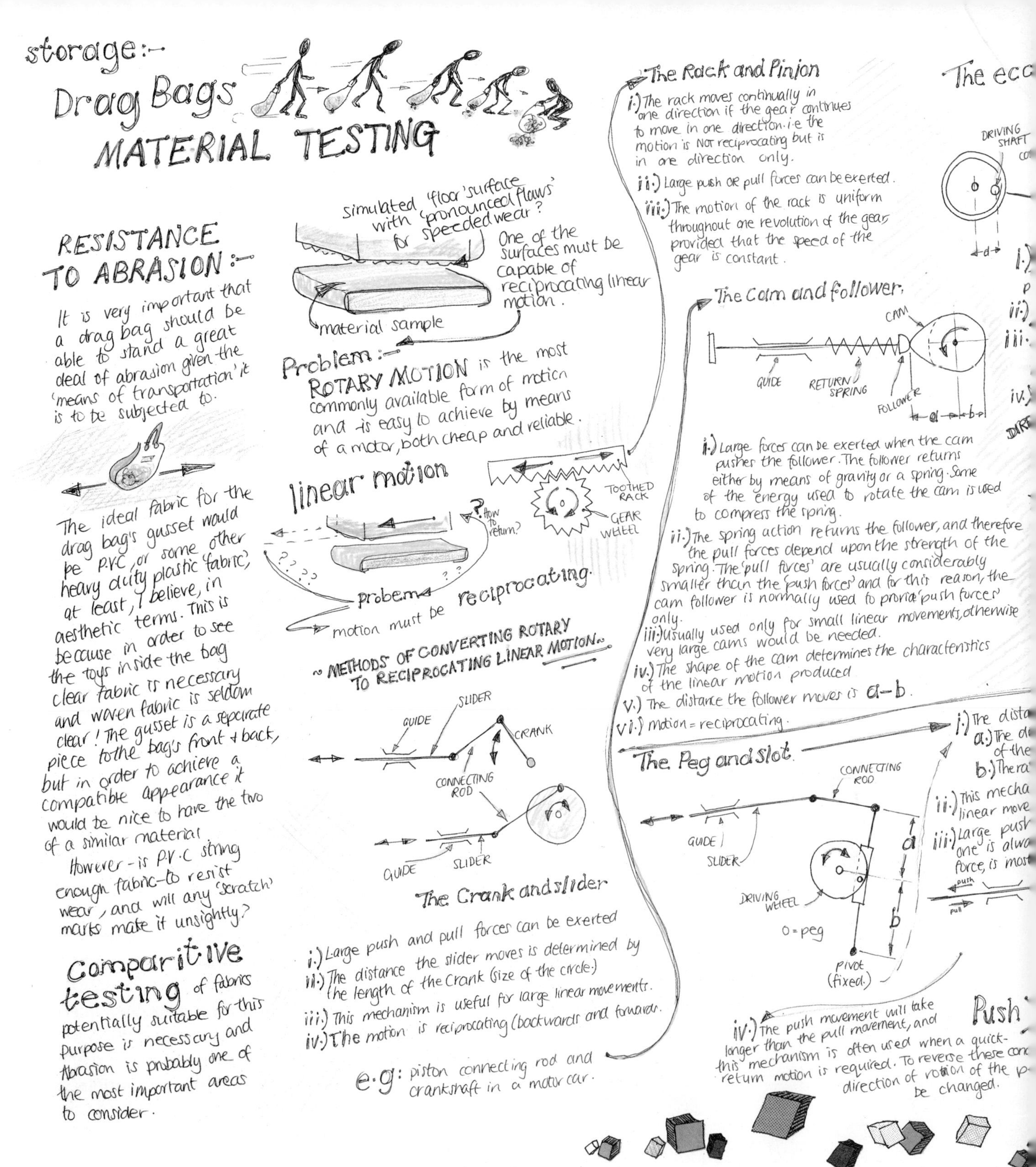

storage:–
Drag Bags
MATERIAL TESTING
RESISTANCE TO ABRASION:–
It is very important that a drag bag should be able to stand a great deal of abrasion given the 'means of transportation' it is to be subjected to.
The ideal fabric for the drag bag's gusset would be P.V.C, or some other heavy duty plastic 'fabric', at least, I believe, in aesthetic terms. This is because in order to see the toys inside the bag clear fabric is necessary and woven fabric is seldom clear! The gusset is a seperate piece to the bag's front + back, but in order to achieve a compatible appearance it would be nice to have the two of a similar material.
However – is P.V.C strong enough fabric – to resist wear, and will any 'scratch' marks make it unsightly?
Comparitive testing of fabrics potentially suitable for this purpose is necessary and Abrasion is probably one of the most important areas to consider.
simulated 'floor' surface with 'pronounced flaws' for speeded wear?
One of the surfaces must be capable of reciprocating linear motion.
material sample
Problem:–
ROTARY MOTION is the most commonly available form of motion and is easy to achieve by means of a motor, both cheap and reliable.
linear motion
How to return?
TOOTHED RACK
GEAR WHEEL
problem
motion must be reciprocating.
METHODS OF CONVERTING ROTARY TO RECIPROCATING LINEAR MOTION.
SLIDER
GUIDE
CRANK
CONNECTING ROD
GUIDE
SLIDER
The Crank and slider
i.) Large push and pull forces can be exerted
ii.) The distance the slider moves is determined by the length of the crank (size of the circle)
iii.) This mechanism is useful for large linear movements.
iv.) The motion is reciprocating (backwards and forwards.
e.g: piston connecting rod and crankshaft in a motor car.
The Rack and Pinion
i.) The rack moves continually in one direction if the gear continues to move in one direction. i.e the motion is NOT reciprocating but is in one direction only.
ii.) Large push or pull forces can be exerted.
iii.) The motion of the rack is uniform throughout one revolution of the gear provided that the speed of the gear is constant.
The cam and follower.
CAM
GUIDE
RETURN SPRING
FOLLOWER
a
b
i.) Large forces can be exerted when the cam pushes the follower. The follower returns either by means of gravity or a spring. Some of the energy used to rotate the cam is used to compress the spring.
ii.) The spring action returns the follower, and therefore the pull forces depend upon the strength of the spring. The 'pull forces' are usually considerably smaller than the 'push forces' and for this reason, the cam follower is normally used to provide 'push forces' only.
iii.) Usually used only for small linear movements, otherwise very large cams would be needed.
iv.) The shape of the cam determines the characteristics of the linear motion produced
v.) The distance the follower moves is a–b.
vi.) motion = reciprocating.
The Peg and slot.
CONNECTING ROD
GUIDE
SLIDER
DRIVING WHEEL
0 = peg
a
b
Pivot (fixed.)
iv.) The push movement will take longer than the pull movement, and this mechanism is often used when a quick-return motion is required.
The ecc
DRIVING SHAFT
Push
push
pull

Working out methods of testing is sometimes a design problem in itself!

Secondary sources of information, such as reference books and experienced people, are perfectly sound ways of gaining the information you need. It can be very time consuming to conduct your own tests all the time. Indeed, professional designers often rely on available data relating to materials.

> ***Collecting data on materials***
> *Write to manufacturers for detailed information on materials and select from the literature they send to you the particular data which is relevant to your designing.*

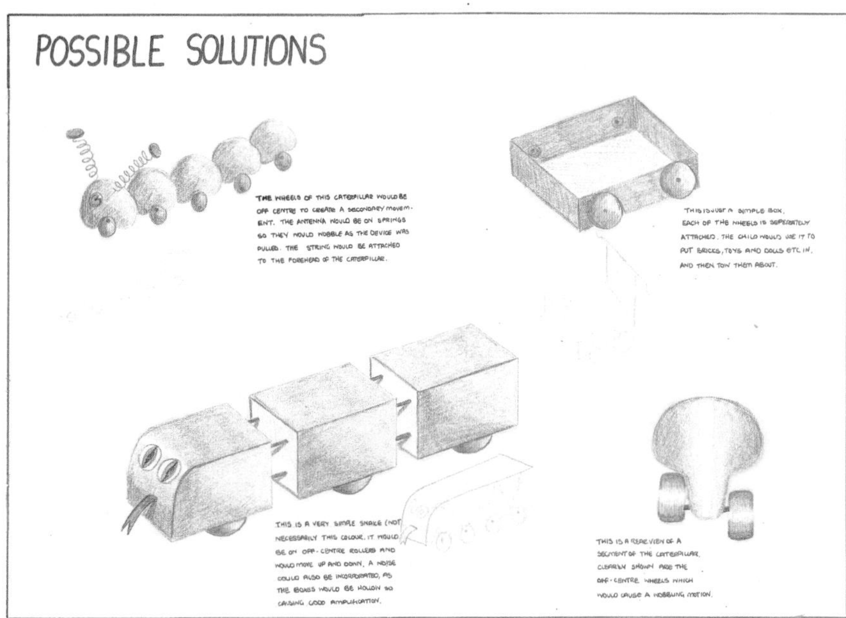

Examples of toy idea sheets

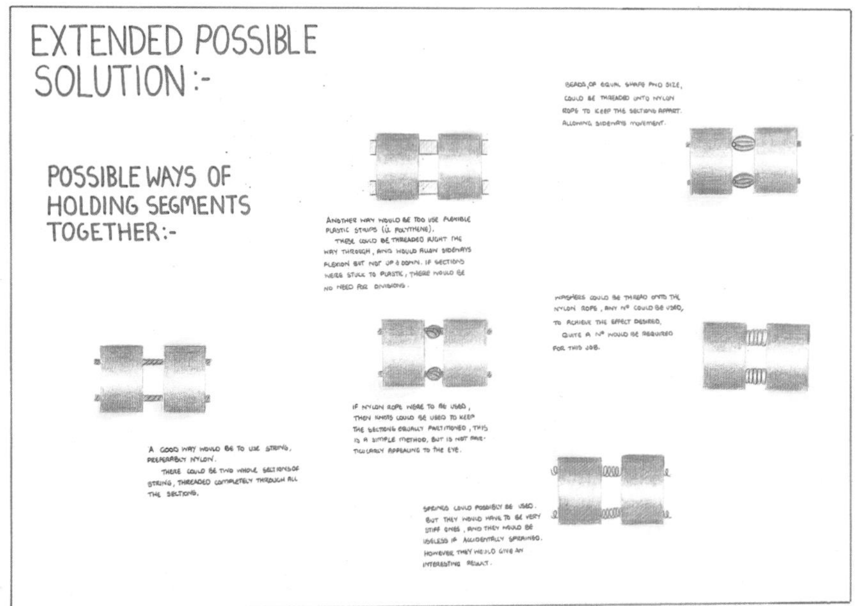

Snake toy methods of connecting

Ideas for a solution to your design problem

It is essential for your own designing that you thoroughly explore possible ideas for an answer to the design brief you are working to. If your work is for an examination in design, a good proportion of marks will be allocated to the skills you can show in thinking about and recording these ideas.

Your initial research and investigations will have already focused your mind on certain approaches; you will also be aware of certain constraints such as safety.

Annotated sketching is an excellent way of recording and also for clarifying ideas. One idea often leads to an improved or entirely different solution. Sometimes you will be inspired to examine one idea in some depth, or one particular aspect in some detail.

Here are some suggestions for proceeding:

- Concentrate on one approach at a time, e.g. ideas based on vehicles.
- Work on ideas related to a particular kind of play, e.g. educational toys.
- Explore ideas that make a particular type of secondary movement, e.g. up and down.
- Develop ideas for play in a particular situation, e.g. the bath.
- Work in an open minded way, exploring design ideas of various sorts, following lines of enquiry as they occur to you.

> **Beware!**
> *It is unlikely that your first ideas will be your best. Even if they turn out to be so, exploring other possibilities will serve to confirm it!*

Developing the design of your chosen idea

Having investigated and recorded alternative ideas for a design that will meet the original brief, select one idea that you consider to be the most satisfactory, both in terms of your considerations and your personal preference. Be prepared to justify your selection.

The work now is to refine and develop your chosen idea. Details need to be thought out, materials have to be selected, dimensions of the design and its components have to be established. Mechanisms previously investigated have to be incorporated to give the required secondary movement.

The examples shown illustrate some of these aspects.

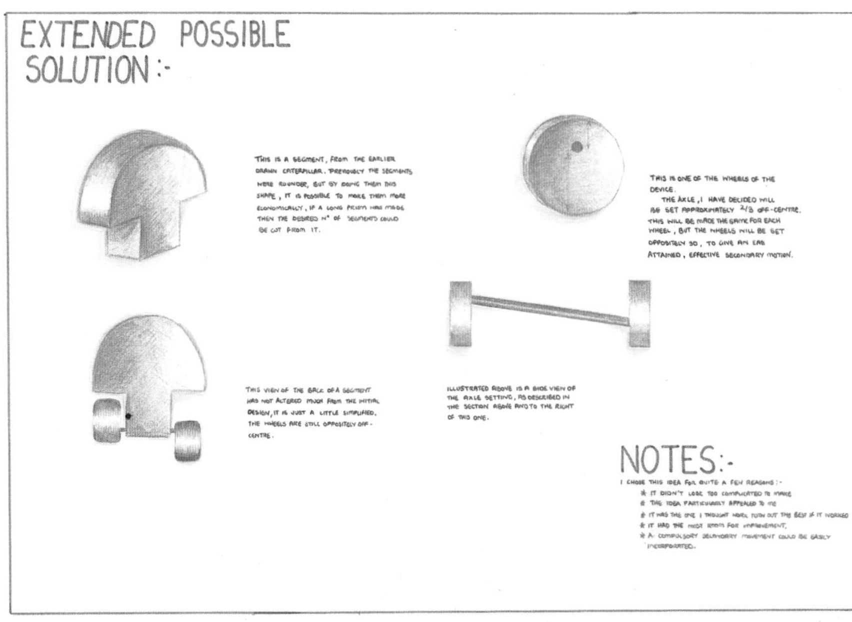

Plan of action

However you prefer to present your final idea, you need to show clearly how it is to be made with complete specifications. Possible methods are:

- a working drawing, drawn to scale
- an isometric drawing
- a neat dimensioned pictorial sketch – perhaps with details shown separately
- an exploded drawing
- a prototype modelled from easily worked material
- a list of components with their dimensions and type of material shown
- a combination of all or some of the above.

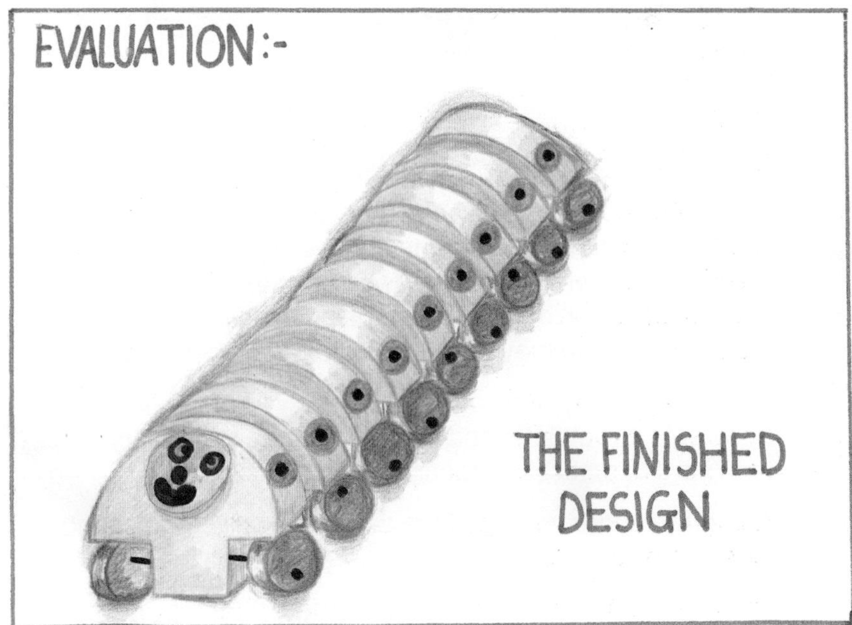

Making your design: the realisation

Proving that your design ideas and decisions work can be very exciting. Do not be disappointed or surprised if you find some aspects of the proposed design need to be modified; in fact you should expect to make modifications. It is a good idea to make a note of modifications and the reasons for them.

In design examinations credit is usually given for the manner in which you handle and work the materials you use. A well-made, attractively finished toy design will be much appreciated by the user as well.

Final touches

Assembly

Evaluating the toy design

Firstly, test the toy yourself and then give it to a child to use. Play with the child and, by observing and talking, see how the child reacts. Record what happens; if you have the use of a camera, take a photograph of your design being used. If the child is old enough, he or she may be able to talk to you about the toy.

Compare your toy with your original analysis of the brief. Is the toy as safe as you intended? Does it make a secondary movement? Is it attractive in appearance?

Recognise shortcomings of the design as well as indicating aspects that work well.

Rarely is the prototype of a design perfect. You may have the opportunity to modify and remake the toy. Failing this, note what modifications are necessary.

Use sketches to illustrate your evaluation, it often makes a point easier to explain. If you have made modifications during the making and have not noted them, an explanation at this stage is advisable.

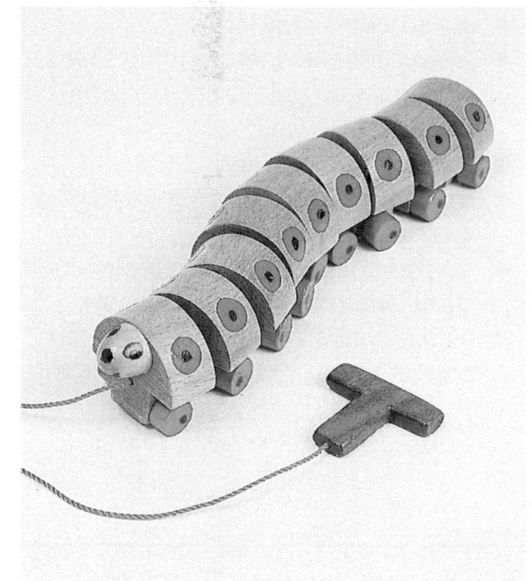

A finished toy

A student's evaluation of her caterpillar design

Good points
The device has a free moving action and readily moves. It has a clear secondary motion and does answer the design brief quite precisely.

The device is fairly attractive to the eye and does resemble a caterpillar. Also, all of the segments move independently and wobble successfully. The nylon rope is very strong and the glue fixing it in position is also very strong.

As a whole, I think the device is quite successful and very pleasing. There are no sharp edges incorporated and all rough edges have been filed smooth, including the handle.

Bad points
The main bad point is that a small child's fingers could become trapped between the segments, but pain would only occur if pressure was applied.

If for some reason the nylon rope holding the body together is cut, the whole device will collapse and small washers will spill out everywhere. These would be a danger to small children. The head isn't really what I wanted and does not quite match the body. Perhaps I could have done some research into the handle shapes i.e. shapes and sizes children find most desirable to hold. I am a little ashamed of some of the body paintwork, as it is rather shabby.

Modifications I would make
If I had more time I would have liked to have completely painted the device so that it was more attractive and would attract a child's attention more easily. Also I would have preferred not to have the knot showing as this is a danger point for nicking the nylon rope and so weakening it.

I would have preferred a more evenly matching head which didn't look like a last minute addition. If I could find some way of blocking in the segments so fingers couldn't get trapped, I would, and a major modification I would make would be to not use washers as dividers. If the device comes apart a mess and possible danger occurs. Perhaps I could also use one long length of rope, not three.

Problems I encountered
I had already attached the head so drilling was a little difficult. The paint was also a problem as it ran and caused a mess. Some of the segments dragged on the ground when the wheels were in their lowest position. I had to file them to overcome this problem.

Final presentation

Do take the trouble to review your work to make sure it is clearly understood by other people; make sure the order of your work is clear and that the presentation is your best.

Constraints in designing

Some designs are constrained by specific factors which determine what they should be. Other designs are 'open-ended' and left to the imagination of the designer. Is the design and construction of a boomerang constrained in any way?

Designing and throwing a boomerang is a test of your skill. Boomerangs have been developed from throwing clubs used by Australian aborigines since Stone Age times. Boomerangs are now thrown for sport and competition for the longest flight and distance thrown. The Boomerang Association of Australia, Strathfield, NSW may supply you with further information.

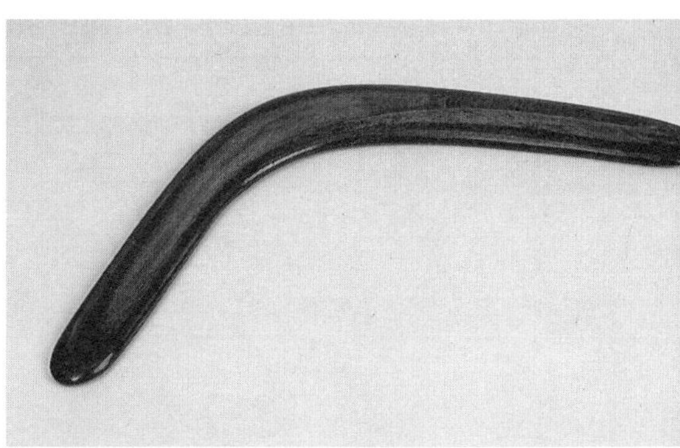

Design, make and test a boomerang which will break the world record for distance thrown on a outward flight and/or for the longest flight.

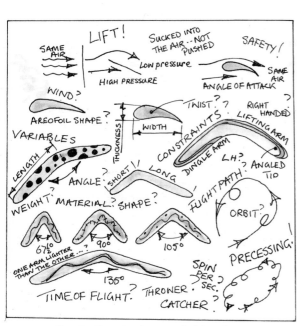

Study the design variables for a boomerang.

How a boomerang works

The flight of a boomerang is caused by both its aerodynamic qualities, due to 'lift' and 'precessing', a gyroscopic force. Lift is caused by the way air flows over the curved surface of the two arms of a boomerang.

Try a simple experiment of blowing along the top of a strip of paper, which can act as a crude aerofoil. What happens to the paper? You should observe lift. Lift is caused by air travelling along the top surface faster than below; the shape causes this to happen. When air travels quickly it is less dense. Thus, the air below is more dense, and the boomerang is sucked into the air, not pushed. The better the shape of the aerofoil, the better its flight characteristics.

A spinning boomerang is like a gyroscope. When it is thrown, it spins, but also curves back on itself, as it flies in an orbit. The precessing force causes the boomerang to come back. This force is rather like that which acts on a spinning bike wheel, when its spindle is held and the wheel spun round. Spin a wheel and try to move it from side to side. It will be reluctant to move away from its vertical plane. This is the force of precessing and a simple gyroscope also acts in this way. Use this information to design your boomerang.

How does a boomerang return?

Can you predict its orbit?

What should it be made from?

Are there any constraints in this design activity?

DESIGN BRIEF

(with specific constraints)

A simple puzzle ornament

A very effective puzzle ornament can be made from 12mm pine, which can be hung by a cord or thong, or mounted on a plinth by a dowel. You must cut your ornament from one piece of wood, after selecting a knot-free piece of wood which can be smoothed with glass paper as preparation for your design to be drawn in place. Use a paper template for your design. You will need a coping saw, glass paper and a hand drill, as well as something suitable to colour and decorate your design, such as a wood stain. Base your design on a theme of your choice. How important is it to have constraints to your designing?

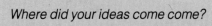

Where did your ideas come come?

How can you transfer your ideas from paper to wood?

Do any saw cuts make the puzzles' picture?

What finish can you give the ornament?

Where will you display it?

Radio design

Technology is the application of scientific knowledge and design is an important process by which such knowledge can be found and applied. The design and construction of an AM radio will engage you in many issues and skills.

Initially, as a designer, you may consider either the re-styling of a radio known to you, or your development of a new concept for a radio. In either case you could concentrate mainly on the styling for your new product as a project in its own right. However, you will need to produce a design folder full of design sketches and drawings using all your drawing skills; and this folder should include detailed research of examples of radios found in photographs and books. You may even consider modelling your ideas or basing your design on something unusual.

Will your design in anyway determine how 'good' your radio will be? To what extent will the function of your radio affect its 'attractiveness'? Will you use 'hard lines' or 'pretty lines'; will your radio be a plain box or something interesting to own? Your choice of materials will help in this regard, especially if you can think of any new materials which would produce a novel design. Also, how well you make your radio will be very important to the quality of its performance. To test these ideas you would have to be prepared to live with, and use, your own designs. Design and innovation in electronics industries are crucial to commercial success, where the use of the new materials and production techniques which are available encourages many creative opportunities for designers.

Outside design

Should a radio look like a radio? One of your starting points for this activity may be your consideration of what your radio will look like. Can your radio be hidden within another object? How does the outside of the design relate to its inside?

Produce a series of drawings of your designs. Explore your ideas by producing sectional drawings which show how various parts fit together. Think about where the radio will be used and by whom. How does it switch on and off; where is its tuner for different radio stations, and so on? Your choice of materials for this project will be very important. Acrylic can be very useful for the casing of the radio. Aim to produce a design of quality; one which will be pleasing to use and own.

Inside design

Acquire the components listed here and use the printed circuit board (PCB) layout and component diagrams to design and assemble the inside of your radio. Look up the colour codings for the different resistors and capacitors to ensure you have the correct components.

Part of the design has been started for you; this can be found in the 'component location' diagram. Think about the best positioning of items like the aerial, batteries, switches and tuner. Consider the problem of replacing the batteries because this affects both the inside and the outside of your design, as well as how well the radio performs generally.

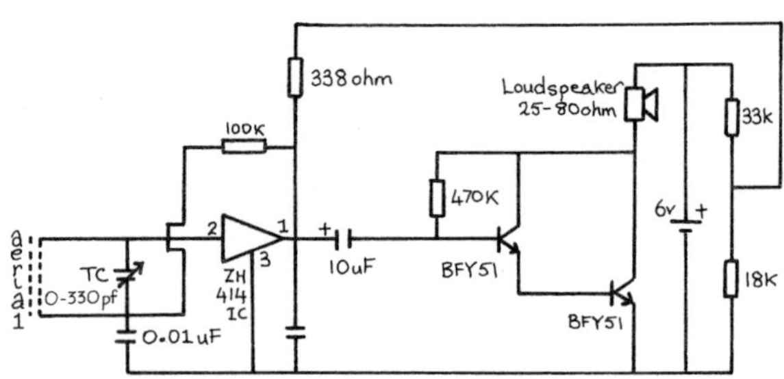

In what ways is technology a feature of designing?

If it is the 'appliance of science', is designing the same or distinctly different?

How can technology be the science of industrial arts?

Which comes first – the inside or the outside; the need for a design or its function?

DESIGN BRIEF

Design, make and test a simple AM Radio using the notes provided. The circuit opposite will serve as a basic introduction to the use of electronic components in a radio. At a later date you may consider developing your radio so as to achieve a higher output, better signal to noise ratio and better discrimination (the ability to pick one signal up as opposed to another), with the aid of more specialised components for the circuits.

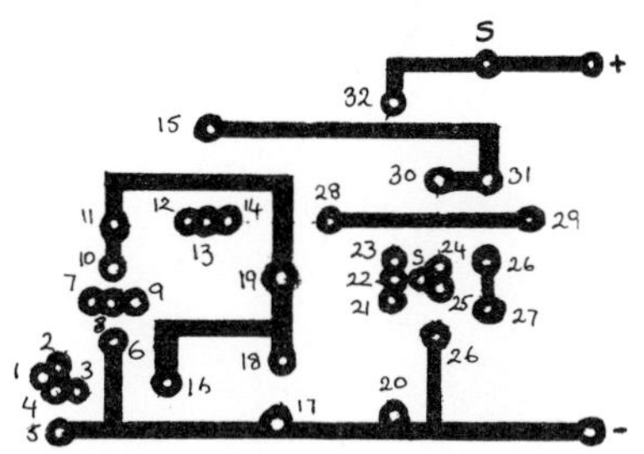

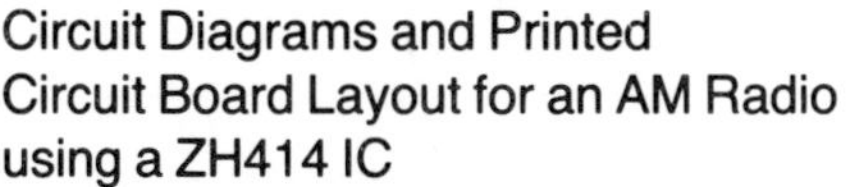
Circuit Diagrams and Printed Circuit Board Layout for an AM Radio using a ZH414 IC

Etching a printed circuit board requires specialised equipment. It is rare for just one PCB to be made in industry since an electronics company producing radios would buy the required PCBs from a specialist manufacturer.

A PCB layout is derived from a good quality drawing of the required circuit on an acetate sheet using opaque ink. The ink side of the acetate sheet is placed on the 'positive resistance' side of a copper clad board after its protective coating has been peeled off. This board is then placed upside down in an ultra-violet exposure unit for four minutes. It is reversed to avoid ultra violet diffusion during the circuit's manufacture. Remove the board to a bath of sodium hydroxide until you can see the blue film coming off and the circuit being revealed. Protect your hands, eyes and clothes during these processes. Finally place the board into an etch tank containing a solution of ferric chloride and leave for fourteen minutes; remove, wash with cold water and then dry. Your PCB is now ready to accept the components for soldering. To do this drill the holes required for the components and solder them into place.

Throughout this study create a portfolio which will contain all your notes, drawings and the technical information you have been given, and which you have found during your designing. Use this portfolio to present your total study and include in it a full evaluation of your radio. Does it work? Does it work well? Does it look good? Does it look like a radio?

PCB Layout and Component location

Resistors
(No polorisation: check colour codes)
1 330ohm 19–22
1 10k 20–21
1 33k 23–32
1 100k 3–16
1 470k 13–15

Capacitors
(Check colour codes)
1 0.01uF (Disc ceramic) 4–5
1 0.01uF (Disc ceramic) 17–18
1 10.0 uF (Electrolytic) 11–12
1 Tuning capacitor 2–7
(0–330pf)
Semi-conductors
2 BFY51 Transistors 28(e), 29(b), 31(c)
25(c), 26(e), 27(b).
1 ZN414 AM Receiver 6, gnd, 8, i/p, 10, o/p(vcc).

ZN414 Pin
GND—3
i/p—2
o/p(vcc)—1

Other Items
1 Aerial 1–9
1 25-80ohm speaker S–S

Aerial: 50 turns of 24 gauge enamelled copper wire on a ferrite core.

uF = micro Farads (non polorised)
Electrolytic Capacitor (polorised) has to be connected correctly to + and −; check for +sign. IC = Integrated Circuit (A Chip)

The PCB layout formed from tape. Notice that it is reversed, since it has been found necessary to do this to avoid ultra violet light diffusion during the circuit's manufacture.

Designing for a special occasion

The first step towards designing an object for a special occasion is to identify the occasion. An excellent way to do this is by a group 'brainstorm'. This will generate many alternative ideas, some of which you may not have considered as an individual.

Having put down as many ideas as possible each student considers what objects might be designed: cards, pictures, coins, mugs, stationery are just a few ideas.

On starting her project, Naomi made two decisions. The first was that her special occasion would be 'Leaving School' and the second was that she would design a card. Having produced several alternative ideas, Naomi selected the one that she liked the best.

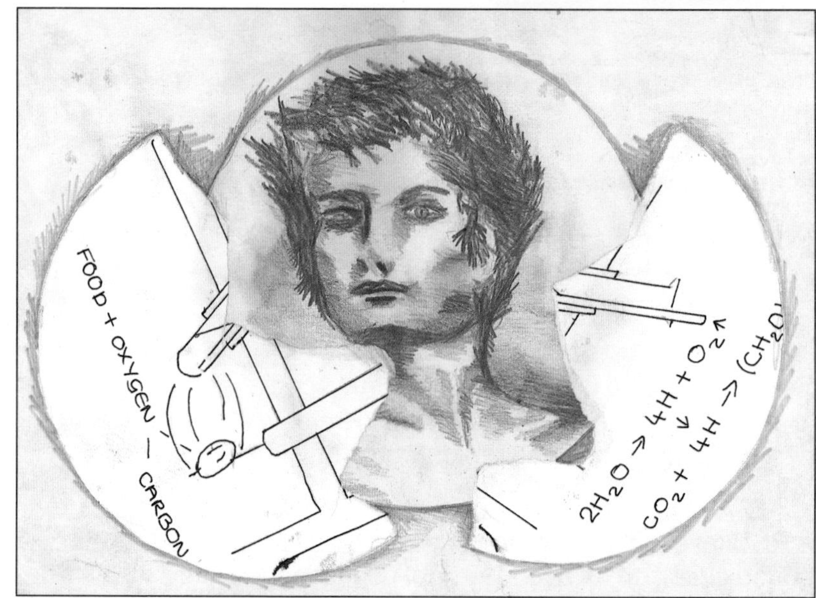

The design changed from being circular to square (more or less) because the circle was hard to draw and less prints could be fitted on it. Despite this, the main idea of using a girl and science equipment was carried out throughout the project.

There are many possible solutions to this problem. Other students produced objects as varied as:
Cake in a box to deliver it in.
Stamps for the Birmingham Olympics.
A poster to advertise a group.
A set of stationery.
Novelties for a stag party!

Experimentation

Once the decision about the composition (what was in the picture) had been made, Naomi then went on to experiment with different methods of printing.

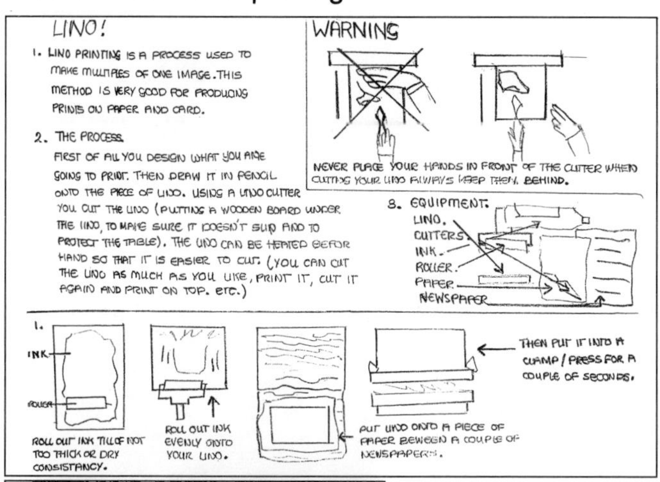

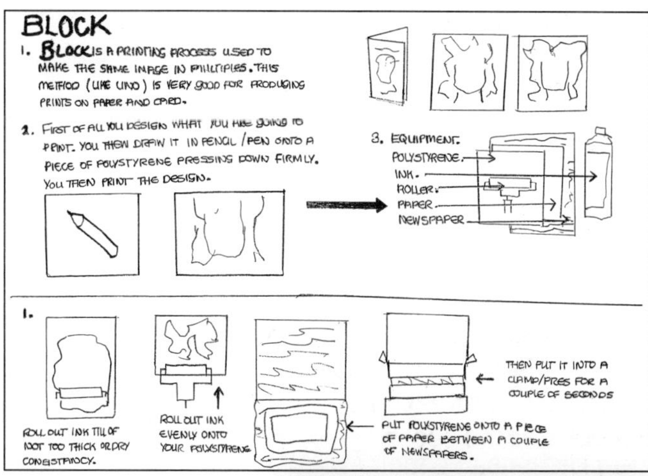

From these two prints, I had to decide which one to use; in the end I chose the print using the block method because I preferred the size and general effect.

I had to modify my final design because of the results of my prints and their sizes.

I developed the science equipment further because I thought that it did not fill up enough space and looked bare.

My finished piece was a lot different from the original statement of the problem. My first idea was to produce a small card but in the end I found myself producing a fully mounted print/picture.

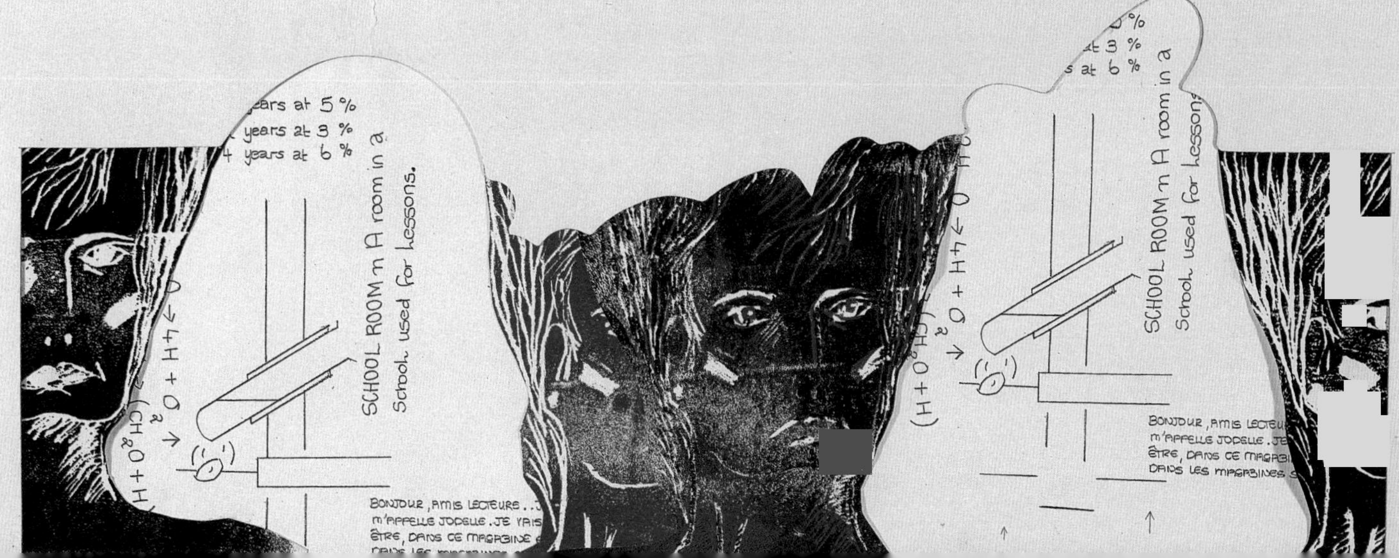

Kitchen planning

Few parts of our homes have been studied more closely by designers than the layout of the modern kitchen. However, when we look at the futuristic layout of the Edwardian all-electric kitchen in 1908 (illustrated opposite), we begin to realise that only in the last four decades has a well designed and fitted kitchen become a desirable consumer durable. Indeed, the re-fitting of a kitchen is probably the most expensive purchase that you will make for your home, and as such it will become your most valuable asset should you wish to re-sell your property.

There are many companies who specialise in the design and installation of new kitchens and their expertise can cost you thousands of pounds even for a kitchen of average size. Alternatively, you can design your own layout and buy the units either ready built or in a 'KD' (knock-down) form, ready for assembly at home.

The kitchen is one of the busiest and most dangerous rooms in the house so the design of its layout needs very careful consideration.

The Edwardian all-electric kitchen of 1908.

Philips 90 series combined built-in oven and microwave.

Open fire, pots and pans – the way it used to be.

DESIGN BRIEF

This design project can be tackled in one of two ways:

1. Re-design the layout of your own kitchen at home, where you have to clearly identify the design requirements of your own family, as well as keeping to a strict budget.
2. Look at the plan of the room below which has been specially selected by the Kitchen Specialists Association. Meet the design requirements of their family whilst keeping within a budget of £6,000. This amount is to include all cabinets, worktops, built-in appliances, sinks, etc. but not decoration, flooring, plumbing costs or small accessories.

Produce at least three different design layouts of your selected kitchen using a scale of 1 : 20. Mark in all the major features of your designs, e.g. cabinets, furniture, appliances, sink, etc.

Evaluate your alternative ideas and then produce a 1 : 20 model of your final selected kitchen.

KSA plan

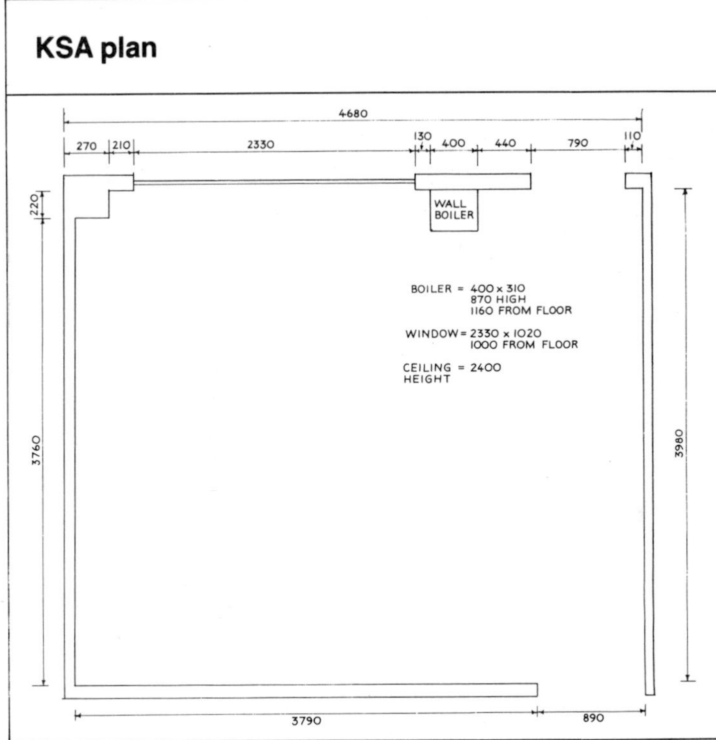

Family profile

The kitchen is to be designed for a two parent family with a daughter aged six and a son aged thirteen. The house does not contain a separate dining room or utility room. The family require a safe, practical working kitchen in which they can entertain their friends.

A budget of £6,000 is to include cabinetry, worktops, sinks, taps and appliances. The position of the doors, windows and wall mounted boiler must not be changed. The kitchen has a concrete floor. Gas, water and electricity are available in the kitchen. It is your responsibility to decide where they will be positioned.

Remember

Whichever kitchen project you select, costing is a very important consideration. You must design your layout, select your units and appliances to keep within your budget.

Making a start

Most kitchen specialists use a 1 : 20 scale when producing plans, and it is a good idea to keep to this scale for both your drawings and final model. Begin by drawing the outline of your kitchen on graph paper, marking in the position of fixtures and fitting which cannot be changed. This may include the following:

1. The internal measurements of the kitchen walls, including the position of door frames and windowsills as well as the height of the ceiling.
2. Door positions and their opening areas.
3. All window positions, their height and width.
4. Water supply and drainage points.
5. Gas and electric points.
6. The position of the central heating boiler and radiators.

Once this has been done it is a good idea to double check your measurements, and then make several photocopies of your plan, which will save you a great deal of time at the initial planning stage.

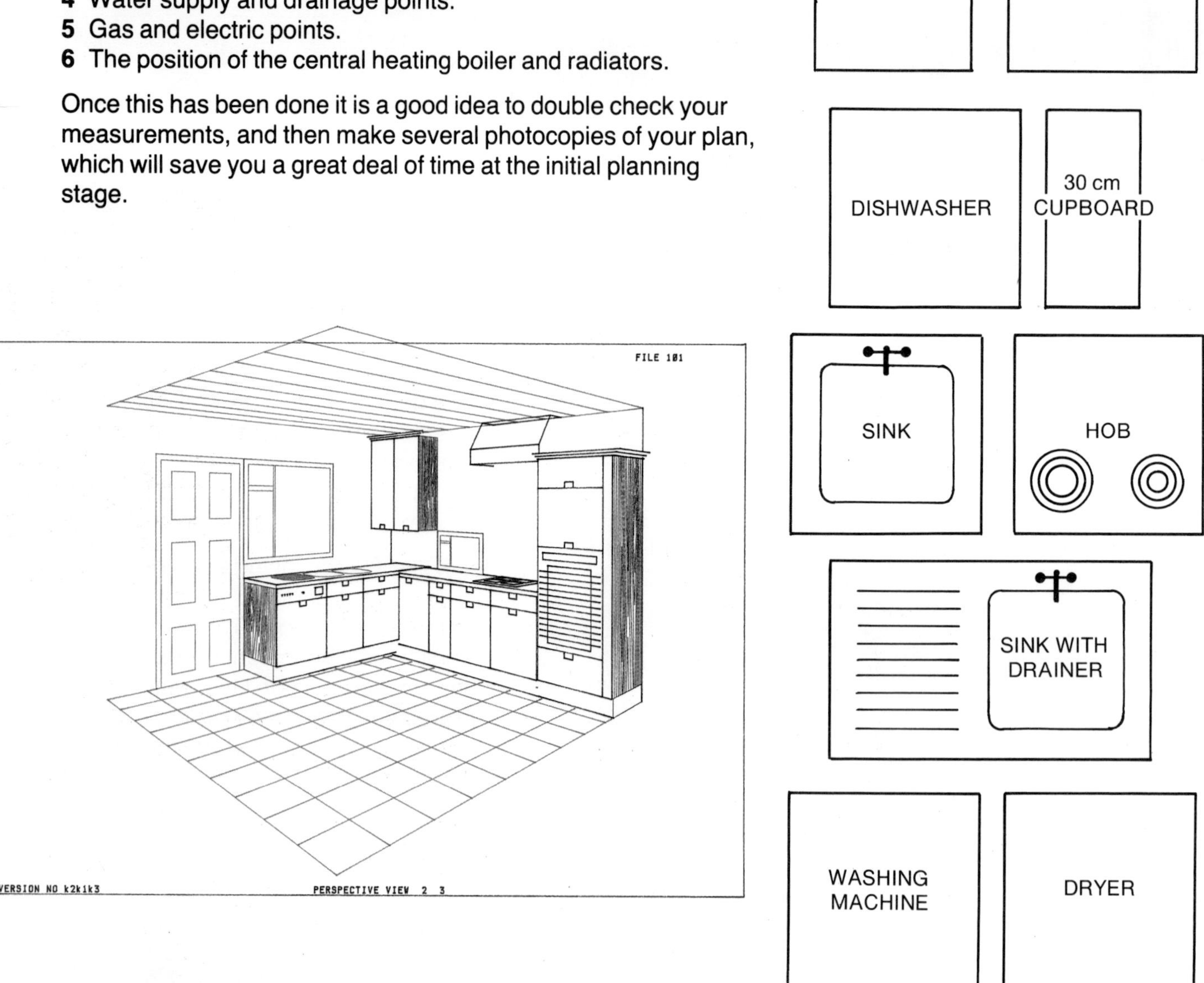

Trace around the 1:20 plans above, which can then be used to place on your kitchen outline.

Visit a kitchen planning centre. Look at the range of units and appliances available. Some centres offer customers a CAD service.

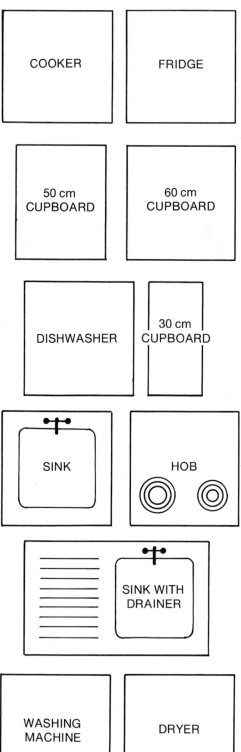

What do you want from your kitchen?

Kitchens can be used for many things. Everyone's requirements for their kitchen will vary tremendously. Consequently you can begin by writing down a list of the design requirements for *your* kitchen. The checklist below may help:

1. Do you want to eat in the kitchen?
2. If so, how many people will need to be seated at the table?
3. Where will you site the table?
4. Will you have a table or breakfast bar? Will you use chairs, stools, or benches to sit on?
5. Will you have to provide facilities such as a high chair for young children or toddlers?
6. What special precautions are needed to make the kitchen safe if young children are around?
7. Do you have a separate room in which you can do the laundry (a utility room) or will you want to include a washing machine and perhaps a tumble dryer within your kitchen layout?
8. Remember to have a storage cupboard, to keep bleaches and dangerous chemicals out of reach of young children.
9. What facilities do you want for washing dirty dishes? Will your 'dishwasher' be human or electrical?
10. What major appliances are you going to have in your kitchen, e.g. cooker, hob, fridge, freezer, microwave oven, etc.?
11. What are the storage requirements you will need for food, cutlery, pots, pans, brooms, mops, etc.? The size of the family and the amount of space available in the kitchen will be big factors here.
12. Do you want to watch breakfast television in the kitchen?
13. What small accessories such as toaster, kettles, deep fat fryers, food mixers and coffee makers do you want to make allowance for. Where will these smaller appliances be stored? Do you have adequate electrical points to cope with them?

There may be many more requirements which you need to consider. Try to ensure you have identified them all before you start on your plans.

Mothercare safety hob guard.

The units available

Manufacturers of kitchen units offer a variety of standard sizes of base units and cupboards. The most common sizes available are illustrated below. However, not all manufacturers will offer such an extensive range and you must check to ensure that the cabinets you select, and your matching fitted appliances, are available in the measurement you require. If in doubt check with the manufacturers' specifications to ensure that the units and appliances are compatible.

Planning your ideal kitchen in an awkward shaped room

The way you tackle the layout of your kitchen will be determined partially by the size and shape of the space you have available. Do not be disheartened if you find that what you want will not fit in, simply persevere and try a variety of solutions until you find the one which is most suitable.

Listed below you will find conventional solutions to the shape of some of the more common kitchen arrangements.

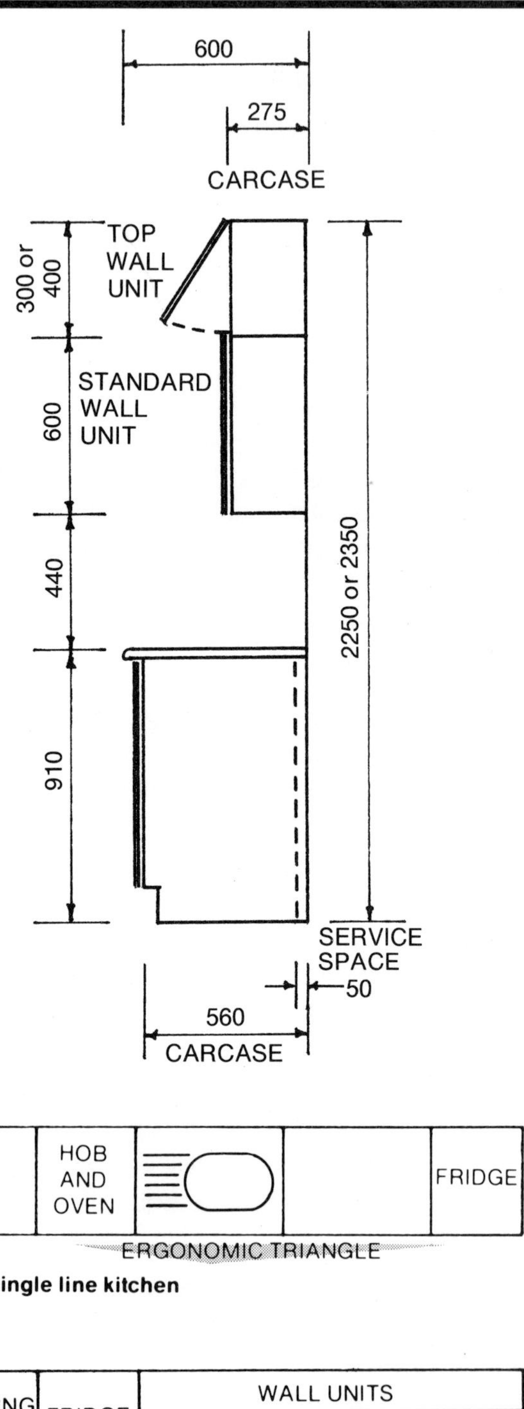

The single line kitchen

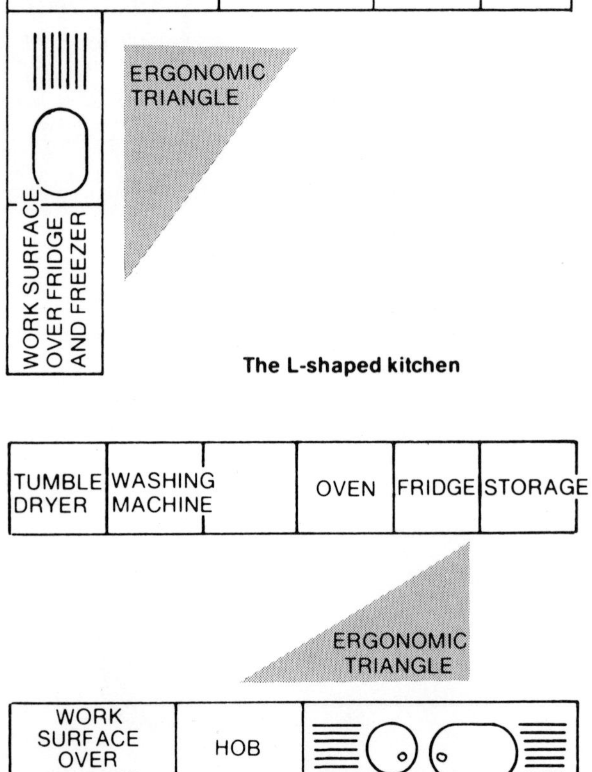

The L-shaped kitchen

The parallel or galley kitchen

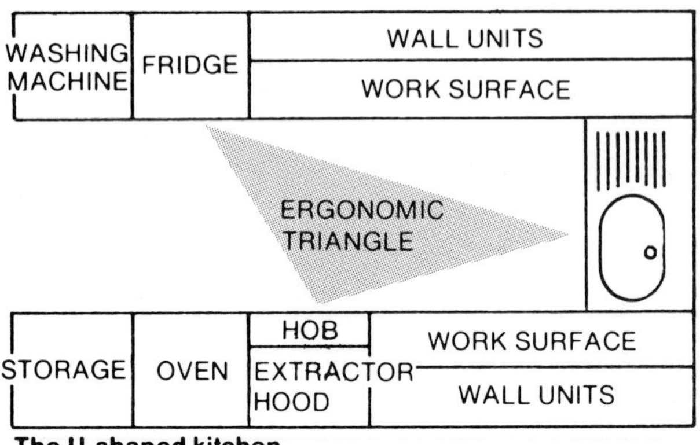

The U-shaped kitchen

The ergonomic triangle or safety zone

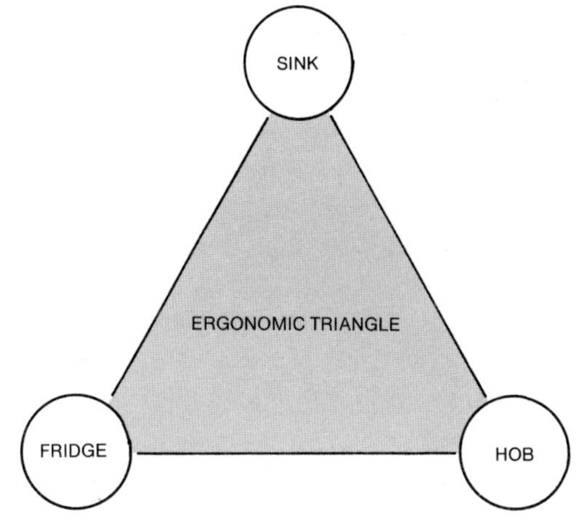

Whilst the term 'ergonomic triangle' may sound complex, it is much easier to understand when explained with the illustrations of the various kitchen layouts.

Research has shown that the three most commonly used centres of activity in the kitchen are:

1 Food storage area, fridges for perishable foods, and cupboards for dry and canned foods.
2 The sink, for washing and preparation.
3 The cooker.

When the three centres of activity are joined together they form the *ergonomic triangle* or safety zone.

To improve kitchen efficiency and to cut down on the amount of walking between these three centres, the total combined length of the distances between them should not exceed 6 metres. The ergonomic triangle should also be a safety zone and walk ways through the kitchen should not pass through it, so that the cook carrying hot dishes from the hob to the sink does not come across a small child on their way out into the garden.

However, this 'triangle' is only hypothetical. In the 'single line kitchen' opposite, the three centres of activity will be in a straight line. In this case the rule to remember is that right-handed people should always have the cooking side to the right of the sink, so the sequence of events should read from left to right:

STORAGE SINK COOKER

If you are designing a layout for a left-handed person you would reverse the sequence.

Having established these simple rules of efficiency and safety, you are now ready to site your cabinets and appliances.

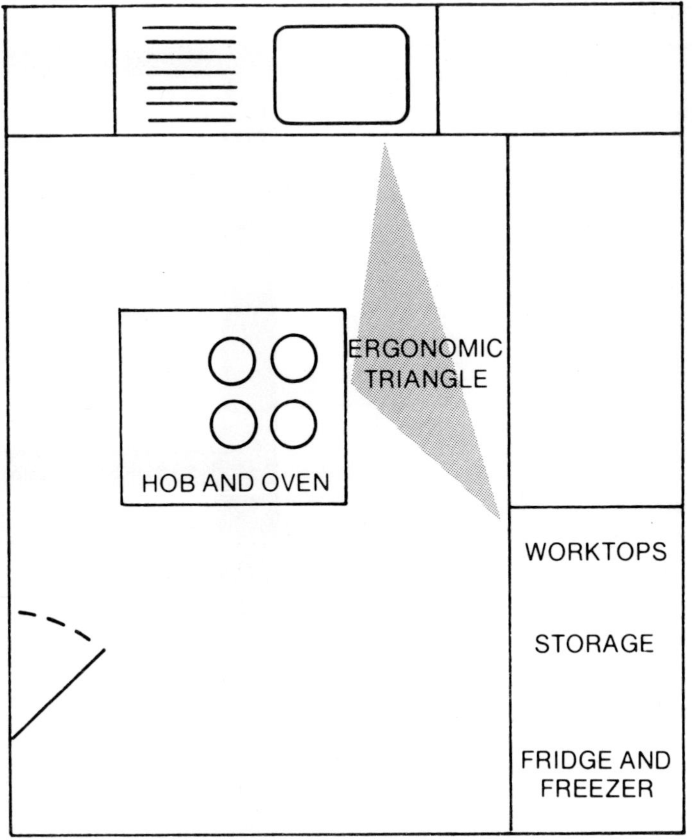

The island kitchen

The do's and don'ts of kitchen planning

Do

- Provide as much worktop space as you can.
- Try to site your sink under a window, so that you benefit from the natural light and the view.
- Ensure the sink has a work surface or draining board upon which vegetables can be prepared and where crockery and utensils can be stacked after washing up.
- Place tall units at the end of a length of base units, rather than in the middle, thus ensuring a maximum uninterrupted working surface.
- Use corner units to avoid wasted space, the use of 'carousel' racks can also help you to store items in inaccessible corners.
- Ensure that there is a work surface of at least 300 mm either side of the hob.

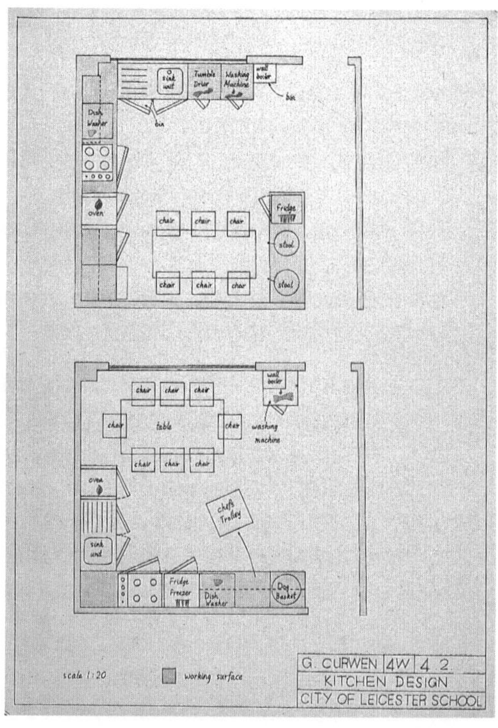

Don't

- Site a fridge or freezer next to a free-standing cooker (unless this cannot be avoided or the appliances are extremely well insulated), otherwise the fridge or freezer will have to work overtime to cope with the heat from the cooker.
- Place a cooker hob under a window.
- Fix wall cupboards above hobs and cookers unless they are on top of an extractor.
- Position lines of units too close together. In the galley kitchen plan there should be at least 900 mm to allow the cook move around and cupboard doors to be opened.

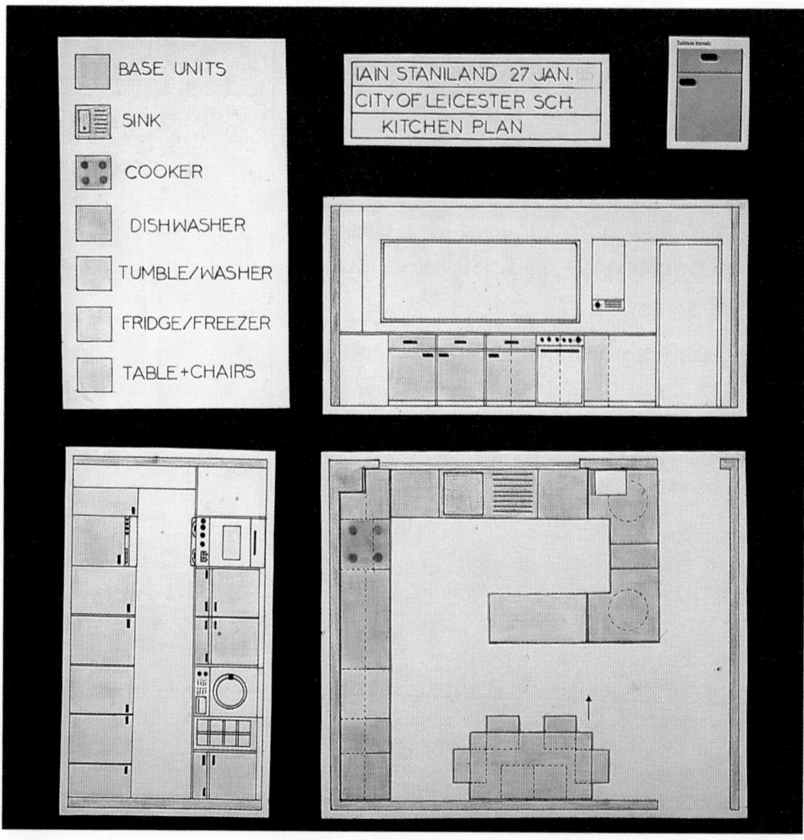

You should now be ready to put your first layouts down on paper. Produce at least three different ideas, evaluating their advantages and disadvantages as you go along. Remember not to design your layouts in isolation – discuss the possible alternatives with the person who is going to use the kitchen most frequently. Ultimately you should choose the layout which they feel will be the most efficient and pleasing to work in.

Below you will find a variety of possible solutions to the KSA kitchen mentioned at the start of this section. Which of these designs do you feel is the most successful and why?

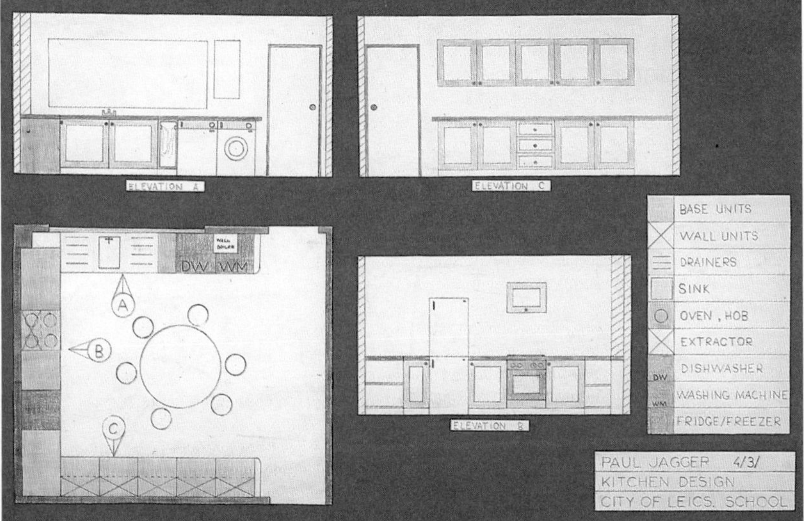

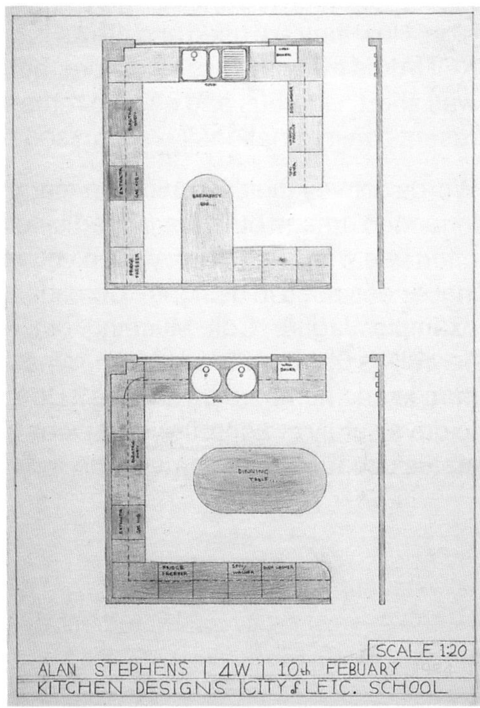

Once you have arrived at what you believe to be the most satisfactory solution on paper, produce a 1:20 model to see whether your ideas work in practice. The model will also communicate your ideas better to the person who is evaluating your design, and will be helpful to you in sorting out colour schemes for floors, walls and worktops.

Examples of 1:20 scale models of the KSA design brief.

Designing with words

Words, letter styles and calligraphy are used a great deal in design. How they are used and drawn is an art in itself. For example, KODAK is meaningless as a word, but was chosen because it was short, vigorous and easy to remember and spell; it now represents an internationally recognised photographic company.

Words convey their meanings in many ways, one of which is innuendo. Image builders, advertising agencies and designers often use words in this way. Can you read the images and innuendos used in designs? Consider the names of cars, for example: Jaguar, Colt, Mustang, or Civic, Accord, Polo and Golf as well as 5, 11 or 25 and so on. What is the innuendo in the names and numbers given here? Do the names encourage you to drive safely or aggressively? Does owning a car give you status because of its name or the way that name is written?

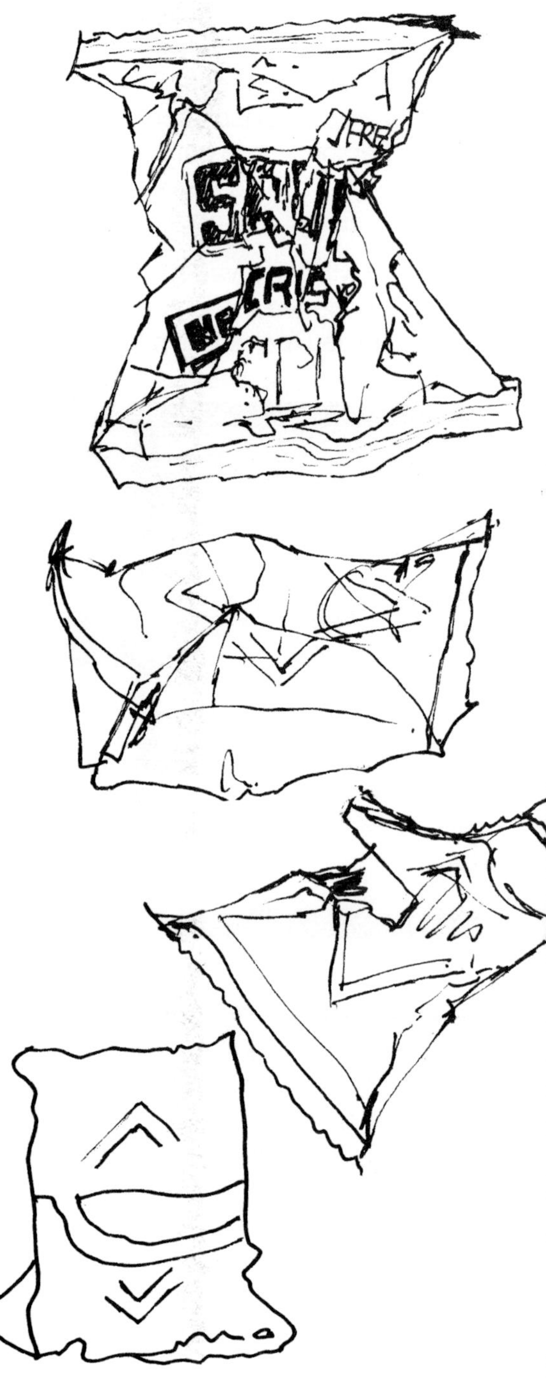

Design a new crisp product and packet, including its name and typography. Use observation drawings of crisps you know about to help you with your research.

Work out the information for your packet by listing: the name of your product, a trade name, the flavour of the crisps, the size, shape and type of crisps, made from potato or corn, the packet size, colour scheme and design, a price and other written information which should be put on the packet. Consider also the proper trades' descriptions required.

Study the examples of lettering in the 'tone' examples on which you can base on your own handwriting. Make several drawings of your packet and illustrate it. Study the use of your observed drawings of crisp bags and use tracings of these to place your new design in a realistic setting.

What's in a name?

What are calligraphy and typology, and what are their roles in design?

DESIGN BRIEF

Using the copy of the 'Helvetica Bold' letter font, draw and cut out a short word ten times larger than the letters in the copy. The aim of this design exercise is for you to explore letter spacing and positioning, as well as to use cut-out letters to form an abstract design. Why are rounded letters like 'o' slightly taller than the other letters?

ABCDEFGHIJ
KLMNOPQRST
UVWXYZabcd
efghijklmnopq
rstuvwxyz 123
4567890&?!ß
£$(;)«»

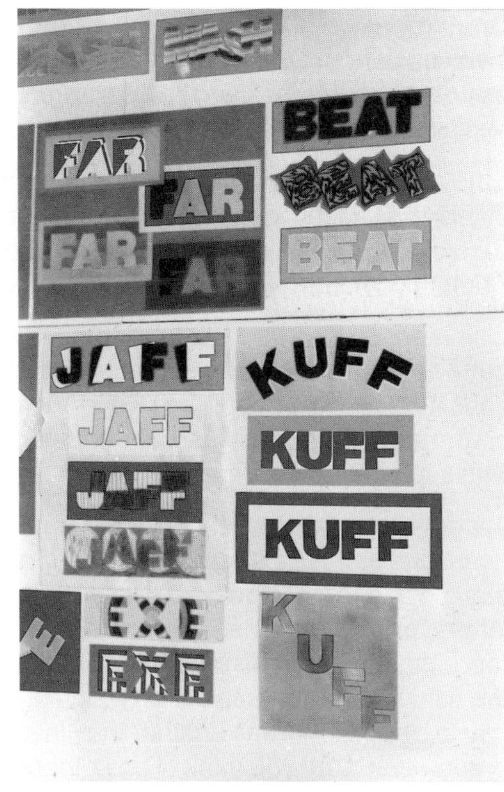

Examples of student work using Helvetica Bold.

The essence of pictorial art is design. This is usually called 'composition' in painting; in graphic design or commercial art it is called layout design. The art of pictorial composition, layout or design is to achieve a pleasing effect by using the elements and information given in a brief to their best advantage.

The following activity is a simulation of the tasks you as a designer might undertake for the following brief.

DESIGN BRIEF

Product: a toothpaste, name to be thought up by the designer.
Information: based on a product which emphasises its ability to clean teeth really well; price; ingredients.
Items: the toothpaste tube and its packet.
Size: 165 mm × 40 mm, maximum size of the tube.
Colour: use no more than four.
Instruction to printer: quantity.
Promotion: new product, whose name reflects its newness, cleanness, brightness and so on.
Required: tomorrow, roughs in colour and full size.

Layout design

Graphic design is essentially the art of visual communication and involves bringing about 'something novel and new' visually. The use of initial sketches and roughs is very important, especially to explain and develop your ideas to other people.

Study and investigate the different ways in which a company displays its 'identity' or 'image', by colour, logotypes and so on. Collect examples, which may include photographs or drawings. Present your study so that it has impact!

Comment on how successful, or otherwise, you think the company has been in making itself identifiable to the public. How well does it project its image? Why do companies wish to put over a corporate identity? Is it just commercial companies who bother with such enterprises?

A logotype may be produced typographically using standard typefaces or special hand-drawn lettering. Alternatively a logo may be a 'one-off' signature with a paint brush. It is a word or letters formed into a design. A logogram is a sign or character representing a word in shorthand. The style of a logo depends on the actual requirements of the design brief. One logo may take a day to design whereas another may involve several weeks of preparation. Can you think of any other devices of this type?

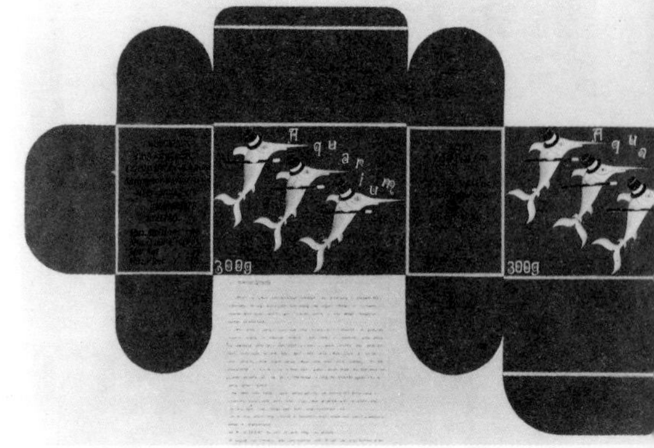

DESIGN BRIEF

Design a logotype for a record company. This design is a very important aspect of record sleeve design generally. You have to create an image so that the public can recognise the graphics on the record sleeve as well as on promotional and commercial material.

What is the function of a programme or advertising handout?

What information is communicated in these designs?

Collect examples of this type of design.

This activity will give you experience of designing using pictures, especially photographs, and lettering. It will require you to research, take photographs and find your own information for your design.

Professionally, this design work would be prepared for printers to print from. This is often called 'camera ready artwork'. Sketch several examples of designs so as to explore alternatives. Work out the actual shape of the finished design, including background shapes, your use of colour and use pictures to layout your work.

Your study should show an understanding of shape, proportion, letter styles, layout of drawings and photographs and your full use of illustrative techniques.

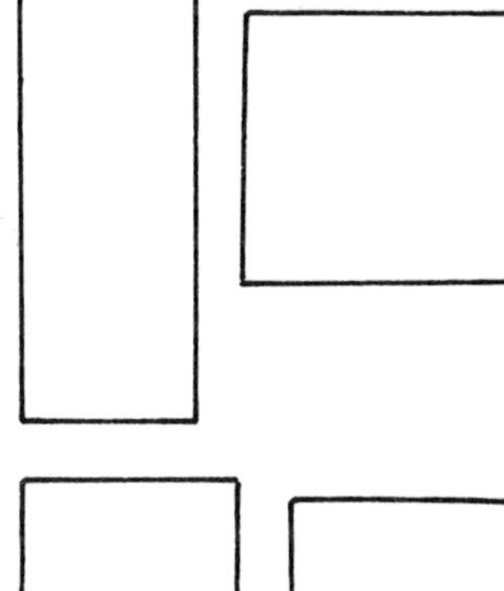

Design, illustrate and layout a programme cover, advertising handout or poster for a specified sports or entertainment event.

Your design should include the title of the event, information about it, background colours and design. You should also use pictures and lettering techniques, either by hand or the use of rub-down letters. Indicate where your design will be used. You may wish to extend this study by designing a whole programme or series of handouts. This will involve you in designing and editing material to see how well it reads, is used and puts over its messages.

Set up a photographic session, maybe with friends, depicting a scene which will be of use to your design, such as an action picture from a game or a posed picture.

Functional design

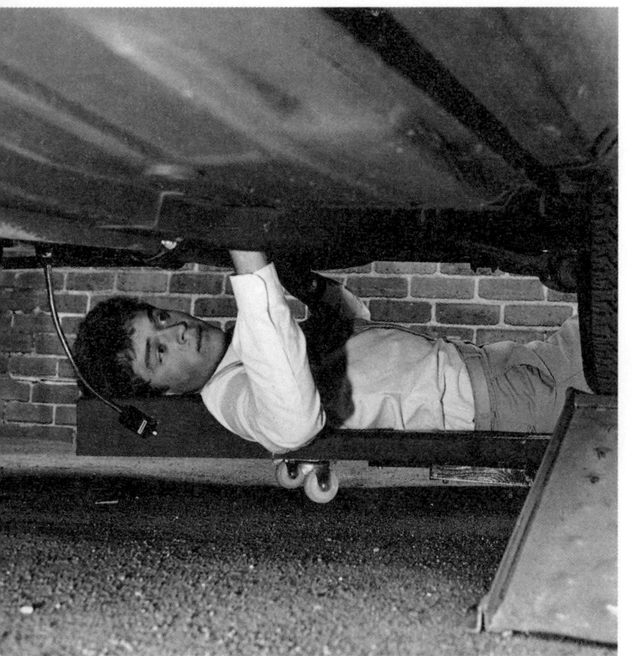

Tim Harris's design for a mechanics' trolley.

When a car is supported on ramps and you need to get underneath it to change the oil or inspect the brake pipes, your job will be made much easier by using a 'car crawler'.

The typical device currently available from motorist's shops consists mainly of a slatted wooden frame and headrest running on four castors.

As his entry for The Design Council Schools Design Prize, Tim Harris, decided to design an improved version of the 'car crawler'. He was very interested in renovating old cars and had found the equipment currently available for getting underneath vehicles was inadequate. He began designing his improved version by first considering the ergonomics: he traced the outline of several people of different sizes before deciding on the size of the trolley and the height and position of the head-rest. He also considered several ways of attaching tool boxes to the trolley before adding them at hand level on swinging hinges. A small battery-operated light was then attached to the headrest to make inspection easier.

Tim used glass reinforced plastic for his initial design realisation, though he considered ABS (Acrylonitrile Butadiene Styrene) might be the most suitable material if the trolley could be manufactured commercially.

If you wish to consider tackling this particular design then you will need to take into account the following requirements for your 'car crawler'.

Ergonomics: Find out the requirements for comfort of the body whilst lying down, particularly the need to support the head in a comfortable position.

Anthropometrics: Body sizes – how long and how wide does the trolley have to be to accommodate the majority of people who may use it?

Ease of movement: Which type of castors will be most suitable to use on your trolley? It is most unlikely that castors designed for furniture will be adequate for the trolley to run over rough concrete floors.

Ease of cleaning: Regardless of how careful you are, from time to time oil and grease are likely to be spilt on your trolley. Consequently you should use materials which will best meet these requirements.

Storage of tools: Ideally you should have a storage compartment attached to the trolley in which you can keep the tools you need for the specific task in hand.

Provision of a light: Attaching a light to the trolley can allow you to set it in a required position, leaving your hands free to work with the necessary tools.

Look at the variety of solutions illustrated below. They were all designed and made by fifth year pupils as part of their design course. What do you think are the advantages and disadvantages of the various designs and materials used?

A solution using laminated plywood and a loose PVC covered cushion attached by velcro.

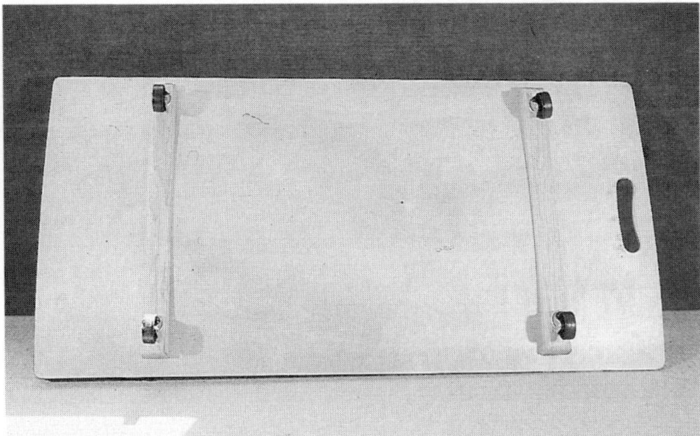

The underneath of the laminated design showing the castors. Why do you think the design includes a handle?

A tubular steel solution using rubber webbing and a loose PVC cushion.

Details of the headrest. Why is it at an angle?

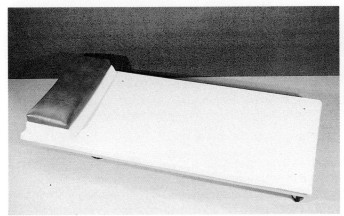

A solution using a GRP shell and a wooden underframe.

The wooden 'plug' and GRP mould for the design illustrated opposite.

Storage problems

Problems in storage are all around us: imagine a kitchen without any designed storage for crockery, utensils, food, cleaning requisites, pots and pans. Well-designed storage gives order and efficiency to our lives and meets the needs of accessibility, safety and hygiene, preservation and protection.

Storage in the home

As a student of design it is probable that at some time you will be given a brief that is related to storage as the problems are so wide and varied. The following examples may be helpful in getting you started.

Margaret had been given an open storage brief by her teacher. She recorded her thoughts:

> 'The main aim of racking and storage is to keep things tidy, organised and protected. A storage place needs to be sturdy and durable. For the design to be effective, easy access to the items being stored must be possible. It should be functional and compact; in many cases there will need to be protection for the contents and for the user. Dual or multi-purpose solutions are often useful. Safety must be considered – perhaps a means of locking will be required if the stored items are dangerous e.g. medicines.
>
> Internal corners are traps for dust and dirt and are best avoided. Items stored should be easily accessible but space should be used efficiently. Any solution should look nice.'

Margaret then considered actual storage problems in the home. Having identified a number of problems, she considered several ideas for solving some of them. In each case she sketched her ideas in such a way as to communicate them clearly. She also recorded her own reasoned comment about each, sometimes quite critically.

Analysing storage problems and considering some existing designs.

Being critical

Evaluation is not only an important final part of designing; if you are designing your work thoroughly, you will make critical comment about your own ideas as you go along – recognising both good and weak aspects and giving reasons for your opinion.

Margaret selected one of her ideas – a racking unit that would be useful for several purposes:

> 'The design consists of three slots which get taller towards the back. This, with slight shaping of the dividers, could give the impression of a landscape – adding interest. It could be used to hold cleaning equipment, books and spices, tins and packets. Cleaning might be a problem so it should be "Wipe-proof" and possibly made so that it can be dissembled.'

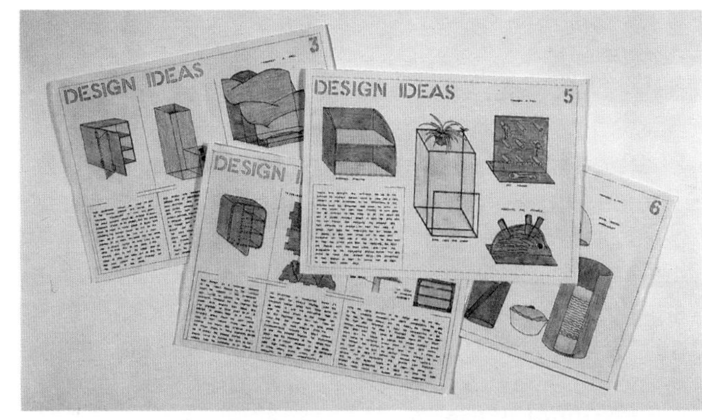

Exploring possible solutions.

Designing was by no means complete. Margaret developed the idea, considering a number of forms and constructions, as well as materials and finishes.

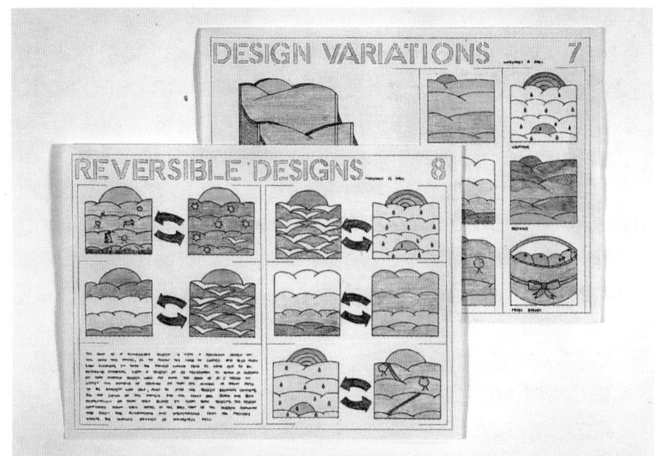

Developing a chosen idea.

Construction detail. The construction and finish was planned so explicitly that no detail of manufacture was omitted.

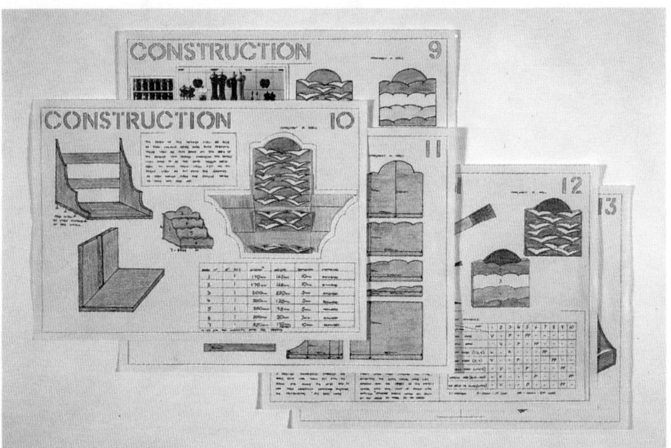

Margaret's solution.

Evaluation. Once the storage rack was made, Margaret was critical of the finished design. She was careful to compare the realisation with the original brief and her own considerations, as well as using the rack as intended. She reported her findings, suggesting possible modifications.

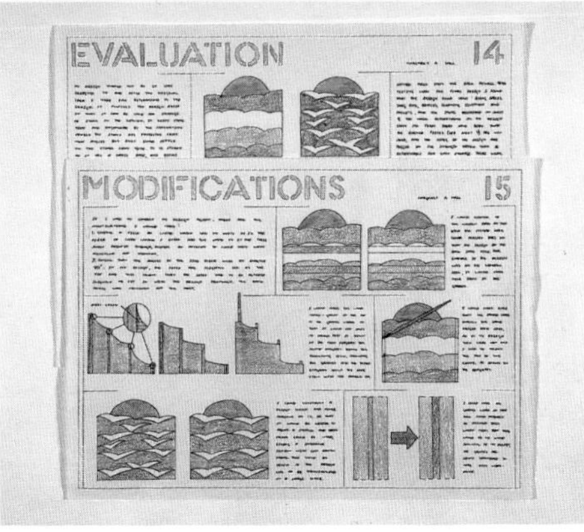

Storage at a playgroup
The design work on the previous two pages was conducted in the personal style of one student. There is no fixed way of communicating design ideas; the real necessity is to be clear and to present your work in a style that attracts people's interest. The student's work that follows is recorded in a fresh, flowing style that is immediately understood by the reader – as if you are looking into the designer's head!

Sarah identified a storage problem at a local playgroup. She joined the playgroup for several sessions and noticed how the adults cleared up nearly all the equipment at the end. There was no easy or interesting way in which the toddlers could tidy for themselves. Sarah therefore set out to meet the problem and to design a storage system for the equipment, and one in which the children would be actively involved. The project earned Sarah an award in the Design Council 'Schools Design Prize' competition.

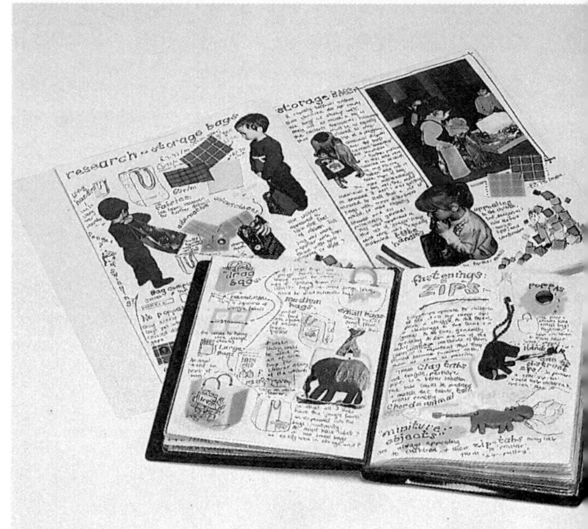

Sarah kept a log of visits, ideas and experiments.

Several mock-ups of the 'drag bags' were made to evaluate all aspects of the design, including materials, construction, colour and applied decoration.

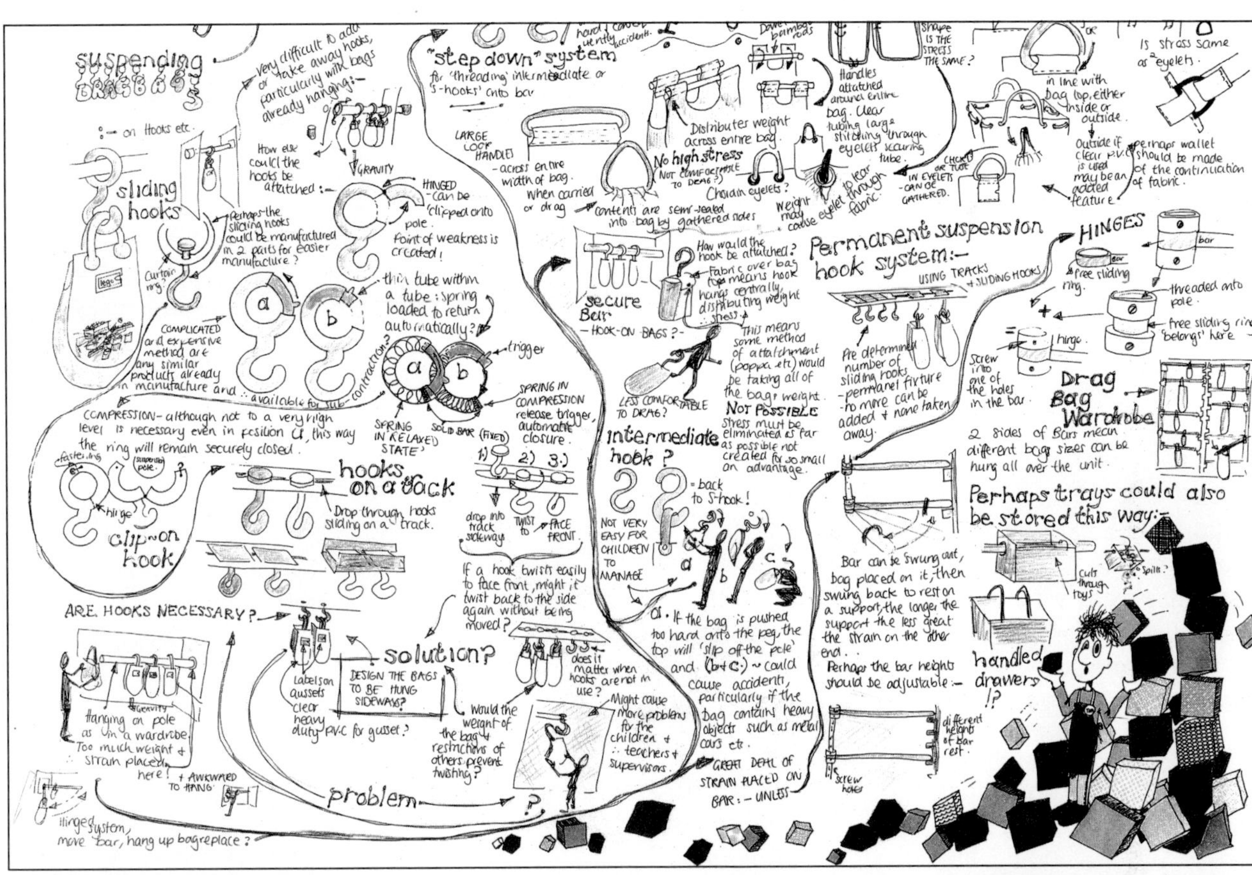

suspending bags

Very difficult to add or take away hooks, particularly with bags already hanging:-

:- on Hooks etc.

How else could the hooks be attached:-

gravity

sliding hooks

Perhaps the sliding hooks could be manufactured in 2 parts for easier manufacture?

Curtain ring

HINGED - can be clipped onto pole. Point of weakness is created!

COMPLICATED and expensive method are any similar products already in manufacture and :. available for self-contraction?

thin tube within a tube: spring loaded to return automatically?

trigger

SPRING IN RELAXED STATE

SOLID BAR (FIXED)

SPRING IN COMPRESSION release trigger, automatic closure.

COMPRESSION - although not to a very high level is necessary even in position a, this way the ring will remain securely closed.

fastening

suspending pole

hinge

clip-on hook

hooks on a track

Drop through hooks sliding on a track.

1.) 2.) 3.)

drop into track sideways

TWIST to FACE FRONT.

If a hook twists easily to face front, might it twist back to the side again without being moved?

ARE HOOKS NECESSARY?

gravity

Hanging on pole as in a wardrobe. Too much weight + strain placed here!

+ AWKWARD TO HANG

Hinged system, move bar, hang up bag replace?

Labels on gussets clear heavy duty P.V.C. for gusset?

DESIGN THE BAGS TO BE HUNG SIDEWAYS?

solution?

does it matter when hooks are not in use?

Would the weight of the bag + restrictions of others prevent twisting?

Might cause more problem for the children + :. teachers + supervisors.

problem

"step down" system

for 'threading' intermediate or 'S-hooks' onto bar

LARGE LOOP HANDLES - across entire width of bag. When carried or drag

contents are semi-sealed into bag by gathered sides

Distributes weight across entire bag.

No high stress

Not comfortable to drag?

Chafing eyelets?

Weight may cause eyelet to tear through fabric.

Handles attached around entire bag. Clear tubing large stitching through eyelets securing tube.

IN EYELETS - CAN BE GATHERED.

Shape is the stress the same?

in line with bag top, either inside or outside.

Outside if clear P.V.C. is used may be an added feature

Is stress same as eyelet.

Perhaps wallet should be made of the continuation of fabric.

Secure Bar - HOOK-ON BAGS?

How would the hook be attached? Fabric over bag means hook hangs centrally, distributing weight. stress

This means some method of attachment (popper etc) would be taking all of the bag's weight. NOT POSSIBLE

Stress must be eliminated as far as possible not created for so small an advantage.

LESS COMFORTABLE TO DRAG?

intermediate hook?

= back to S-hook!

NOT VERY EASY FOR CHILDREN TO MANAGE

a. If the bag is pushed too hard onto the peg, the top will 'slip off the pole' and (b+c:) - could cause accidents, particularly if the bag contains heavy objects such as metal cars etc.

GREAT DEAL OF STRAIN PLACED ON BAR: - UNLESS

Permanent suspension hook system:-

USING TRACKS + SLIDING HOOKS

Pre determined number of sliding hooks - permanent fixture - no more can be added + none taken away.

HINGES

bar

free sliding ring.

threaded onto pole

free sliding ring 'belongs' here.

hinge

screw into one of the holes in the bar

Drag Bag Wardrobe

2 sides of Bars mean different bag sizes can be hung all over the unit.

Perhaps trays could also be stored this way:-

Cuts through toys

Spills!

Bar can be swung out, bag placed on it, then swing back to rest on a support, the longer the support the less great the strain on the other end.

Perhaps the bar height should be adjustable:-

different heights of bar rest.

Screw holes

handled drawers !?

CANVAS?

P.V.C.

In wardrobe storage, this is a major disadvantage.

Fabric

P.V.C. is advantageous, easy to clean, resistant to stains (paint etc). Tears easily when perforated (by stitching etc)

Popper or eyelet rips plastic easily when pressure is applied to it. This may be a major problem if this HANDLE design is continued.

handle

eyelet

NYLON BINDING

added strength from weight

alternatives

drawstring

children will not be able to discern the bag contents, other than the labels information.

lego

"is this enough?"

SIZE PROBLEM:-

2 squares = 390mm, space available in wardrobe housing is 305mm, unless shelves are recessed or bags are very flexible.

Face applied by shutting unit.

P.V.C. (Jungle) from Jessops Blue, Yellow, White & grey P.V.C. £4.95

P.V.C. - also available in plain yellow & blue: Cut to 3 basic sizes.

pencil pocket

A square + P.V.C. clear front.

B 4 squares P.V.C. clear gusset

C 6 squares + clear P.V.C. gusset

Animals could be QUILTED

added depth

storage problem? nice to the touch. Added workload, would it be necessary to quilt all animals?

TOO DISCONNECTED

button up pocket?

Quilted & as a pocket?

should seams be sewn or welded?

Simple shapes can be cut from plain fabrics and attached directly. small emblem?

zip-up?

large zip

May help children to learn about fastenings, but what could be stored in the pockets?

elephant

stitching

COTTON

PERFORATION

The size difference is too great for this allowance. Perhaps the larger drag-bags should be hung differently.

clear fronted

animal backing showing - too complicated, draws attention to animals not toys. Coloured back (blue or yellow)

Pocket view - would it obscure view of toys too much? Perhaps a quilted emblem (animal) would link back & front.

clear fronted? Animal back:

label front

clear sides? coloured P.V.C. - blue or yellow

lining

FABRIC SHOULD BE LINED for ease of cleaning.

not wipe clean

problem

backboard - thin ply? not strong enough to support bags - change backboard?

CONSTRUCTION of bags:

experiments have shown that poppers pull through animal fabric too easily but are relatively stable in coloured P.V.C. should a reinforced panel be applied or is a lining necessary - aesthetically & practically?

WHITE FABRIC BACK SHOWING.

reinforced

lined?

LARGER BAGS FOLLOW CONSTRUCTION A. (clear front - coloured back & gusset.

B. - medium sized bags coloured front & back - clear gussets.

C. = small bags.

SEAMS here are in different position for different sizes

BACK

gusset

FRONT

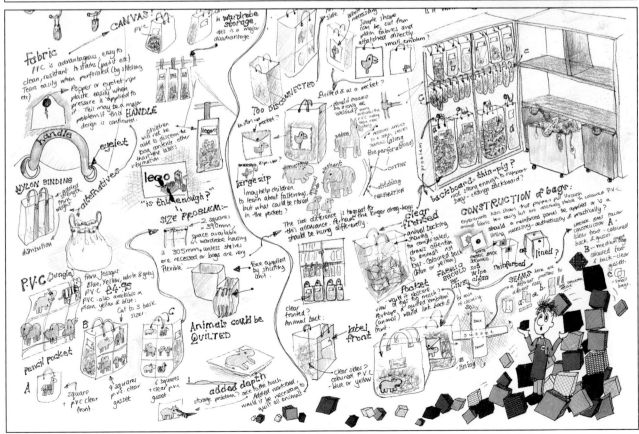

Design through drawing

First hand experience of things is very important to good designing. These design activities emphasise the value of your personal response to your experiences through drawing. Imaginative and observational drawing involves you in recording, analysing, thinking, speculating and communicating information and feelings. The essential information in these cases will be your designs.

Exploratory sketches to establish personal drawing techniques.

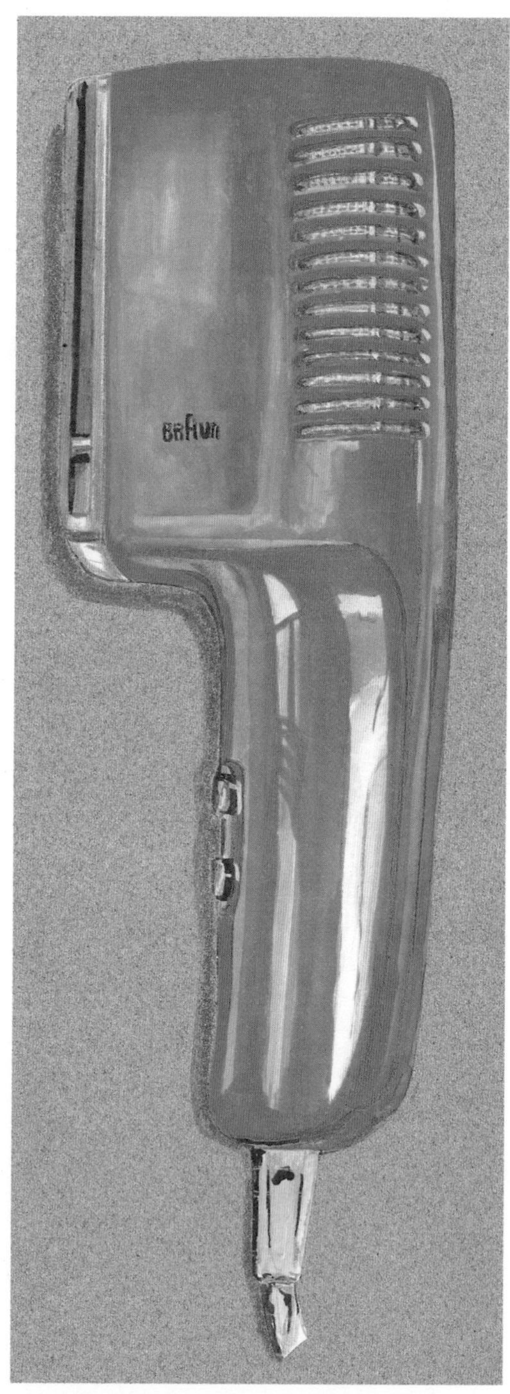

A freehand observed illustration.

Draw, paint and illustrate a small common object, for example, a hair dryer, a calculator or a telephone. Present the whole study to show:

1 Your initial freehand drawings which are intended as loosening-up exercises and the exploration of the form of the object, as well as the choice of view for the main illustration. Refer to photographs, especially those produced by the manufacturers, so as to obtain their information about what the device does, how it can be used and how it is assembled and maintained.

2 Your painted illustration executed on coloured paper to demonstrate techniques of highlighting light and dark in a picture.

3 A context for the use of your illustration.

This study suggests starting points for using your drawing talents.

How is observational drawing useful to your designing?

Can you draw from memory?

What is imaginative drawing?

Is drawing the only way to design?

Designers who can draw well are able to bring about many options and choices of design ideas. This is especially important when they wish to convince other people of the merits of their designs. Modelling is also a useful means by which prototypes for products and devices can be designed. Designers use presentation drawings to influence clients, the people who may make, use or sell their design. Creating 'visuals', the jargon for design drawing, passes through several stages of development before a final version is produced. The drawing is one very useful way in which design processes can be employed to their full effect. The quality of your design drawing is for you to control; and you may draw before, during or after making something.

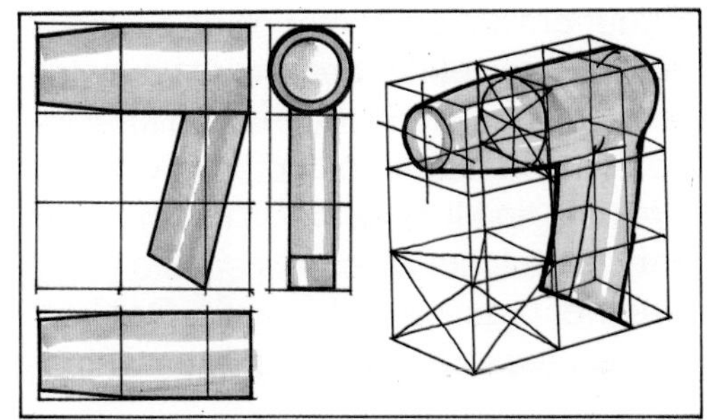

Orthographic views of a design idea for a new hair dryer. Freehand perspective grid to help establish the three-dimensional form of the design.

DESIGN BRIEF

Use drawing to design the new styling for a common household appliance, such as a hair dryer. This design activity invites you to consider the form and function of your design.

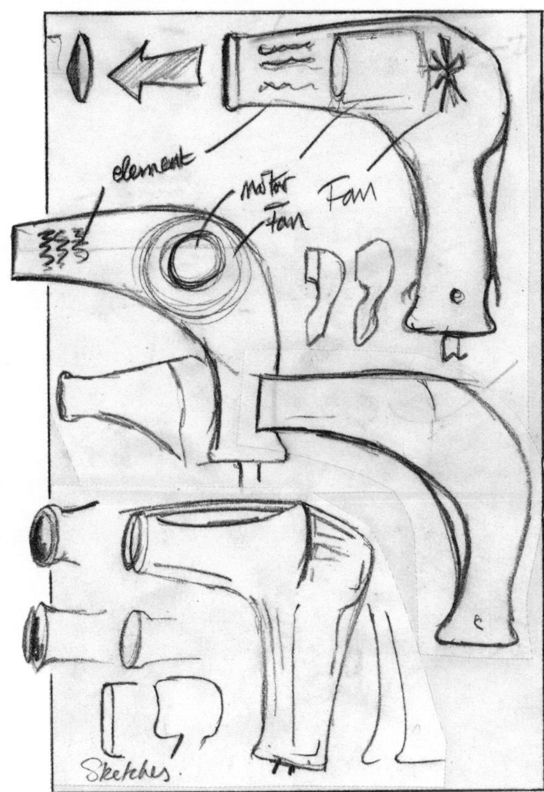

Sketches for both the design of the product and its illustration.

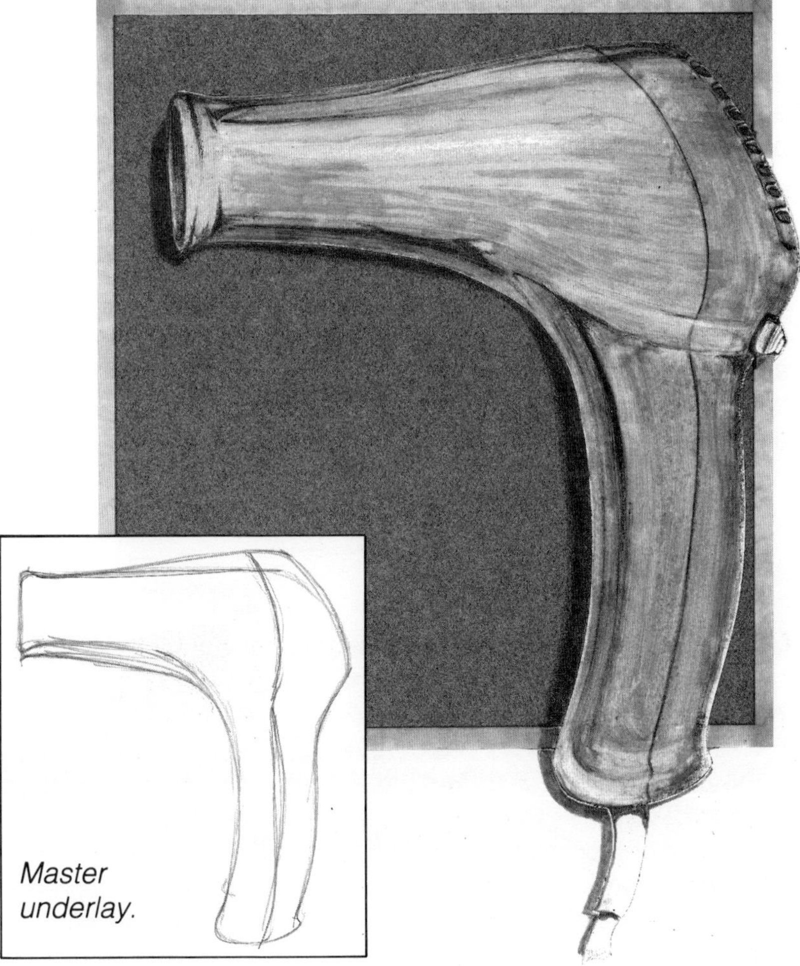

Master underlay.

Final drawing based on master underlay pencil drawing, using wet edge technique with a marker, including talcum powder for pastels to be layed on top and rubbed away in places to create highlights, also pencil work for shadows and white gouache for extra highlights; finally the drawing was cut out with a scalpel and remounted on coloured card.

Imaginative drawing and modelling

If your drawing and modelling skills are versatile, and you are able to use your experience of drawing familiar things to create new designs, then you may be able to design what you *want* to design and not be restricted to what you think you can draw. Drawing, in all its forms, is not the only way to design, but it is a very useful tool which will enable you to express your ideas, whether practical or fantastic. Don't worry about making mistakes – explore the possibilities which your imagination brings about!

Stylisation in illustration

These illustrations utilise the designer's skills of observation and developed drawing techniques. Using imagination and their illustrative skills, stylists can design the cars of their dreams.

The style of a car determines its reputation and success. It is your first contact with the car. Notions about comfort, reliability and qualities of handling, although important, are not identified by motorists until they use the car.

Styling has important technical consequences for a car. Its shape and styling establish how practical a car is in everyday use. Getting in and out of the car, visibility, wind noise, deflection of rain, how dirt stays on the body, dust penetration and drag coefficients are all technical matters influenced by body shape. Protection against rust, regulations for bumpers, headlights, rearlights, panel curvatures and projecting parts, accident protection and so on, are other general features of car development.

Is there any scope for the designer's own ideas in styling?

Which technical factors determine styling?

How does 'public taste' affect car design?

Are there any national elements in car design?

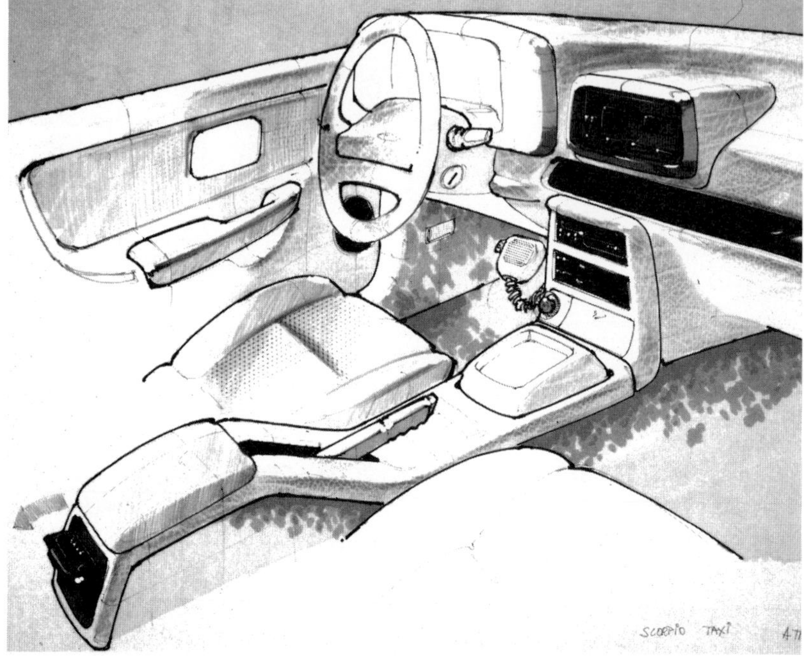

DESIGN BRIEF

Design, illustrate and model a car body. This is an exercise in styling and 3-D representation. Invent your own specifications for a car, for example, 'a family car', 'a sports car' and so on. Use information supplied by various car companies.

The production of a scale model using clay to form a three-dimensional representation. Prepare the clay into a block large enough to cover your model from. (Clay shrinks between 8–12% so for your model to be the correct size when finished make it 10% larger.)

From your working drawings transfer your front, plan and end views on to the corresponding planes of the block of clay.

After your drawing has been transferred to each corresponding plane, begin to carve away the clay one plane at a time.

If you have curved surfaces each plane should be worked individually. Once the block has been carved to the essential form required, begin to carve in extra detail.

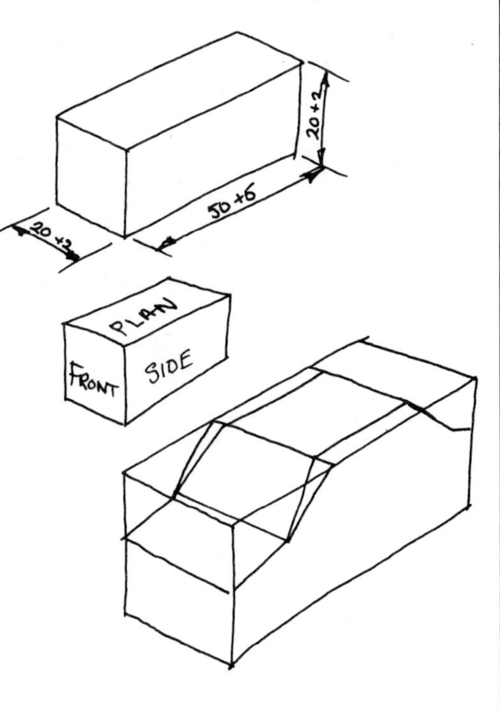

Care of the clay

1. Make sure the clay is wrapped up well so that no air can get to it between design sessions. If wrapped up correctly, the clay will stay in a workable state for weeks.
2. Once all the surface detail has been carved on to the clay surface, turn the model over and hollow the inside.
3. Firing at 1060°C then prime the clay with white emulsion (silk).
4. Decorate with sprayed enamel paints.

Designing the fantastic!

This activity gives you the scope to design something fantastic! It will involve all your drawing and modelling skills and techniques; and will help you develop your skills of visualising your designs. Most importantly, if you are to create and design something which is unreal, or a new concept in space travel, then the more imaginative you are, the more successful your design will be.

If in doubt, exaggerate! Think first, change your mind, maybe even make 'mistakes', but explore the different possibilities which your imagination brings about. Find everyday things which you can draw from or adapt for your designs.

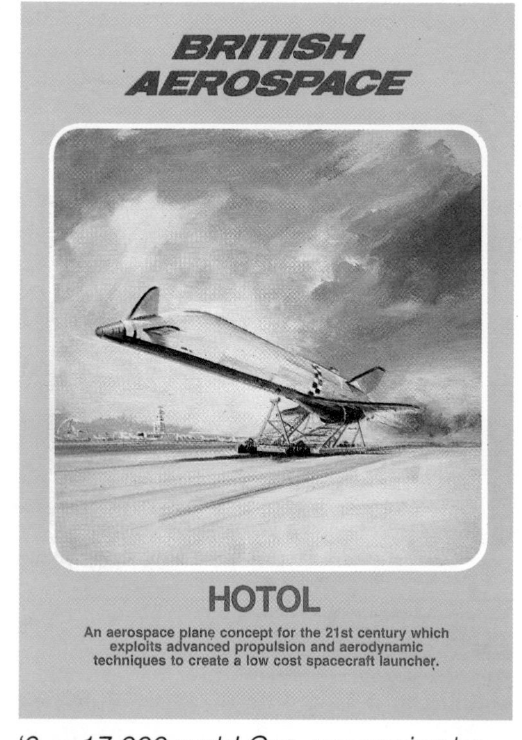

BRITISH
AEROSPACE
HOTOL
An aerospace plane concept for the 21st century which exploits advanced propulsion and aerodynamic techniques to create a low cost spacecraft launcher.

'0 → 17,000 mph! Can one engine be designed to do this?

Design, draw and model a spaceship, either as a fantastic vehicle or as an all-purpose re-entry vehicle from space to earth.

Sketch and draw a series of freehand perspective drawings of the spaceship, including full use of pencils and coloured pencils for rendered effects. Use any objects as reference material for drawing techniques, for example, tones, surfaces and light and dark.

Present a fully rendered drawing and then repeat this by drawing a reverse view of the vehicle.

Produce a space effect background on to which your drawings, previously cut out, can be mounted. Use multi-media illustration techniques for your background.

Model your vehicle and display your work. Balsa wood, plaster of Paris, plastic remnants from model making kits and household containers are all useful materials for 3-D modelling. Some foams, for example, 'Styrofoam', are easily shaped, painted and glued but require technical information and workshop facilities for their safe use. Always work safely!

Freehand perspective drawing.

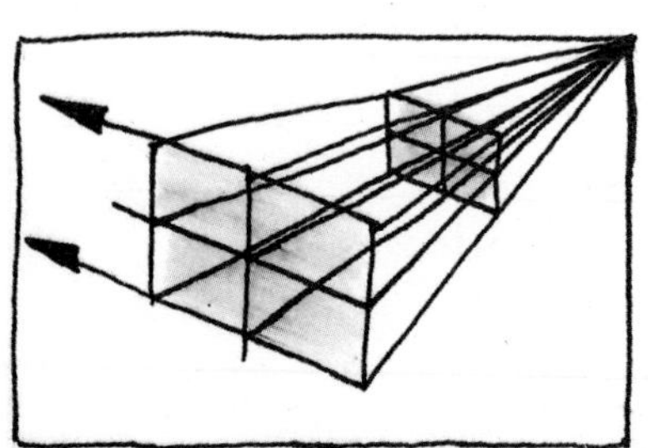

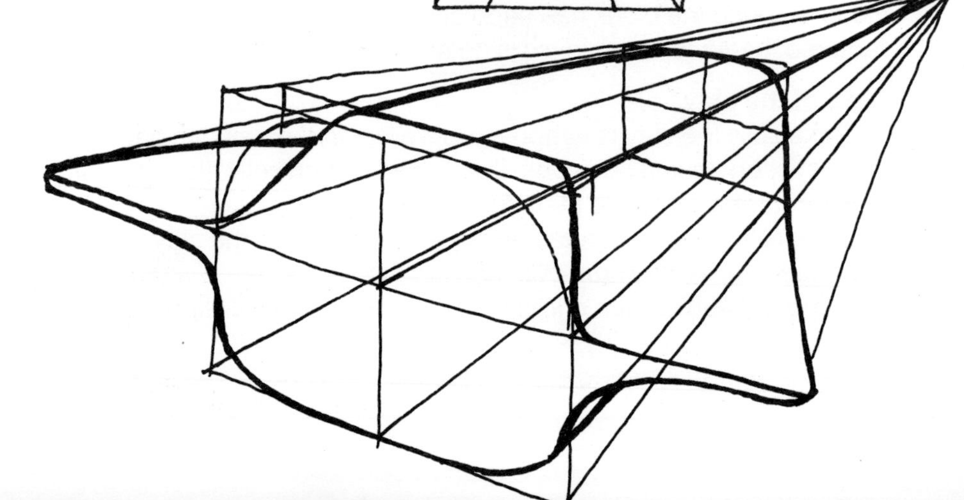

Full pencil rendering, going and coming back . . .

Student example

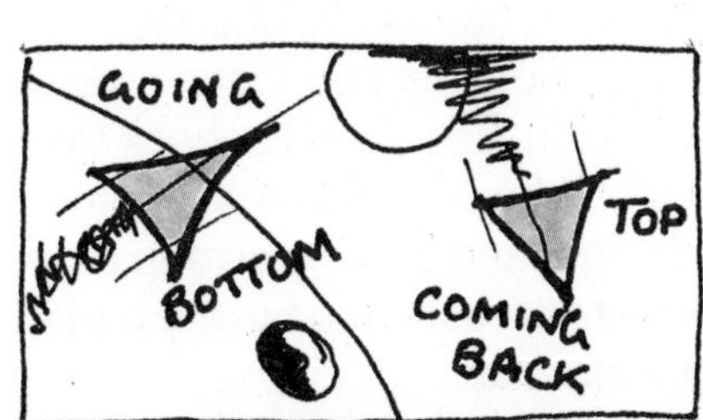

Did you stick to your original idea or did you change your mind?

What influenced your designs?

What other activities could you apply these ideas and skills to?

Could you have made the spaceship without drawing?

Time for design

With the development of low cost, highly accurate quartz movements similar to those illustrated below, it is possible to design clocks in a much more imaginative way.

> **DESIGN BRIEF**
>
> As a starting point, it would be a good idea to decide *where* your clock will be used. It might be one of the following:
>
> - a kitchen clock
> - a clock for a young child's bedroom
> - a 'cartoon' clock for an older child's room
> - a formal clock to be used in the living room
> - a bedside clock

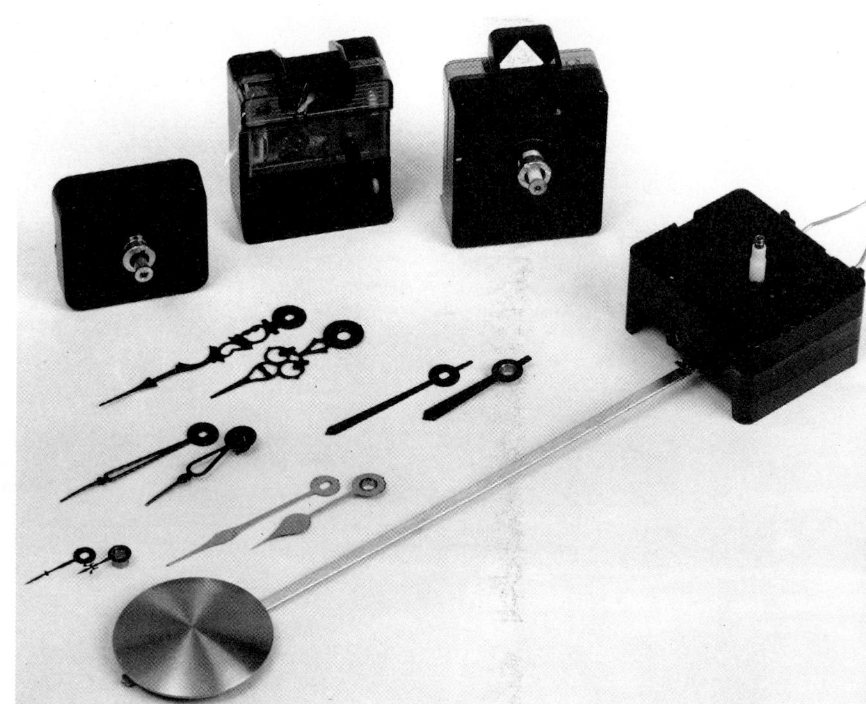

A range of movements and hands which are available from suppliers.

You should consider the following elements in your design:

Movements

A wide variety of movements are available ranging from a simple unit, to others which include pendulums and chimes.

Hands

The style of the hands you choose should be complementary to the style of your clock. You also need to check that the size of the hands fits in with your overall design, and that the sweep of the hands is not restricted by any part of the face or case.

Controls and batteries

Ensure that the design of your clock allows you easy access to adjust the hands and change the batteries if required.

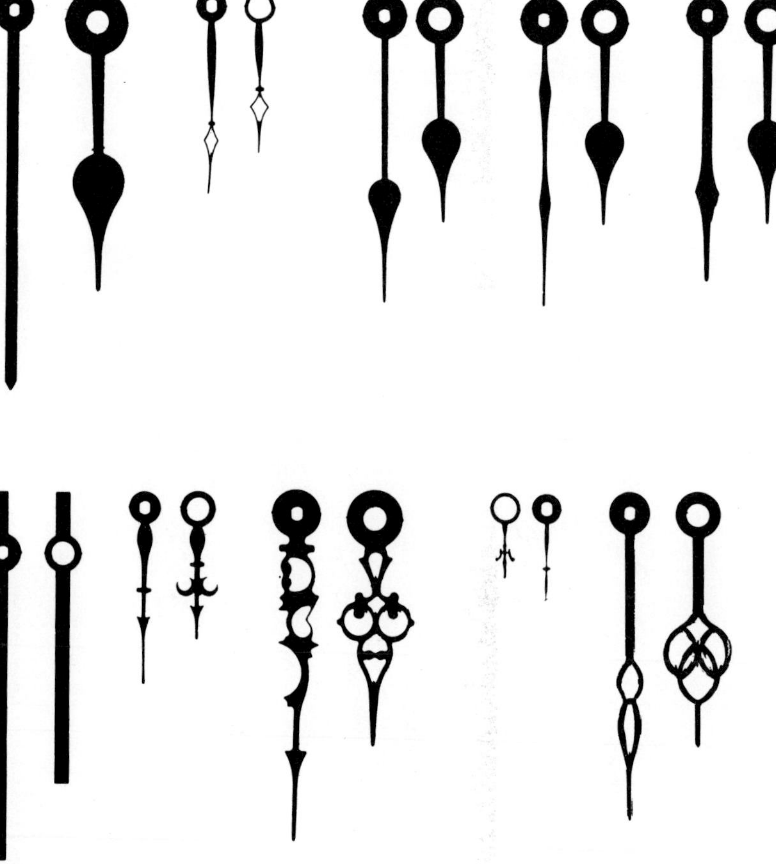

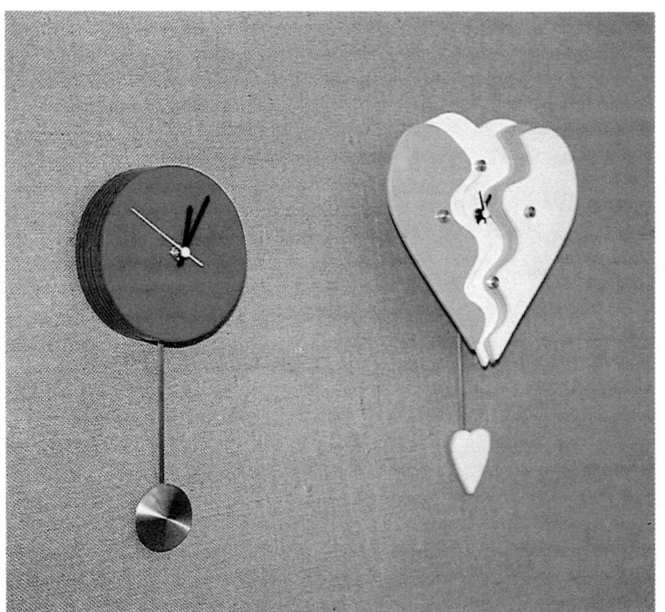

A variety of designs and approaches.

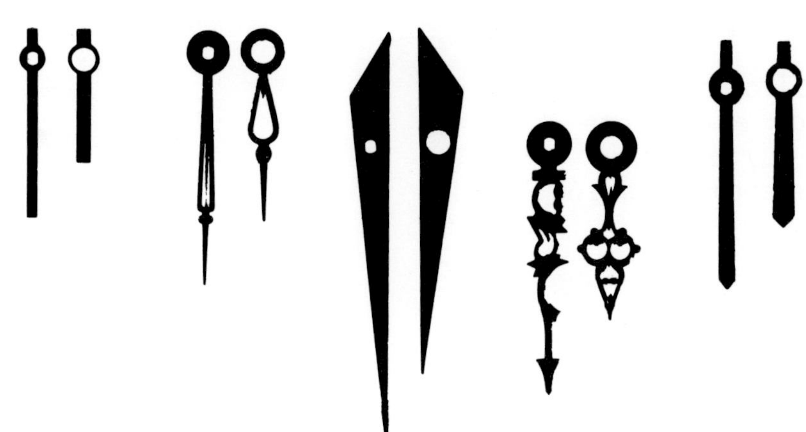

Movements and hands can be obtained from a variety of outlets. If in difficulty contact:
C and L Clocks,
Kings Hill Industrial Estate,
Bude,
Cornwall.
Tel. 0288 3351

Bathroom fittings

The design brief below can be used as a starting point for looking at the design of bathroom fittings and accessories. It is quite specific in what it asks you to do. However, you could write your own, more generalised brief to give you broader scope in tackling this particular area of study.

The Allibert SAPONA range of bathroom fittings.

DESIGN BRIEF

You are employed as a designer by a company who specialise in the manufacture of bathroom fittings. Their present range of products includes the following items:

- mirror
- soap dish
- toilet roll holder
- towel holder
- shelf
- toothbrush holder.

Your brief is to design a new product range which may include the items listed above. However, you may develop and add to the range by introducing new products.

Your response to the brief must take the following form:

1 Analyse the market competition by looking at the existing range of bathroom accessories produced by other manufacturers. This analysis should take the form of a research sheet illustrating existing products on the market, plus your comments and reactions to them.

2 Design four products within your range, paying particular attention to:
  a Appropriate use of materials and methods of construction.
  b Developing within your designs a style or theme which relates your designs to one another. This may be done by choosing a dominant colour, shape, form or combination of materials.

3 Choose two of the products from your range and manufacture them to the highest possible standard.

4 Produce an evaluation report for the two products you decide to make.

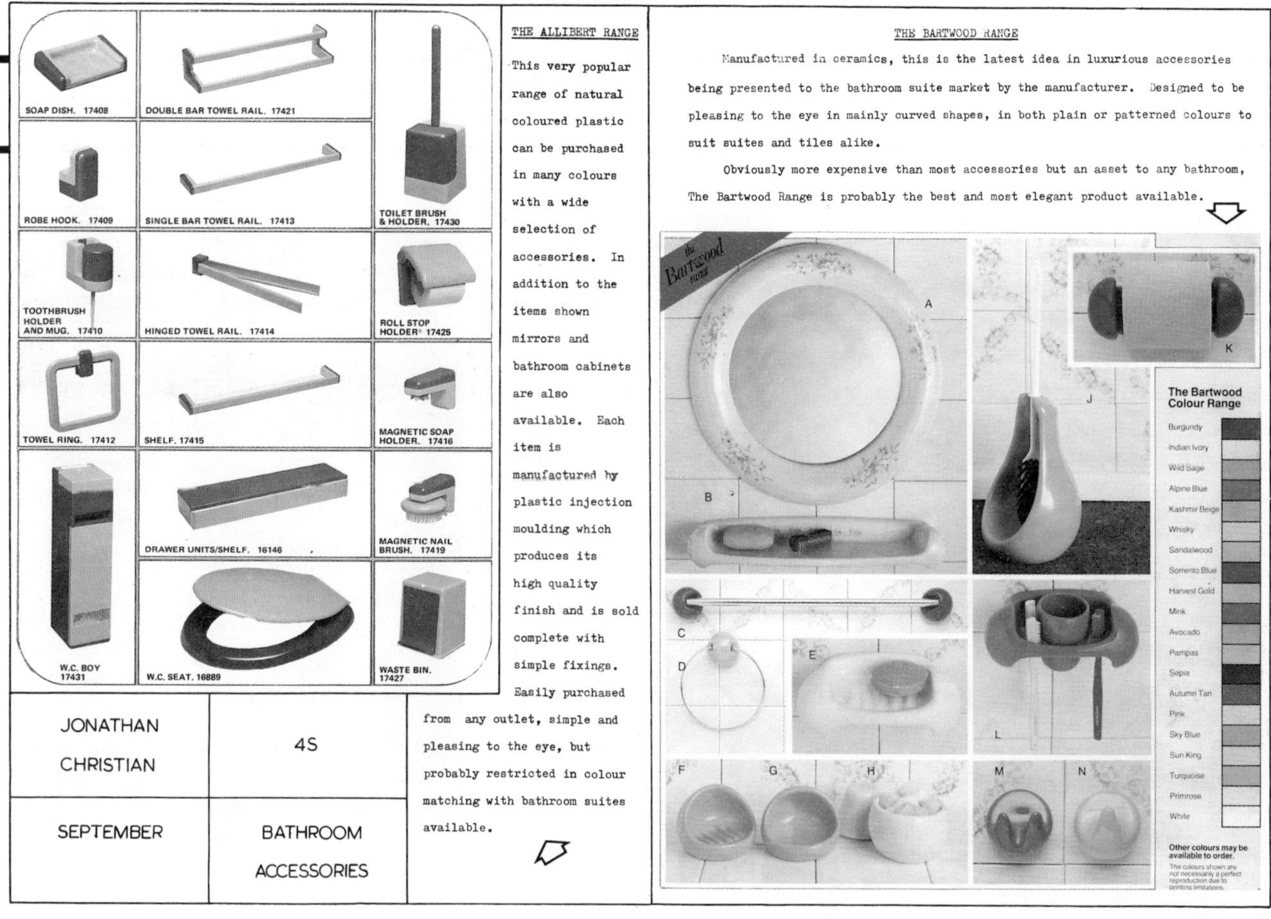

Examples of pupils' research sheets.

Making a start – design investigation

When you begin to look at the range of bathroom accessories available to the consumer you soon realise that there exists a wide variety of designs, manufactured in many materials and offered for sale to the consumer at differing prices.

There are many ways of comparing the designs of one manufacturer with another. Here are some starting points:

- Visit the shops in your area which are likely to stock these products and compare designs.
- Collect promotional leaflets which advertise these products and build up a sheet of illustrations of varying designs.
- Write a polite enquiring letter to several manufacturers explaining your project and asking for assistance.

Throughout your period of investigation remember to record your findings through notes, illustrations and your own personal comments about the designs you see around you. You could produce a product evaluation sheet, similar to the one below to help you record and assess different designs. As well as recording your reactions to the products it would help if you had either a sketch or photographs of the design to support your comments.

PRODUCT EVALUATION SHEET

Name of Product	Name of Maker	Cost	Materials used	Method of Production	Advantages of Product	Disadvantages of Product	Rating A–E

One of the companies who specialise in the design and manufacture of bathroom accessories is Allibert. Examples of their products are shown above.

Designing your products

Once you have looked at the variety of bathroom accessories you will begin to appreciate some of the shapes and forms used by manufacturers, and can now begin to put pencil to paper. Remember not to copy the ideas you have seen. Concentrate simply on producing forms and shapes which seem visually interesting and practical.

In these early stages it may be useful for you to produce a list of design requirements which your accessory should fulfil. Refer back to this list as your ideas develop to ensure that your design is not deficient in any way. As a guide a list of possible design requirements for a toothbrush holder are included opposite. You may add to these if you feel it is appropriate.

As you investigate the commercial design of bathroom fittings, there are several points which you may consider as possible areas of interest for more study.

How do industrial designers develop their ideas into products?

Is there any significance in the fact that many of the companies who specialise in bathroom fittings are French or Italian rather than British?

What factors determine the selling price of commercially produced goods such as those illustrated above?

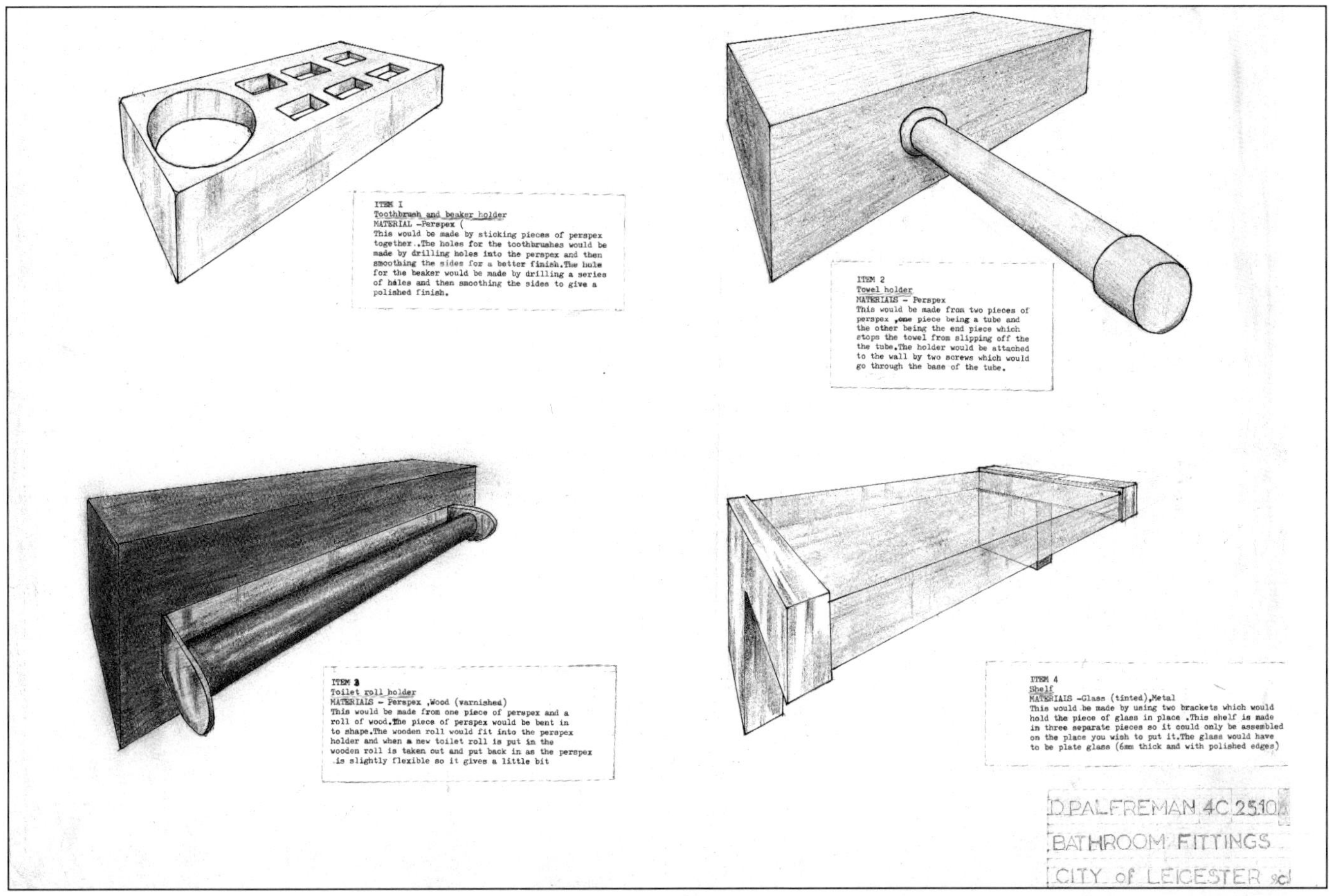

Example of pupil's design drawing sheet for bathroom fittings.

Initial ideas – sketches

These early sketches are 'thinking drawings'. Do not worry if some of these ideas turn out to be unsuitable. Simply let your mind explore all the varieties of shapes and forms that are possible and available to you.

Developing your ideas

Try to specify the materials and methods of construction you hope to use. These should be included as small detailed notes added to your sketches.

If you are in doubt about the suitability of materials or processes discuss this with your teacher. Remember that, unlike industrial producers such as Allibert, you will have to take into account the limited range of materials and production facilities available in your design department.

Design requirements for a toothbrush holder

How many toothbrushes do you wish to store? What are their sizes? How will you support them?

Should you allow for the storage of a beaker or drinking glass. If so, what size?

Will the holder be wall mounted or free standing?

If you wish to store a tube of toothpaste, how will you accommodate the awkward shape?

What materials will best cope with the condensation problems of the bathroom?

Your unit must be able to be easily cleaned to maintain hygiene standards. What other requirements can you think of?

Designing around the materials

As your design ideas become more detailed you need to become aware of the problems involved in making your product. Restrictions will be imposed by the materials you choose and the processes available to you in your school to work them.

All materials have advantages and disadvantages which must be carefully considered before making your final decision. Illustrated below and described opposite is a selection of some of the materials you may use in this project. However, there are many more such as clay, glass and other forms of plastics. As technology develops new materials, they will become available to the designer. The choice is yours!

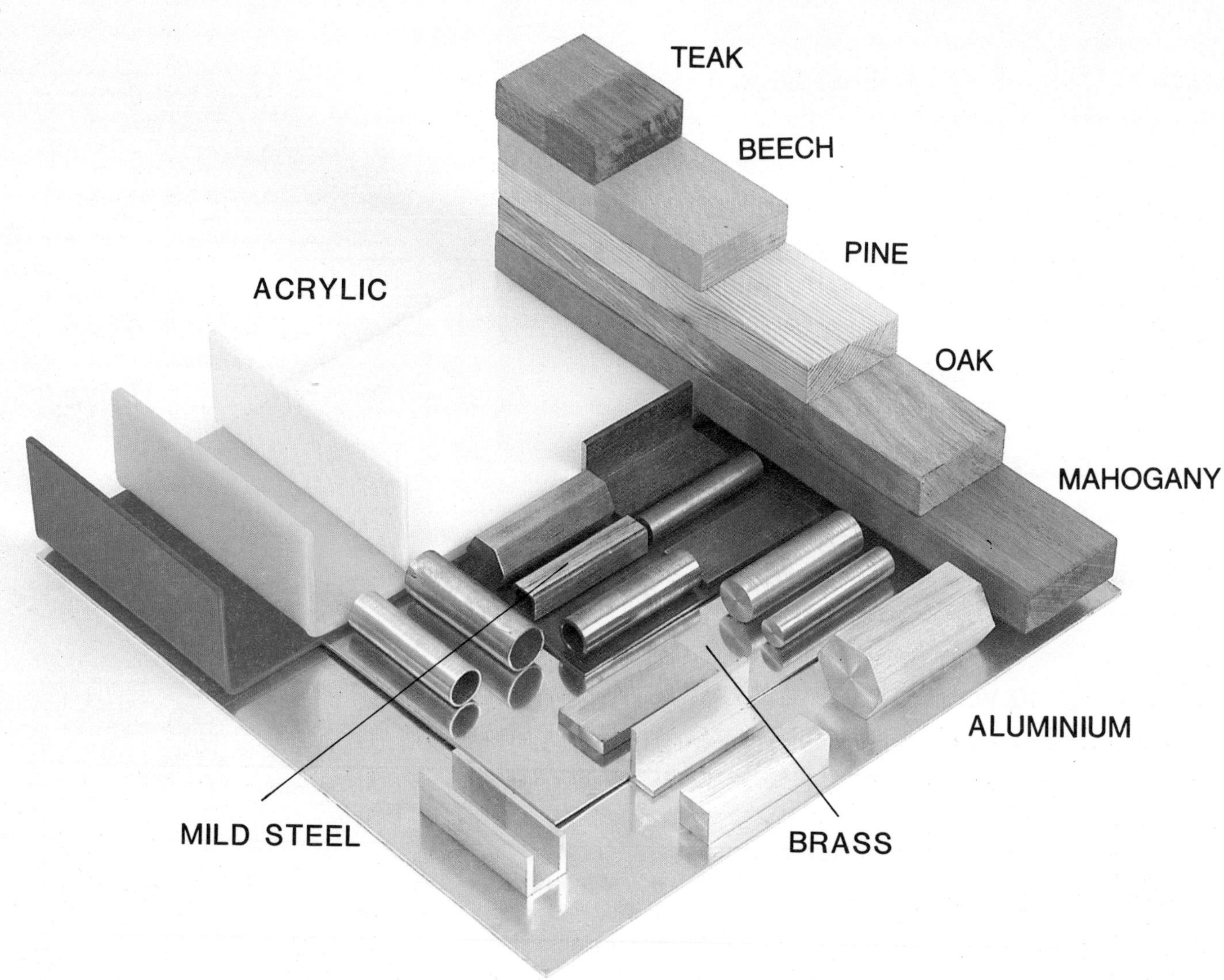

MATERIAL	USEFUL PROPERTIES	BEWARE!
MILD STEEL *Alloy of iron and carbon*	Easily worked and machined. It can be joined by brazing, welding and the use of screw threads and rivets. It is inexpensive and available in many forms: thin rod, tube, strip and flat sheet.	Easily rusts and will not withstand the condensation problems of bathrooms unless it is either chromium plated, plastic coated or protected in some other way.
ACRYLIC *Polymethyl Methacrylate*	Stain and moisture resistant. It is easily worked and shaped and can be formed by heat. It is attractive and available in a variety of colours, being easy to clean and therefore hygienic in the bathroom situation.	Acrylic can be brittle, and holes should not be drilled too close together. The edges need to be carefully polished if it is to look its best – can be time-consuming.
ALUMINIUM *Alloy of aluminium silicon, copper and magnesium, though this varies*	Soft, lightweight, easy to work, bend and polish. Its tough protective oxide layer helps prevent discolouring and corrosion, compared with mild steel.	Very difficult to join by soldering or welding without specialised equipment. This may restrict your designs to sheet forms or a reliance on screw threads or rivets.
BRASS *Alloy of copper and zinc*	It machines well and can be used for parts of the project which need precision. Its 'gold' like appearance can provide a pleasant contrast if used alongside wood or acrylic.	Expensive. Easily discolours and tarnishes if not constantly polished or protected with a 'lacquer'.
PINE *Pinus sylvestris*	A softwood which is easy to work particularly if 'knot' free. The timber is light in both colour and weight and has a characteristic pleasant smell.	As with all timbers, pine needs to be sealed extremely well, so as to avoid the wood becoming 'wet' in a damp atmosphere. It is a soft timber which can be easily damaged and bruised.
OAK *Quercus*	A hardwood with a yellow straw colour. A very strong timber which works well particularly if straight grained samples are used. However it is difficult to generalise with so many species.	An acidic timber which will accelerate the corrosion of metals such as steels especially if damp. Use brass or chrome plated fittings to avoid this problem.
BEECH *Fagus sylvatica*	A hardwood with a fine straight grain and even texture. It is a light beige coloured wood with a 'pinky' tone and small dark-reddish brown flecks. Excellent for bending, laminating and it also turns well on the lathe.	Some beech can be extremely hard, requiring sharp saws, planes and lathe tools.
MAHOGANY *Khaya ivorensis (African)*	A hardwood in which the colour varies from a pink to a deep reddish-brown. The grain varies from being straight to having an interlocking pattern similar to that found in the striped 'sapele' species.	Mahogany with an interlocking grain can be very difficult to plane and finish. Requiring a constantly sharp blade and a fine cut if 'ripping' is to be avoided.
TEAK *Tectona grandis*	An outstanding timber with many valuable properties including its durability, strength and the ease with which it can be worked. Its colour is 'golden brown' which darkens on exposure to the light. It is often figured with dark markings. Teak is resistant to a wide variety of chemicals and its ability to cope with moisture is illustrated by the fact that it is an ideal, though expensive material for boat building.	It is a very expensive timber. It is 'oily' by nature and some problems can be experienced when gluing unless the timber is degreased beforehand. Few polishes penetrate the timber and teak oil is the most suitable finish.

As your ideas become clearer in your mind and your drawings begin to resemble the product you wish to make, you should ensure that the scale of your design is suitable and that the size you have specified is not too big or too small.

The best way to test out your ideas is to produce:
Either; a full-size or scale drawing of your product.
Or; if your design is to be made in a sheet material, a paper or card template which will help you to try out your design before manufacture.
Or; a full-size model.

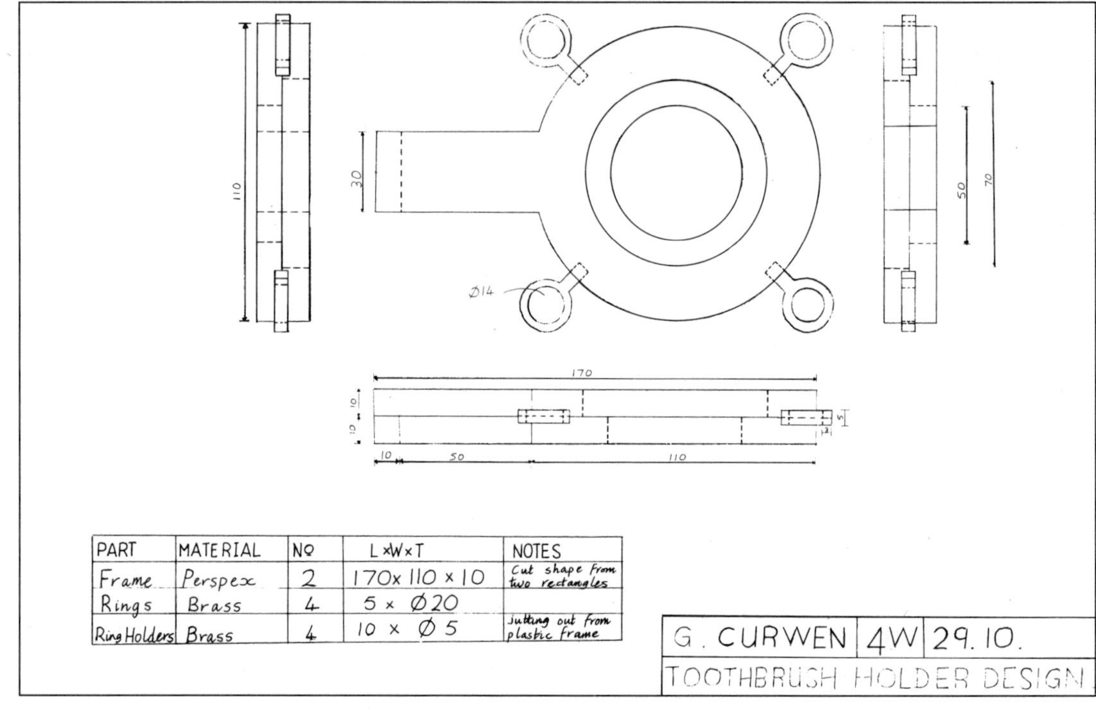

110
30
Ø14
50
70
170
10
50
110
PART | MATERIAL | Nº | L×W×T | NOTES
Frame | Perspex | 2 | 170x 110 x 10 | Cut shape from two rectangles
Rings | Brass | 4 | 5 x Ø20
Ring Holders | Brass | 4 | 10 x Ø5 | Jutting out from plastic frame
G. CURWEN 4W 29.10.
TOOTHBRUSH HOLDER DESIGN

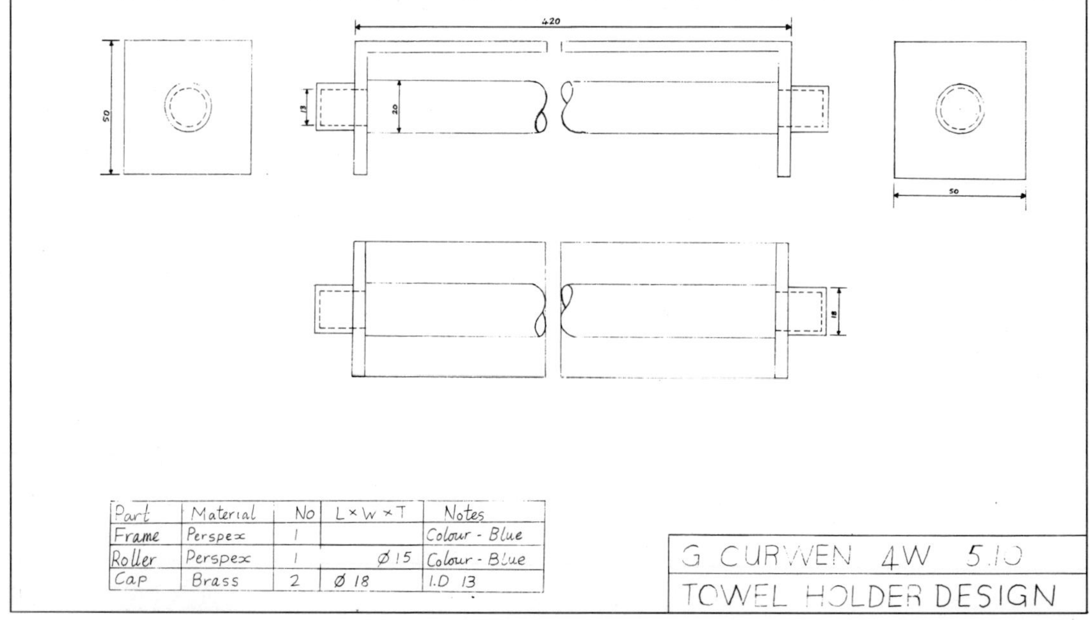

420
50
20
50
Part | Material | No | L×W×T | Notes
Frame | Perspex | 1 | | Colour - Blue
Roller | Perspex | 1 | Ø15 | Colour - Blue
Cap | Brass | 2 | Ø18 | I.D 13
G CURWEN 4W 5.10
TOWEL HOLDER DESIGN

Design realisation – making your product

Once you think you have resolved all the problems associated with designing your product, the next stage is to organise how you intend to make the individual articles – or realise your design.

Mirror-shelf and toothbrush holder in acrylic.

Design evaluation

The final stage in any design activity should be the point at which you look carefully and critically at what you have produced and try to assess how successful you think your solution actually is. This process is called **evaluation** and can be performed by yourself as the designer or by someone who has not been involved in the design but who can offer an independent expert opinion.

Personal evaluation

As your design progresses and your ideas develop you will be constantly making minor changes and modifications. This is a natural part of designing which should be encouraged and is part of the way in which designs improve. For example:

- You may need to modify shapes and forms in your early sketches.
- Sizes may need to be changed in view of models you may make to support and test your ideas.
- Methods of construction may prove inappropriate and have to be altered.

However, when the product is completed you must try to assess how successful you think it is. Personal evaluation is difficult as it is not always easy to criticise your own efforts, particularly if you have put in a great deal of time and energy. However, try to be honest – give praise where it is due and criticise where justified.

Independent evaluation

This is where you take your design to someone who can give it an independent appraisal because of their expertise and background in the area of your design. Listed over the page you will find examples of products and extracts from written evaluations.

Here are some of the points you should consider when writing your
Evaluation report

1. *Are you satisfied with the product you have just completed? If you are not entirely satisfied, are your reservations for visual or functional reasons?*
2. *Having tried out your product, how well does it perform? If not exactly as planned, how could it be improved?*
3. *What modifications did you need to make to the product as the work proceeded? Have these final modifications improved the final design?*
4. *What have you learnt about designing and making from the project, and how will you change your approach in the future in view of your experiences working on this project?*

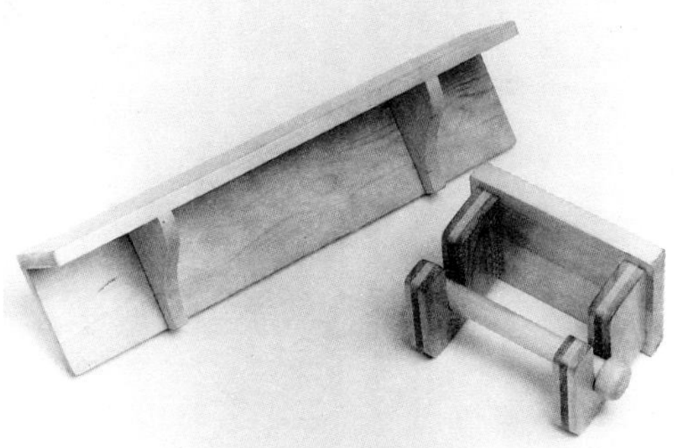

Shelf and toilet-roll holder in pine.

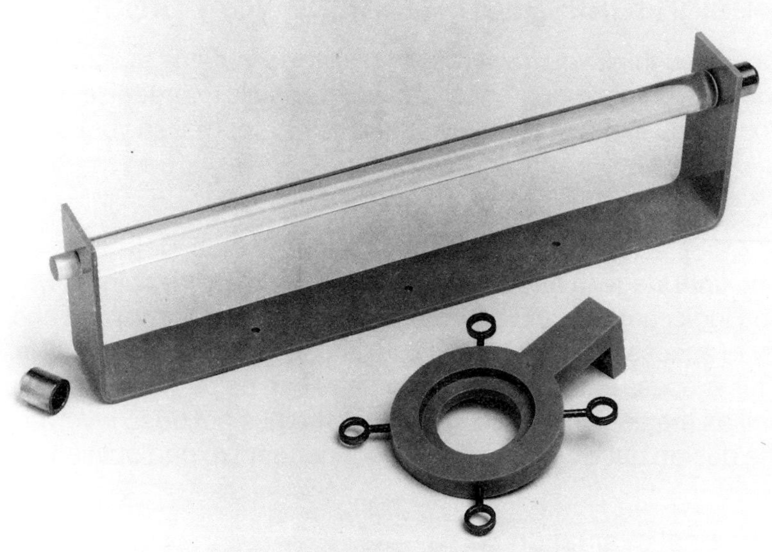

Towel rail and toothbrush holder in acrylic and brass.

Student's personal evaluation

Extracts from a student's evaluation report, relating to the toothbrush holder bottom right:

'On the whole I think the fitting is very good. It is compact, light and would be cheap to mass produce. The material is ideal for this sort of product because it is easy to clean and it doesn't rot. In my opinion perspex looks nicer in these surroundings.

A mistake was made in the positioning of the screw holes though this did not ruin the appearance of the fitting. The screw holes could have been repositioned so that the fitting could hang on the wall instead of being screwed on. If this idea was taken up it would decrease the stress on the screws from the weight of the utensils. The appearance of the fitting would also be enhanced because the screws would be hidden by the bent perspex, giving the appearance of the fitting being stuck to the wall. This would add to the clean and hygienic look of the product.

If I were to choose between the two fittings I would choose the toothbrush holder as being more successful because of its compactness and simplicity. The toilet roll holder is too heavy and bulky.'

How much do you agree with the personal comments expressed above?

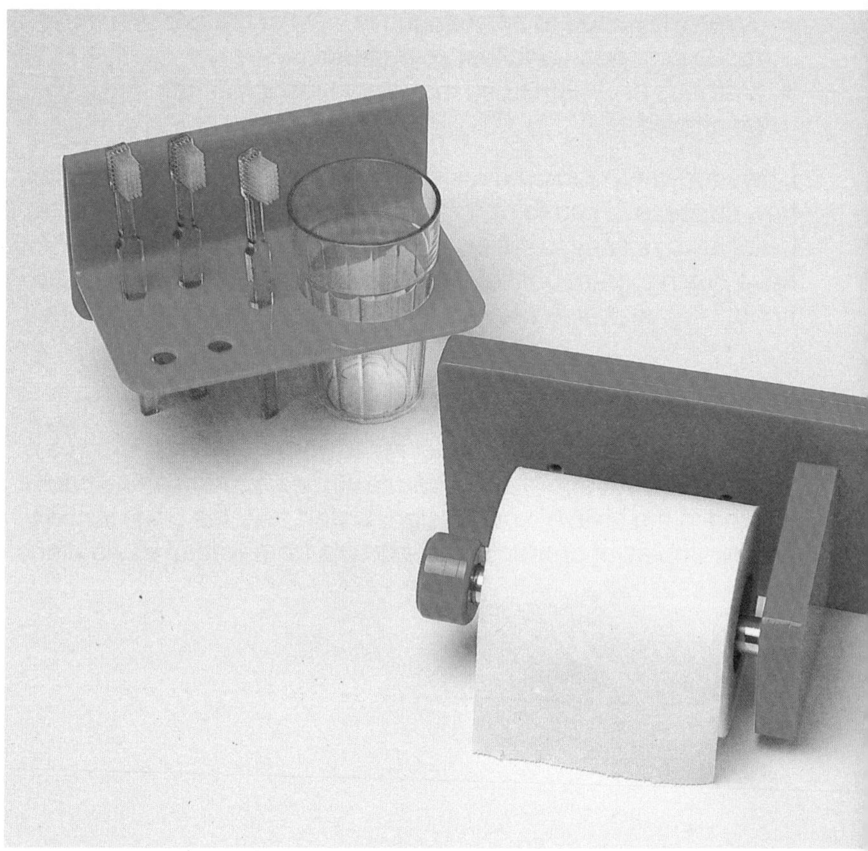

Toilet roll holder and toothbrush holder in acrylic and aluminium.

Playwear design

DESIGN BRIEF

You have been asked to design and make an overall to keep an active toddler clean. You may decorate the garment if you wish.

Analysis of the brief

You first need to analyse the problem, and decide what is really involved in developing a solution. Try jotting down your thoughts about the needs of toddlers.

A student working on this problem wrote:

> 'Age range 2 to 5 years. Children might be painting, using sand, glue, pens, mud. Jumping, climbing, falling over.
>
> Most of the body needs covering. Decoration bright, child-like, e.g. alphabet.
>
> Fastening to be big because of small fingers, e.g. Velcro, big buttons, zips – but not at the back.
>
> Possible decorations: animals, letters, numbers, colour.'

Are there any other people who can help you with your analysis?

Ease of movement?
- running
- jumping
- falling
- turning

Independence?
= a need to dress themselves
∴ fastenings not too small.

Playing – water, sand, mud, paint, glue etc.
How to keep arms clean?
Leg and body protection?

Look at the overalls that are on the market now. Try to work out the advantages and disadvantages. Below is one student's research in this area.

'**Advantages**
In this idea, most of the body is covered. It has an attractive design on it and is brightly coloured. It partly covers the legs and it is easy for the child to move.

Disadvantages
The method of fastening is at the back; the garment might be suitable for a slightly younger age group.'

'**Advantages**
The buttons are large enough for a young child to cope with. The elasticated ankles stop the garment riding up when the child plays.

Disadvantages
It would be difficult to put on over other clothes.'

'**Advantages**
This pinafore covers the majority of the body and could be worn over most clothes.

Disadvantages
The pinafore is too frilly – a boy may not like to wear it. There is no decoration and it would get dirty easily. The fastening is probably a small button and is at the back so cannot easily be done up.'

Research

What research could you do?

Arrange a visit to a nursery or playgroup. Talk to the staff, the children and parents.

Ask questions!

Ask the toddlers about the colours and decoration they like. You could devise a chart to record your findings. You could sketch some ideas and ask the children which ones they like. Ask the adults for their advice, for example, about the kind of fastenings that small children can manage. Which would be suitable? Which would be dangerous?

Watch the children. See if they can dress themselves. Which parts of the body need to be kept clean?

Take your own photographs.

What fabrics would be suitable? Remember they will get very dirty! You will have to consider fabric strength including whether it will tear. What seams will be suitable?

Remember to keep the cost of the overall as low as possible, as young children soon grow out of their clothes.

You might like to do some experiments on the fabric for strength, colour fastness, etc.

You could find out which fastenings children can manage unaided.

Tests of this kind need to be standardised – what does this mean?

Now you are ready to put down your ideas. Jot down *all* your ideas. If you look at the sketches on this page you will see how one idea has developed.

Often the simplest idea is the best.

Whichever design you decide to make it must be the one that best fulfils the requirements of the brief. Make sure your solution is suitable for all shapes and sizes, and can be worn by a girl or a boy.

Sizes?

How do designers of children's clothes take into account the range of children's sizes?

How should you?

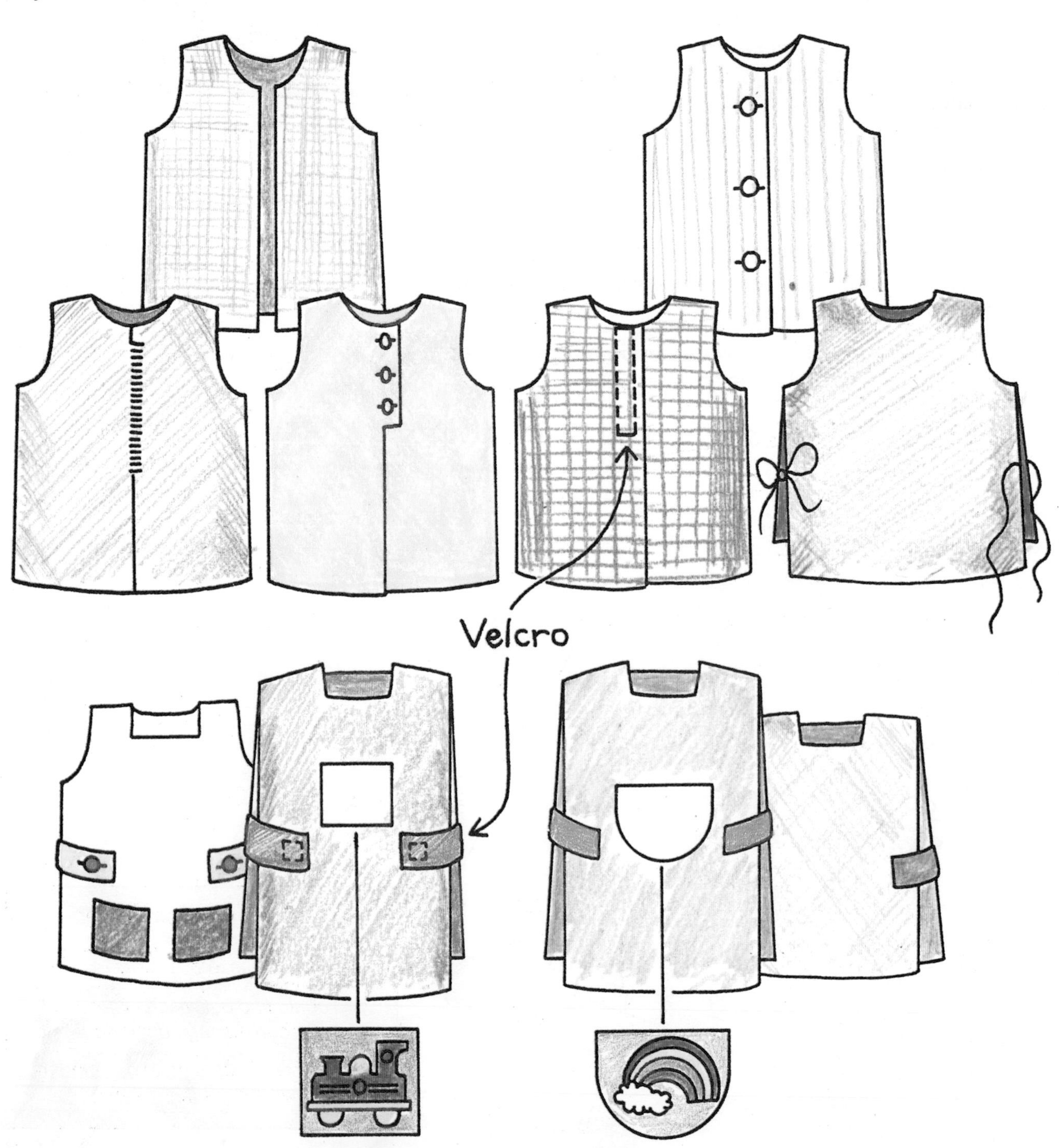

Realisation

Once you have selected the design and any decoration, there are several other problems to be solved.
What seams will you choose to use and why? How will you prevent the fabric from fraying?
If the overall is to be worn over clothes, will you have to draft the pattern a size larger?
What size pattern will be suitable?
How is the decoration to be applied?

Screen prints for mass production?

Evaluation

All designers assess their finished product. How will you conduct your evaluation? You could take the garment to a group of children and ask them what they think about it.

You might like to devise a simple chart to record their responses.

The children might like to comment on the overall: the colour, style, decoration, etc. You could tape-record their responses.

Children's Responses to the Pocket Decoration and Colour of the Overall.

	Like Rainbow	Dislike Rainbow	Like Colour	Dislike Colour
Alice		X	X	
Sally	X			X
Anna	X		X	
Rachel		X		X
Mark	X		X	
Ben		X	X	
Andrew	X		X	

Can the children put on the garment unaided? You could take a series of photographs of a small child putting on and using your final product.

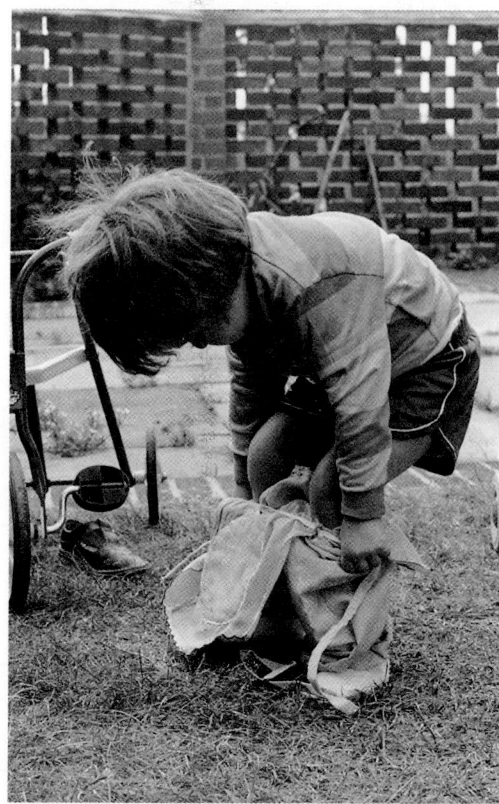

***All** the comments that you receive should be included in your evaluation.*

Keep an open mind!

Throughout the design process, keep an open mind about the possible solution.

Collect, research, ask questions, experiment, jot down results – ask more questions!

Be prepared to collect a lot of information and ideas before you finally select a proposal and make it in fabric.

You will have learned a lot in the process!

Finally assess the product yourself. Refer back to your analysis of the problem. Does your solution answer all aspects of the brief?

In the light of experience, you may decide that another solution would be more successful or that your idea needs modification. Record your thoughts.

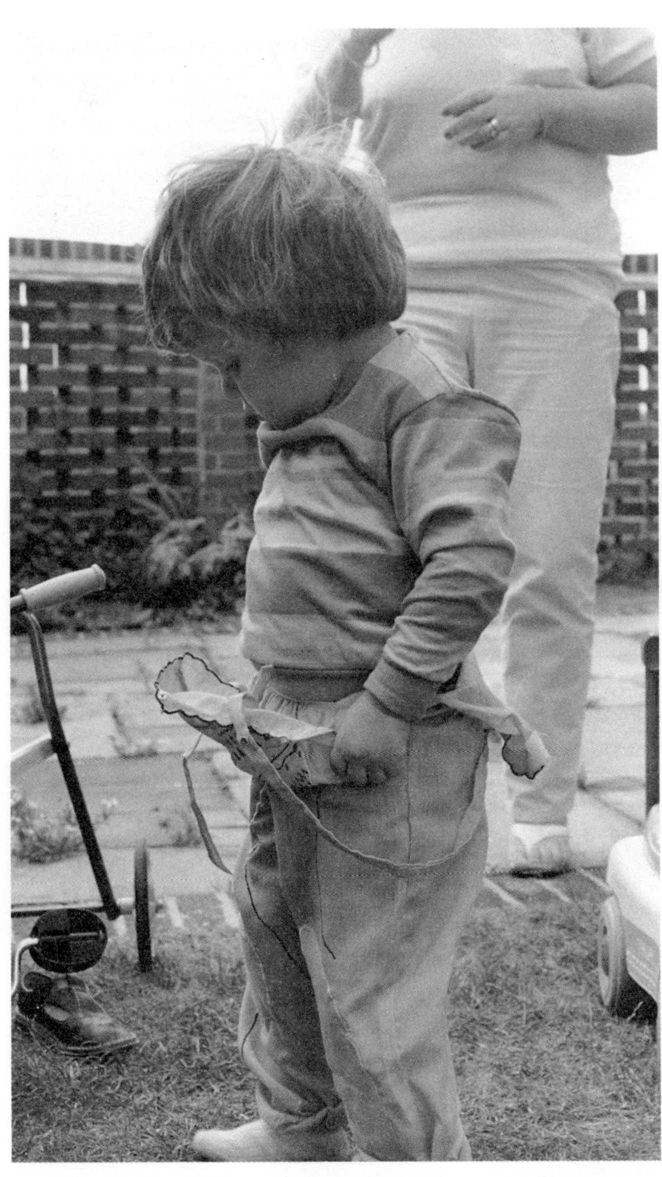

Patterns

The following examples have been devised so that you can develop your sense of shape, line, texture and form, two-dimensionally. They will require you to be able to use all your drawing and presentation skills and techniques.

DESIGN BRIEF

Design a motif for a bedroom wall, so that its style and colouring suits the room's decor. Make sure that you have discussed your scheme with your family. Research decorating with stencils.

Prepare and paint your wall in the usual way. Design your motif so that it will repeat along the wall and cut a stencil. If necessary, adapt motifs from the patterns and fabric designs already in the room. Use a centre line (a chalky string, snapped against the wall for your border design).

Tape the stencil into position and apply your chosen colour paint. Test your idea before you work on your bedroom wall. Use emulsion or stencil paints and check with leading paint manufacturers for any further technical or practical information your require.

Collect and photograph examples of patterning used in everyday life.

What function does patterning have in either man-made things or nature?

What part does it play in design?

If shapes make a pattern randomly do they make a design?

Study the patterns used by different peoples and discuss what a traditional pattern might be.

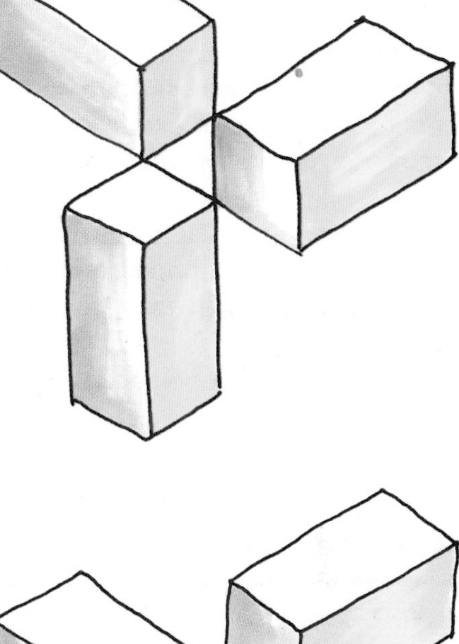

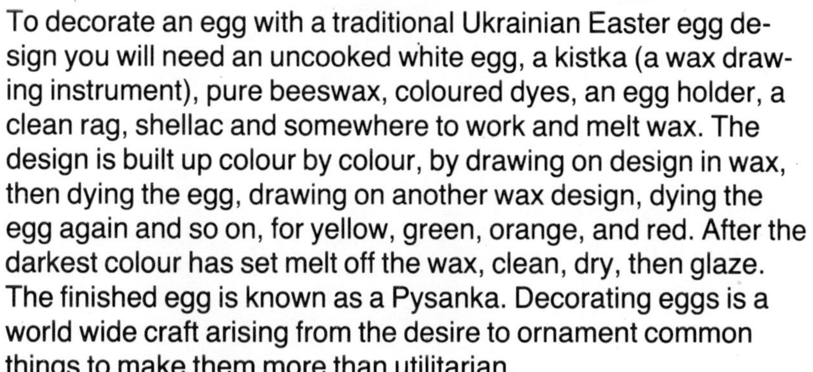

To decorate an egg with a traditional Ukrainian Easter egg design you will need an uncooked white egg, a kistka (a wax drawing instrument), pure beeswax, coloured dyes, an egg holder, a clean rag, shellac and somewhere to work and melt wax. The design is built up colour by colour, by drawing on design in wax, then dying the egg, drawing on another wax design, dying the egg again and so on, for yellow, green, orange, and red. After the darkest colour has set melt off the wax, clean, dry, then glaze. The finished egg is known as a Pysanka. Decorating eggs is a world wide craft arising from the desire to ornament common things to make them more than utilitarian.

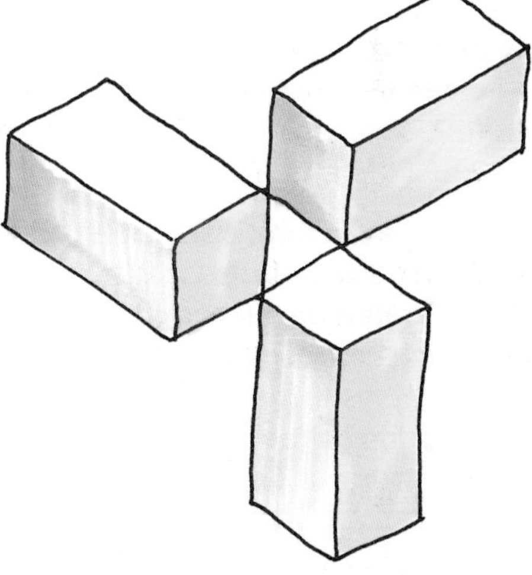

DESIGN BRIEF

Draw a grid, based on 25mm equilateral triangles, on an A2 sheet of paper. Divide the sheet into two, using one half to draw, colour and cut out several motifs. Draw the two motifs, one the reverse of the other, and test the different ways in which they fit together.

DESIGN BRIEF

Design a basic tile using either mechanical drawing or freehand drawing. Concentrate on the optical effect of your design and use this to form a repeated pattern. Make your first attempt after sketching and planning out your design for an ink drawing, to create a high contrast of effects. A technical pen will be useful.

Puzzles and problems

A puzzle is a puzzle! Anyone who can invent a new puzzle will have been successful in the design exercise. A traditional puzzle is based on interlocking shapes, stamped on to a picture. All the parts and shapes of a puzzle can be designed. If a simple shape like a square is used, you will see that very complicated patterns can be designed. A puzzle may have only one solution or many.

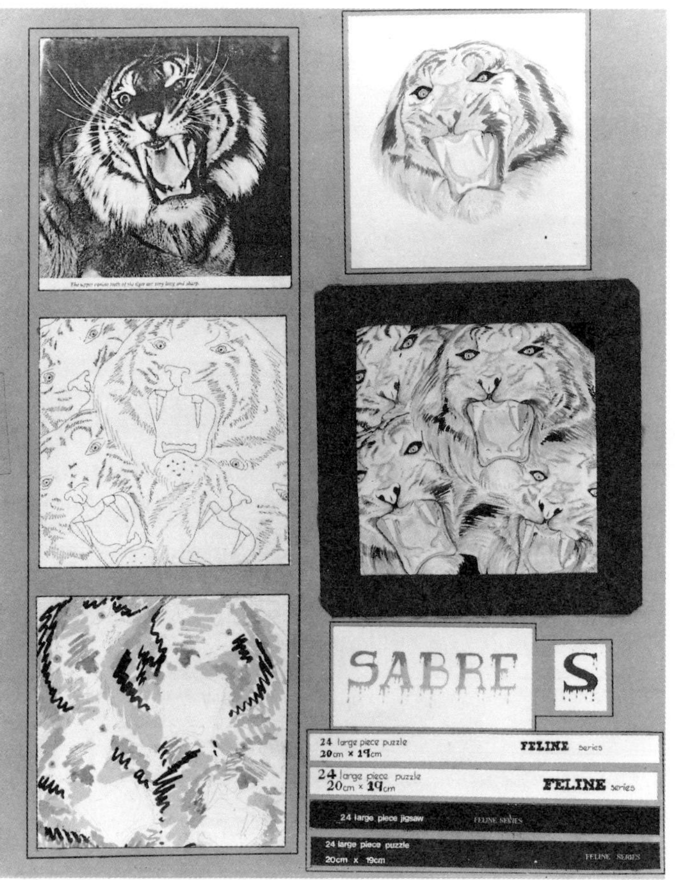

DESIGN BRIEF

Design, make and package a puzzle, which uses squares as the pieces and where each square is illustrated with a pattern or a picture. Use colour throughout your design. Aim to make a puzzle with the appearance of many solutions, but which has, in fact, only one or very few solutions. It may be based on shapes and patterns, colours or a picture.

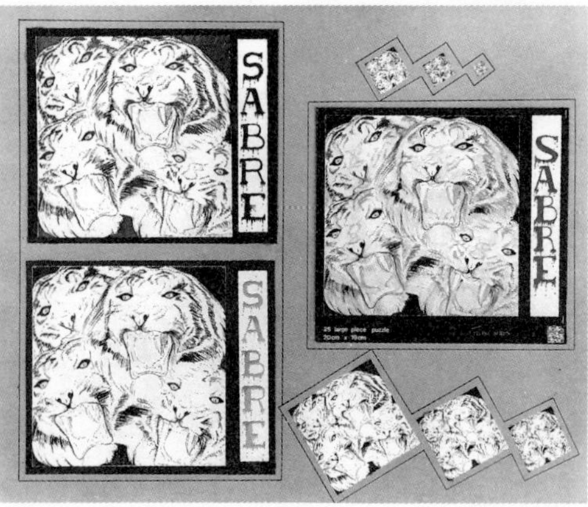

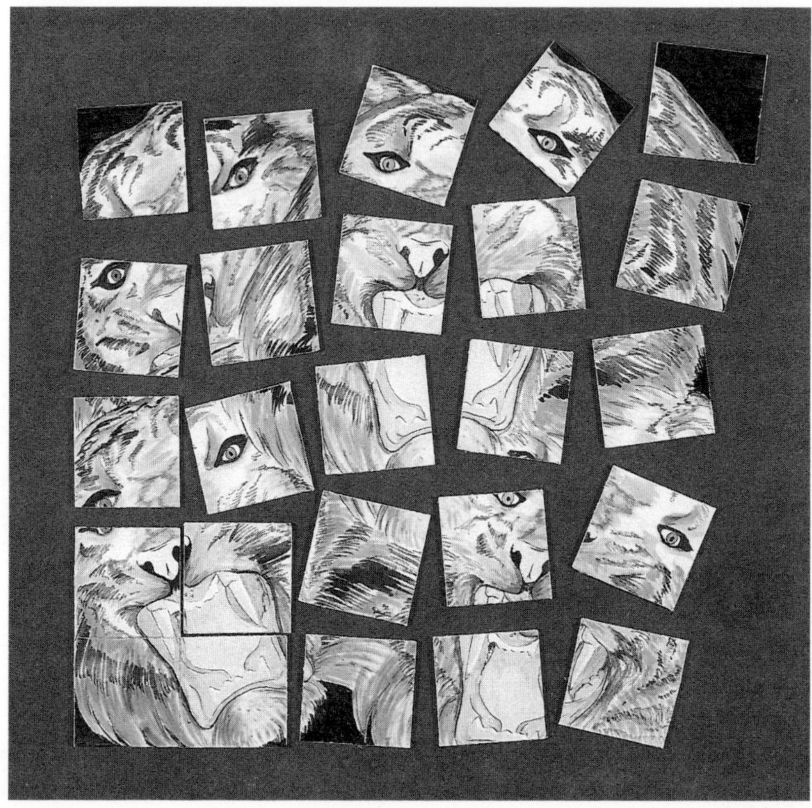

The aim of this activity is for you to try some of the mental and visual skills which designers often find themselves puzzling over. Can you see things three-dimensionally? Can you convert two-dimensional objects into three dimensions? Can you solve problems by picturing their solution? Can you draw out your ideas and proposals for your design?

It should be remembered that, at times, our senses may mislead us, and that they do not always provide us with reliable information. What we see has to be interpreted with caution. We know that there are variations in the results of observations made by different people; for example, we do not all perceive colours in the same way.

Use drawing at any point during your study of these problems:

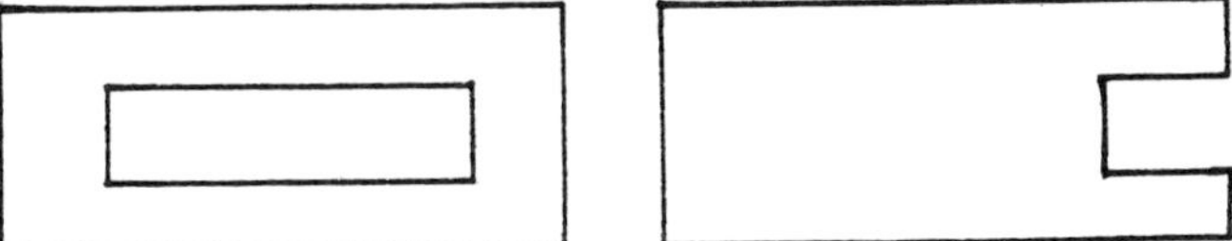

Given two orthographic views of solid objects, use them to draw three-dimensional sketches of the objects.

Draw a diagram so that three points are each connected to three other points, without any connection crossing over another one.

A gardener has ten trees which must be planted in five rows, so that each has four trees in it. Draw the plan of his garden.

Can you see 'Velpreys Isle'?

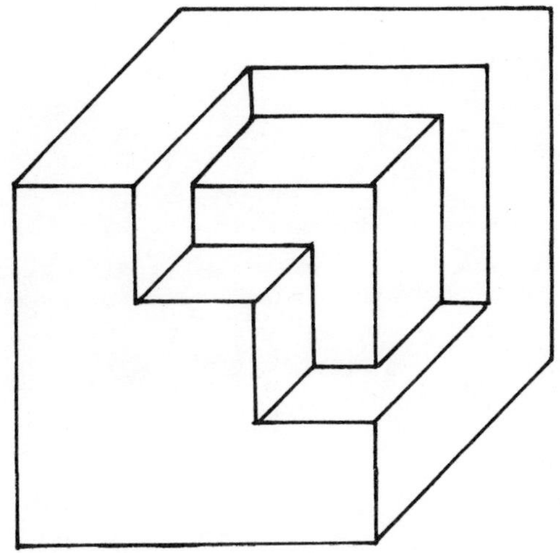

How many ways can you see this drawing three-dimensionally? Use shadowing and colour to interpret the different images. You should be able to find more than three interpretations.

Describe how the apple came to be in the bottle.

Investigate patterns used in puzzles.

What is a 'lattice' and a 'motif'?

How does one work with the other?

Is seeing believing?

Collect examples of illusions and puzzles.

Working together

A computer adventure game

An adventure game is a story in which you act out the action using a computer. To be interesting it should be different each time it is played and a player should make choices or hunches as the action unfolds. You may be on a fantastic journey or escaping from danger. The adventures which you create may be the result of many kinds of problem solving activities. These games will involve colourful graphics and commands based on 'action words', called verbs.

This is an imaginative activity involving the design of characters, situations and actions. Your first problem is to invent a story for your characters to act in. The locations in which the action takes place can be drawn out on a map. Transferring this on to a grid, (for example 8×8=64 squares) is a good way to begin visualising an adventure game. This map should show the different types of location and establish the many routes which can be taken through your game. The story should have a beginning and various ends. If a player gets lost or takes the wrong turn then your game should offer players alternative routes or force them to quit.

You will have to produce an error checking sequence to help you programme your computer. Your game should provide a player with objects or devices to help or hinder progress. There should be incentives, puzzles and problems as the game is played, so that players can accumulate scores or penalties.

Use all your design and graphic experience to draw up a plan in detail before you programme your adventure into your computer. Adventure games are intended to be interactive and are fascinating to design and play. Creating a good story is probably the most important aspect of this type of designing.

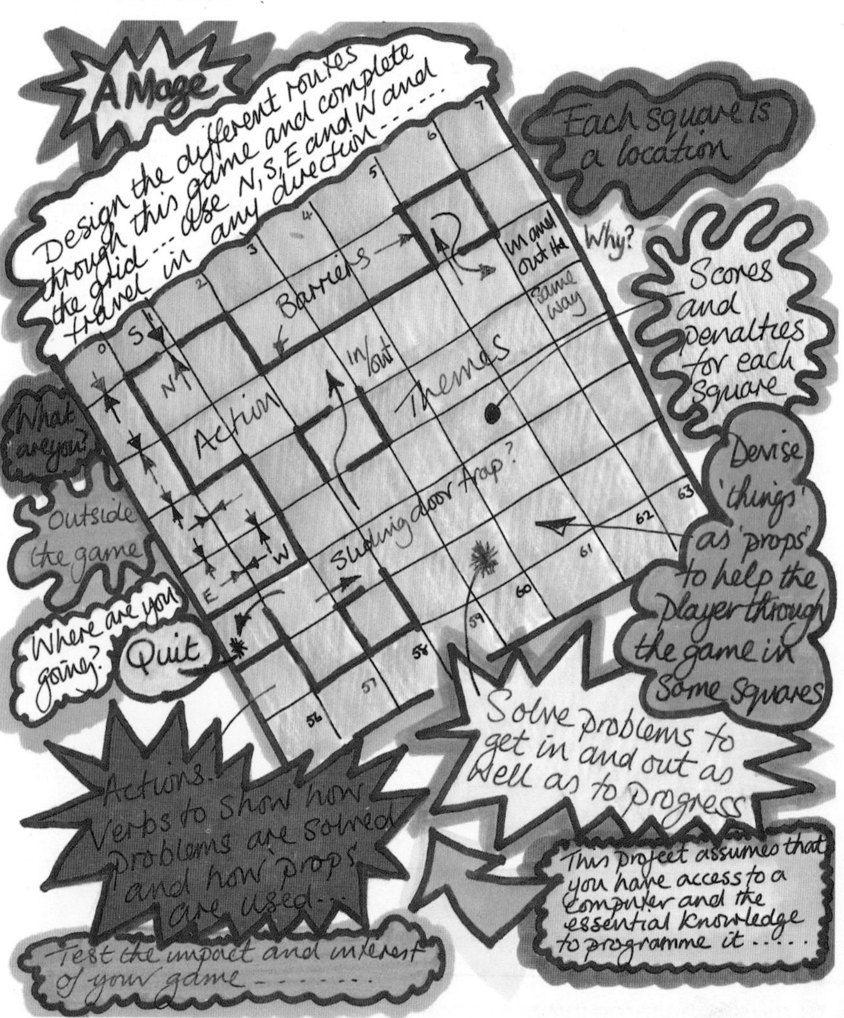

DESIGN BRIEF

Design and create a computer adventure game. Illustrate the game with characters, situations and actions. Devise a storyboard which describes the sequences of problems which are to be solved by a player. Include locations and properties needed to play. Plan the television screen images and presentation of information needed to play the game. Package and promote your game.

What are the products of your designing in these activities?

Can you distinguish between design products and design processes?

Cartoons

Cartooning starts from an impulse to draw and communicate. Leading newspapers and magazines receive many hundreds of cartoons from hopeful cartoonists each week. A cartoonist should have a distinctive view of life, a feeling for drawing and designing with pictures and a desire to put over a certain message. A message may be serious or humorous. It is a personal response to life, and a creative idea or a joke combined with a drawing style makes a cartoon. Find a distinctive style of cartooning which is yours alone!

DESIGN BRIEF

Create a cartoon which explores the humour in this idea: outside a shop is a sign saying DOGS, and below it is hook for dogleads; next to this is another sign saying CHILDREN . . .

Film animation

Producing an animated cartoon is complex in many ways and requires team work and planning for it to be successful. This activity is intended for you to consider the initial problems in cartoon filming: to write a story, sketch out a storyboard, produce artwork for characters, backgrounds and animation effects. If you wish to go beyond that and *make* an animated cartoon you will need access to film equipment. You will also need to know how to use a rostrum camera and how to edit film.

Film animation requires time and team work. You will have to consider maintaining your enthusiasm for a long project. Your abilities to organise as well as to play your part in a team effort are the essential qualities in this design activity.

DESIGN BRIEF

Design and plan a cartoon film. Think about a story, artwork and filming on a rostrum.

Fast food ideas

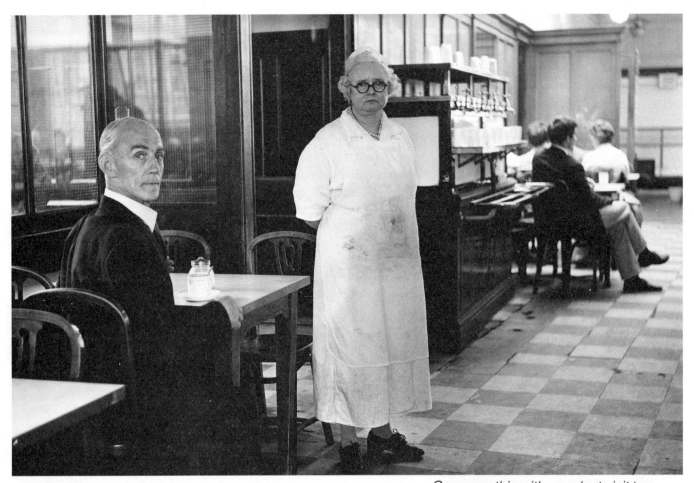

Compare this with your last visit to a McDonalds!

Over the years our eating habits and our attitudes to the foods we eat have changed. New trends in eating habits appear to be towards a more casual, 'snacking' style of eating. Many people now eat more of the easily prepared and pre-prepared convenience foods, eat more snacks than meals and eat food outside the home more often.

According to recent research, undertaken by the British Nutrition Foundation, surveys show that:

- about *three-quarters* of all eating occasions are now made up of snacks
- about *one-third* of all adults buy take-away food at least once a week
- nearly *half* of all meals eaten outside the home were taken, during the day, at casual food places e.g. canteens, cafes, store restaurants, 'burger bars', etc.

In a recent article, 'Fast Food – what's in it for you', *Which?* (February 1985) magazine reported:

> 'As a nation the British have contributed to a take-away food industry that the Government estimated was worth £1.4 billion last year, and a fast food industry which claims to be growing at the rate of 15% a year.'

Trends therefore indicate that much of the food we choose and eat is bought ready prepared. This means that we are less involved in and have less control over the ingredients of many of the foods we now eat. Much of this food contains 'hidden' fat, sugar and salt, things that we are advised to eat less of.

Modern dietary guidelines, based upon the NACNE and COMA Reports, suggest that as a nation we are eating far too much fat and sugar, too much salt and not enough fibre-rich foods. Evidence so far suggests that this type of diet is linked to various diseases and disorders.

If several of our daily meals or snacks are bought outside the home on a regular basis, it is therefore important that we should try to choose those which contain less fat, sugar and salt and more fibre. However in buying take-away food, we also want variety, fast, attractively presented food, which is good value for money, and of a type that can be conveniently eaten anywhere.

DESIGN BRIEF

Design an original, healthy take-away meal or snack which could be sold from a stall or kiosk in:

a the high street
b your school.

City centre fast food outlets.

Initial investigation

Before you can begin to plan your take-away food product, you will need to investigate some of the wider implications of the design brief. For example:

1 Which types or groups of people buy take-away food?
2 Why are take-away foods in demand?
3 What sort of food do people *really* want to buy for a take-away?
4 Which types of food are already available in school and in the locality?
5 Which foods are considered to be good value for money, yet sold at a profit?
6 Which foods are considered to be easy to eat?
7 What is the law concerning food sold in the street?

To find some of the answers to these questions, you may

- conduct a survey
- make a questionnaire
- talk to people – pupils, teachers, shoppers, relatives
- visit the High Street
- use magazines, newspapers, books
- observe eating patterns in school.

To make a healthy take-away product, you will also need out which foods contain less fat, sugar and salt, and more than others, e.g. cottage cheese contains less fat than ch cheese. There are various ways of finding out this informa from your teacher, from food tables, books, leaflets, videc writing to community dieticians, Health Education Officers on.

Recording and documenting the results of your surveys.

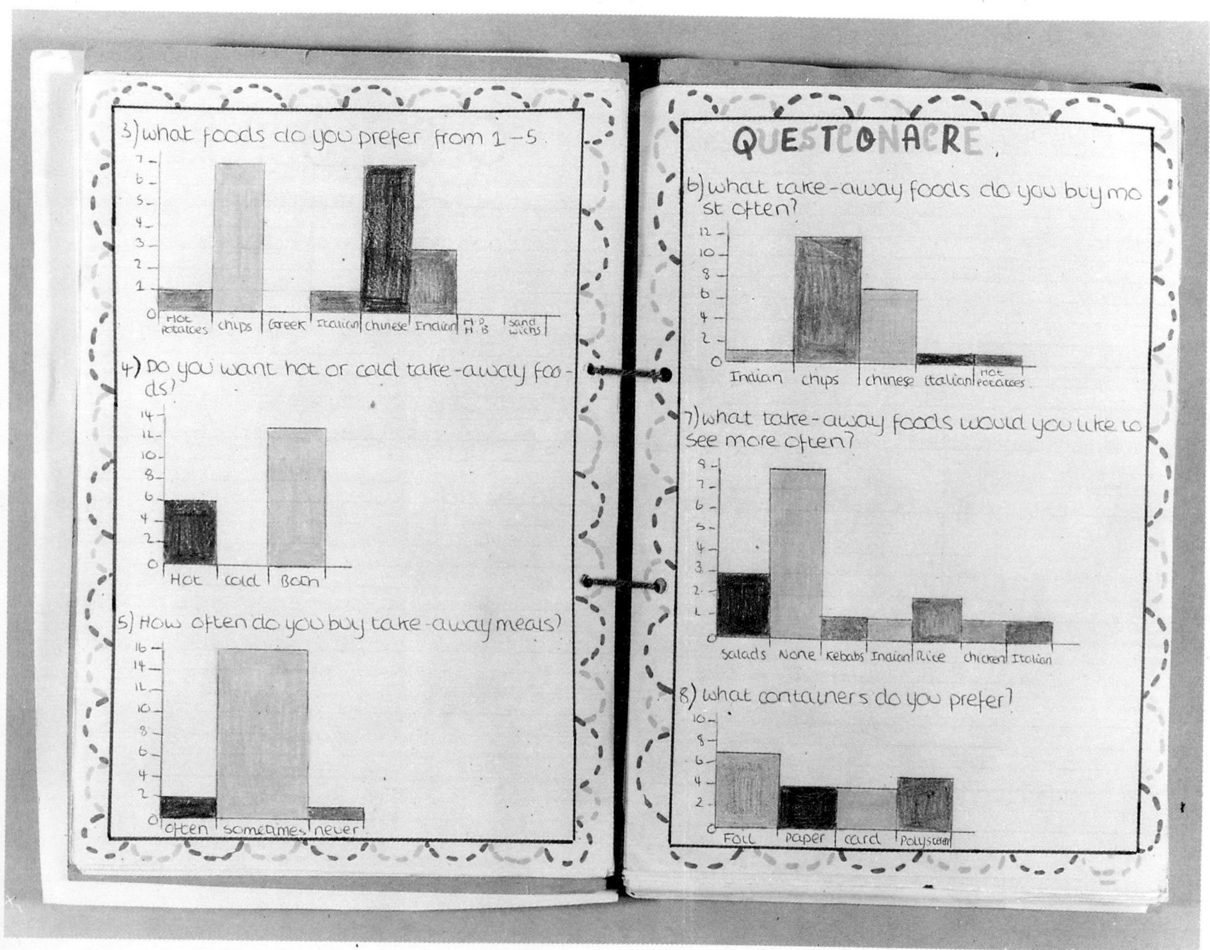

Further investigation

Before investigating further, you will need to make some decisions. The information collected and recorded during your initial research will have sparked off some ideas, and will help you to decide:

- Which type or group of people you are aiming to sell your product to.
- What type of product/s you wish to make.
- How and where you will sell your product.

Having made some preliminary decisions, you may now find that you need to make further investigations. In order to explore, make, experiment, develop and promote your product/s, consideration of the following three broad areas could be helpful:

1 Food materials and treatment
2 Packaging
3 Marketing and advertising

1 Food, materials and treatment

FOOD MATERIALS AND TREATMENT

Are garnishes or accompaniments required? If so, which? How are these prepared? How much do they cost? Are they to be considered optional extras?

Sweet or savoury? Hot or cold? Cooked or raw?

Which foodstuffs are you planning to use? Which main nutrients do they contain?

Are your products healthy? If not can you modify them? How?

Is the food to be precooked and then reheated at point of sale? If so how? Time taken?

Are you aiming at one basic product in a variety of flavours or is your product part of a range?

Which methods are to be used for preparation and cooking? How much time does it take? What equipment is required?

Do the materials require storage? How are they easily and safely stored? Do they require special storage at the point of sale?

What is the cost of the materials used? Do you need to look for cheaper alternatives? Do seasonal changes affect the price? Can the product be sold at a profit?

Are the materials easily purchased? Are they available throughout the year?

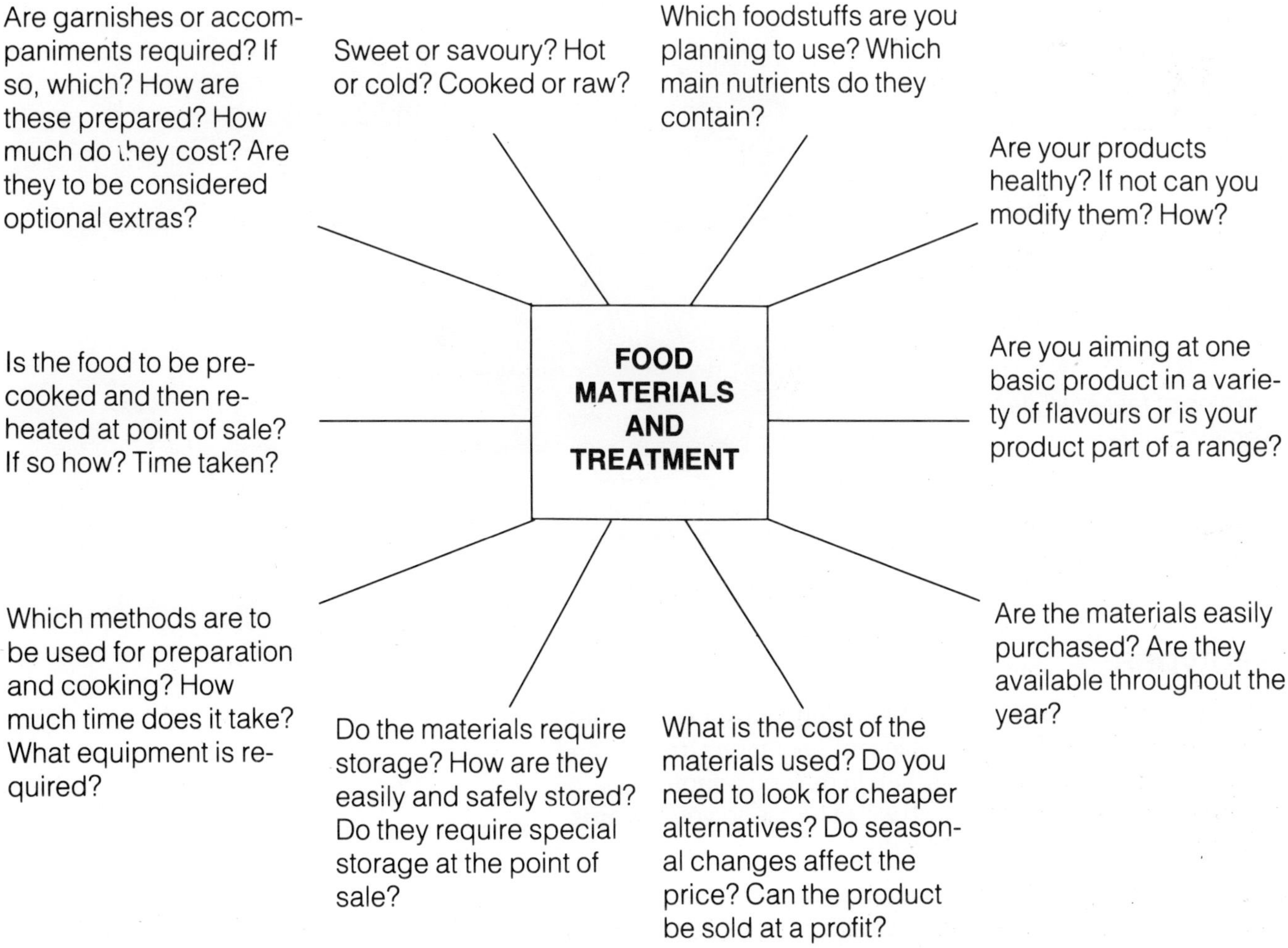

2 Packaging

Remembering that your product should be easy to carry away and to eat, how will you package your product for sale?

Find out which packaging types and materials are used commercially. Decide upon the functions that you want your package to serve. Do you want it to act as a container or a wrapper? Should it keep food hot? Does it need to be water-tight? Does it need to protect the contents? Which materials would best suit these functions? Which shape/size would you choose?

3 Marketing and advertising

Are you planning to advertise your product? If so how? Find out how commercial fast food outlets advertise and market their products. Can you design a theme, logo, slogan and colour scheme for your product? Would you require a poster, carrier bag, etc. to promote this theme?

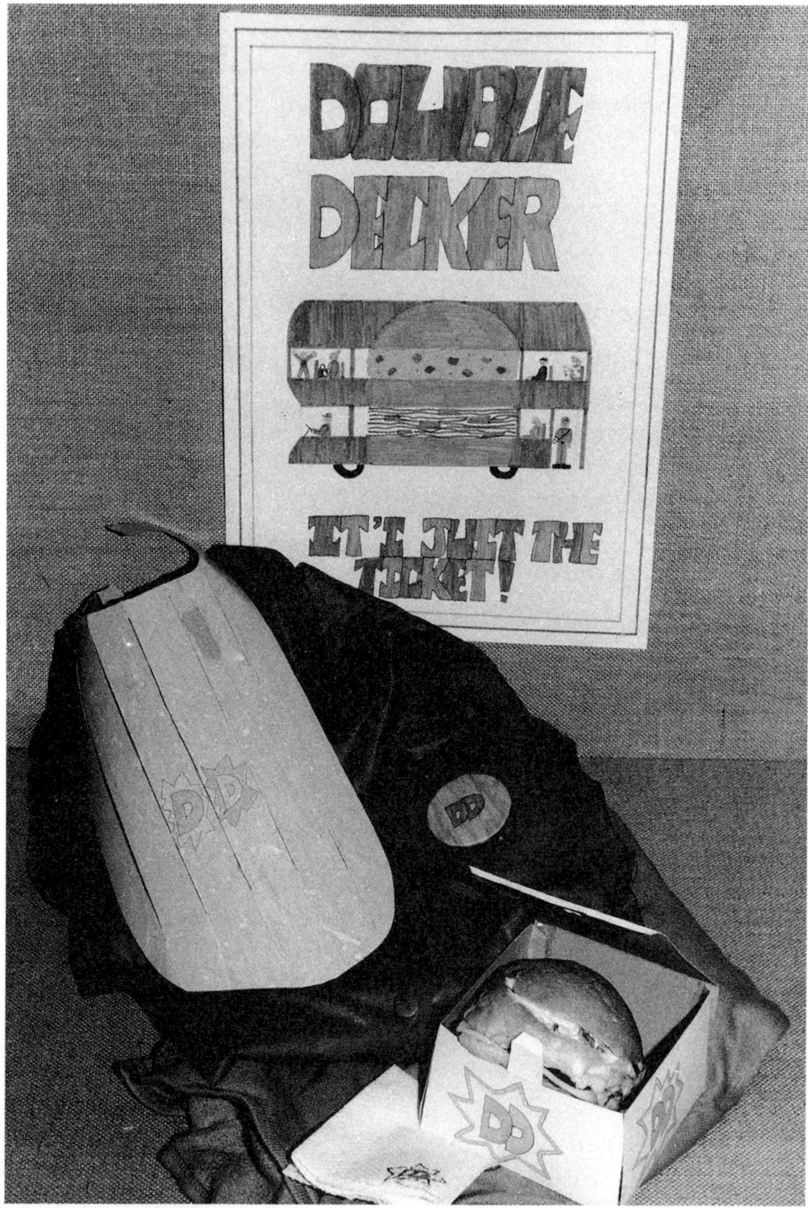

Examples of fast food packaging and advertising.

Prototypes

For every dish that you decide to make during this design brief, you will need to record your activities, observations, results and conclusions. This will then assist you in making adaptations, modifications and changes, which will in turn lead you towards making a well thought-out final product.

An activity record sheet, such as the one opposite, will be useful, and will enable you to make fair comparisons and conclusions.

PRACTICAL ACTIVITY RECORD SHEET

BRIEF: Fast Foods   DISH CHOSEN ....   DATE ....

Chosen materials

Quantity   Type   Cost

Total cost of dish

Preparation methods and sequence

Evaluation of the dish. How successful was the dish? Comment on:

Flavour and texture

Appearance

Suitability

Storage

Timing:	Start	Finish	Total	Total time taken
Preparation	.....	.....	.....	
Cooking	.....	.....	.....	
Finishing	.....	.....	.....	

Analysis in terms of health. Comments

Is this dish:
- low in fat? Yes/No
- low in sugar? Yes/No
- low in salt? Yes/No

Is this dish:
- high in fibre? Yes/No

Food value of dish

Are any food groups/or nutrients missing? Which foods could be added or served with the dish to improve it nutritionally?

Variety

Can alternative flavours be made? Suggestions?

Are accompaniments or garnishes required? If so, what? How much will it cost?

Costing and quantities

Number of portions made ....   Total cost of dish ....

Cost per portion ....   Selling price ....

Profit margin on ingredients per portion, is therefore ....

Could you change any ingredients to make the dish more profitable? How?

Packaging and serving

Would this dish look appetising when portioned and displayed?

Will this dish require last minute preparation, e.g. cutting, reheating, garnishing, etc.

What packaging requirements are necessary, e.g. to insulate, protect, to eat from, etc?

What packaging/serving container are you considering for this dish?

Realisation

When you have completed your research and investigations (through both theory and practice) you should have discovered some of the problems of, and answers to this design brief. You will be in a position now to use these findings to make a final choice.

1 **Final food choice** including: chosen recipe and alternative flavours; preparation methods and sequence; nutritive value of the product; costings – wholesale and retail

2 **Final packaging choice**, including: a sketch or picture; the materials used

3 **Final advertising and marketing choice**, including: theme, colour scheme, logo, slogan; advertising ideas

Final solution

Make your product and display it, in or alongside a sketch of its package/container, together with your advertisement ideas. Photograph your display to record the event.

Final evaluation

- Has this final solution answered the design brief?
- What were your reasons for this final choice? How did the product rate in terms of customer appeal?
- Was the final choice a healthy takeaway? How original was it? Is it commercially viable?
- Can you modify or improve upon this solution, etc?

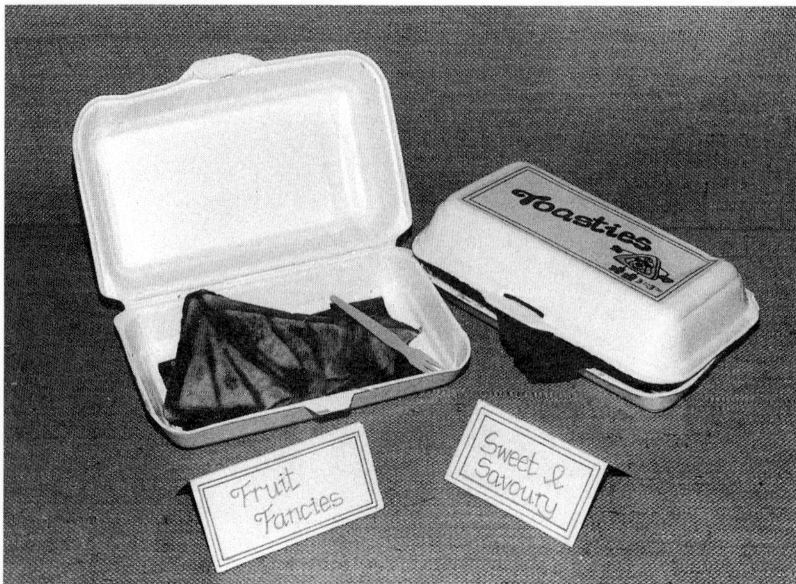

A take-away snack . . .

Display of design sheets and packaging.

. . . complete with dips.